SEMANTIC THEORY
TOWARDS A MODERN SEMANTICS

Kurt Baldinger

SEMANTIC THEORY
Towards a Modern Semantics

translated by William C. Brown
and
edited by Roger Wright

Basil Blackwell · Oxford

First English edition published 1980 by
Basil Blackwell Publisher
5 Alfred Street
Oxford OX1 4HB
England

First Spanish edition published 1970
Second edition, upon which this translation
is based, published 1977
by Ediciones Alcalá, Madrid

British Library Cataloguing in Publication Data

Baldinger, Kurt
Semantic theory.
1. Semantics
I. Title
412   P325

ISBN 0-631-10891-2
ISBN 0-631-11491-2 Pbk

Typesetting by Preface Ltd., Salisbury, Wiltshire
Printed in Great Britain by
Billing and Sons Ltd,
Guildford, London, Oxford, Worcester

Contents

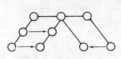

Preface to the
English Edition

Writing an introduction to the study of modern semantics is
bound to be a brave enterprise, since hardly any other branch
of linguistics has developed as much in the last thirty years;
furthermore, studies undertaken have had very different
orientations, from a methodological viewpoint; thus it is
impossible to synthesize all these different trends and perspectives in a unified way, without doing an injustice to some of
them. I have not even tried to do this; I am thus exposing
myself to a charge of one-sidedness, although I can justify
myself by the use of the indefinite article in the title. The kind
of semantics I am dealing with is paradigmatic; it is, in my
opinion, syntagmatically verifiable, and in no way contradicts
syntagmatic semantics; yet even within these chosen limits,
there is a bias determined by my own evolution. I deliberately
intended the word *towards* in the subtitle to be ambiguous: it
should be understood at the same time from a historical evolu-
tionary viewpoint (from Ullmann to Heger, from the triangle
to the trapezium; from my 1957 study on *Semasiology* —
which I would today call *Semantics* — to my present viewpoint) and from a methodological point of view (in the sense
of a progressive refining of the methods towards more complex models); for this reason, this study should be considered
as an introduction to the evolution of the subject as well as a

textbook. Another procedure would have been just as valid; for example, it would have been possible to give a dominant place to the theory constructed by Greimas (treated here very briefly, but published by the author himself in 1966), or to Coseriu's; or to begin with American semantics, which is nowadays primarily based on transformational theory (even so, I shall not discuss this approach, although, of course, I do not doubt its value). Therefore, although the present introduction is only one of several possible kinds, it *is* a possible one, and I hope it will be able to make clear, despite the perspective I have chosen, relations which can lead to a clearer understanding of so complex a phenomenon as language. I also hope, and in this I see its immediate usefulness, that it can serve as a methodological model for both semasiological and onomasiological studies.

Each chapter was first written as a lecture given in the years after 1960 in conferences and seminars in Europe and, during my travels in Latin America, from Argentina to Mexico. I decided to collect it all into a synthesis, wholeheartedly responding to the invitation of my friends Manuel Alvar and Antonio Quilis to give a series of lectures on *Present-day Tendencies in European Semantics*, in Malaga, from July 19th to August 26th 1967, on the occasion of the second Advanced Course on Spanish Philology.

This synthesis formed the essence of the first Spanish edition of this book (*Teoría semántica, Hacia una semántica moderna*, Madrid, Ediciones Alcalá, 1970, 278 pp.). This first edition was well received, and, when it was out of print, I published a second enlarged Spanish edition in 1977 (*Teoría semántica, Hacia una semántica moderna*, segunda edición corregida y aumentada, Madrid, Ediciones Alcalá, 1977, 302 pp)[1], which formed the basis for this first English edition. In the second Spanish edition as well as in the English translation, I could

---

[1]In the meantime, from the same publishing house, had appeared Klaus Heger's book *Teoría semántica II, Hacia una semántica moderna*, Madrid, 1974, xii, 223 pp. which contains Heger's works between 1963 and 1970. This book went to press in 1970.

profit by numerous critical reviews of the first Spanish edition, especially by those of Ludwig Söll [†] (*ZrP* 87, 1971, 349–298 ["The whole book is characterized by its penetration and clarity, by its ample documentation, by a felicitous combination of theory and practice, and by numerous well-chosen personal observations"]), Pierre Gardette[†] (*RLiR* 37, 1973, 216 ["The best of the present introductory manuals to the problems and methods of modern semantics"]), Roger Wright (*Archivum Linguisticum* III (n.s.), 1972, 105–108 ["This book is the best and most interesting on semantic theory to have appeared for some time. The theory is perceptive and of immediate practical value; and for a professional linguist there are many intriguing parallels with modern American traditions"]), Ileana Vincenz (*Cahiers de linguistique théorique et appliquée* [Acad. Rép. Soc. de Roumanie, Bucharest] VIII, 1971, 261–266 ["The book by K. Baldinger is of note for its own semantic theory and for its accurate analysis. . . . It goes beyond the interest it could arouse in semantic theorists and specialists and demands the attention of everyone who wants to enter on the complex study of general linguistics"]), Georges Lüdi (*Vox Romanica* 30, 1971, 318–326 ["Thus, Baldinger's *Semantic Theory*, with its abundance of intelligent observations and suggestions, is an important contribution to semantic investigation, which is in the process of a radical transformation; orientation and guide at the same time"], and Francisco R. Adrados (*Revista española de lingüística* [Madrid] 1, 1971, 203–205 ["The book . . . constitutes, in short, a good introduction to semantics (not complete, the new American semantics is missing and so are the European approaches referred to above)"]). I also want to mention the critical review by Ana María Barrenechea (*Rom Phil* 26, 1972, 346–405), the only one that rejects the essence of the book ["In conclusion I shall say that this book, like all of Kurt Baldinger's works, shows us that he is a philologist of the first rank, with a knowledge of Romance lexicography achieved by very few, with a great sensitivity in perceiving differences of meaning in different contexts, and expressive nuances. We would praise, to use his words, his "esprit de finesse" and not his "esprit de géométrie", since his theoretical presentations are not as good as the intuitions in his concrete analysis"]. In part, at least, Ana María Barrenechea's criticism was motivated by the numerous errata (more than 150) in the first edition, errata which often deform the sense of what I am saying, and for which I am not personally responsible. I hope to have overcome other objections in the second edition (cf. the new chapter 7). The main resistance to the trapezium was based, apparently, on the fear that the specific structure of one language might be "replaced" by noematic systems independent of any particular language, which would quite obviously be absurd. I also want especially to mention the criticisms of the triangular and trapezoidal model made by Helmut Henne/Herbert E. Wiegand, "Geometrische Modelle und das Problem der Bedeutung", *Zeitschrift für Dialektologie und Linguistik* 36, 1969, 129–173; it is probable that their incidental objections have been cleared up in the meantime, with the modifications that Heger (cf. Chap. 7) has made to the trapezoidal model[2]. Also concerned with the trapezium is Estanislao Ramón Trives, "Hacia una descripción integrada de la lengua. Análisis de las tendencias de la Semántica actual en las doctrinas de K. Heger y B. Pottier", in *Anales de la Universidad de Murcia* XXIX, 1970–71, 5–41; "La lengua en su constitución esencial interna", *ib.* XXX, 1971–72, 49–75.

Concerning the fear, occasionally felt by some traditional linguists, of oversimplifying the infinite multiplicity and variety of phenomena which occur in a language, I shall merely point out, in the first place, that, in using the trapezium, no attempt is made to restrict semasiological analysis with all its wealth of possibilities and shadings, and that, in the second place, even given its necessarily simplifying character, consequent on the

---

[2]See also the article "Pleremik: Sprachzeichenbildung", pp. 132–144, by Henne/Wiegand, and "Lexikographie" by Henne, pp. 590–601, in the *Lexikon der Germanistischen Linguistik*, published by H. P. Althaus, H. Henne and H. E. Wiegand, Tübingen (Niemeyer), 1973; H. E. Wiegand, *Synchronische Onomasiologie und Semasiologie – Kombinierte Methoden zur Strukturierung der Lexik*, Marburg, 1970 (Germanistische Linguistik, 3/70).

selection of particular elements, a noematic system provides a much greater number of theoretical possibilities than are actually realized in a given language (cf., for example, the 256 possibilities of combination calculated by Heger in *Monem, Wort, Satz und Text*, 1976, p. 299, for just one presuppositional group – one among many other possible groups). Now, more than ever, I am convinced of the validity of the theoretical conception which, in any case, has its origin not with me, but with Klaus Heger, especially in its revised and expanded version.

I have taken into consideration those objections which I considered justified, for this second edition. Since, as I pointed out above, this book sets forth *one* possible semantic theory and its historical evolution (from Ullmann's triangle to Heger's trapezium), I have limited myself to correcting the errata and the mistakes of the first edition, adding bibliographical data and some examples; and, instead of revising some chapters, – which would have given a false impression of the evolution of the theory –, I have preferred to write the new chapter 7, "The Present Form of the Trapezium". This chapter, in which I reconsider a number of themes dealt with or mentioned throughout the book, is based to a great extent on the introductory chapter of Heger's *Monem, Wort, Satz und Text* (Tübingen, Niemeyer, 1976, 355 pp.). In this new final chapter, which reflects the work done on remodelling the trapezium since 1968, as well as the consequences of such a remodelling for the whole semantic theory, all the assumptions of the model, at the present state of discussion, are dealt with again, and they are justified and given precise terminological status. In fact the changes made, compared with the previous chapters, enable one to measure the progress which has been made in the meantime (for example, concerning the differentiation between *seme* and *noeme*, the definitions of *polysemy, homonymy, synonymy* and *polymorphy*, etc.). I think that, in essence, the trapezoidal model has now been given its definitive form and justification. Its practical value has been demonstrated (cf. Part II, chap. 3, concerning "remember", and in the near future the doctoral thesis of my assistant Karl Brademann on the renderings of "remember" in Old and Middle French which will be published in the Beihefte of the *Zeitschrift für romanische Philologie*).

For higher levels, Heger himself has recently published an analysis of an individual text[3]. Since, from the beginning, this book has been orientated to the semantic theory which leads from the triangle to the trapezium, I have decided against taking into consideration the ideas which are found in the present bibliography on semantics – which has now reached flood proportions –, since this would have had negative repercussions on the unity of this introduction to *one* semantic theory[4].

---

[3]Klaus Heger, "Signemränge und Textanalyse", in Elisabeth Gülich, Klaus Heger, Wolfgang Raible, *Linguistische Textanalyse. Überlegungen zur Gliederung von Texten* (Papiere zur Textlinguistik, 8), Hamburg (Helmut Buske Verlag), 1974, 1–71; cf. also Wolfgang Raible, "Vergleich mit der von Klaus Heger durchgeführten Textanalyse", 127–147.

[4]See the excellent work by J. Lyons, *Introduction to Theoretical Linguistics*, Cambridge, 1968.

On semantics within transformational grammar, cf., for example, "the most ample and coherent presentation", of Jerrold J. Katz, *Semantic Theory*, New York (Harper and Row), 1972, 464 pp. (cf. the review by Christian Rohrer in ZrP 91, 1975). On structural semantics, see Eugenio Coseriu, *Probleme der strukturellen Semantik* (Vorlesung gehalten im Wintersemester 1965/66 an der Universität Tübingen, Autorisierte und bearbeitete Nachschrift von Dieter Kastovsky), Tübingen (Tübinger Beiträge zur Linguistik, edited by Gunter Narr [= TBL], 40), 1973; further *Einführung in die strukturelle Linguistik* (Vorlesung Tübingen, 1967/68; autorisierte Nachschrift besorgt von Gunter Narr und Rudolf Windisch), Tübingen (Romanisches Seminar), 1969; further, Coseriu, *Sprache, Strukturen und Funktionen*, XII Aufsätze, Tübingen, 1970; *Einführung in die strukturelle Betrachtung des Wortschatzes* (TBL, 14), Tübingen, 1970 [= German version of "Structure lexicale et enseignement du vocabulaire" (with the discussion), in *Actes Ier Coll. Int. Ling. Appl.*, Nancy, 1966, and of the article "Les structures lexématiques" in *Probleme der Semantik*, Wiesbaden, 1968]; "Les universaux linguistiques (et les autres)" in *Proceedings of the Eleventh Intern. Congress of Linguists (Bologna-*

At this point, I should like to express my gratitude to all those colleagues and friends who accompanied the evolution of this book throughout the last 15 years or helped me in one way or another – many names which I mentioned in the Spanish editions – ; most of all my friend Klaus Heger, with whom I am continuing to discuss all problems of semantics and general linguistics.

I am further grateful to William C. Brown, Jr. – an American linguist who took my courses in semantics at El Colegio de México in 1972 – for the English translation (from the Spanish edition), by no means an easy task. G. A. Padley (Université Laval, Québec) was kind enough to clarify with me many difficult passages in the English translation. And finally I am very grateful to my colleague Rebecca Posner (University of York), who undertook a revision of the complete translation, and to Roger Wright (University of Liverpool) who was charged by the Publisher Basil Blackwell to take care of the publication and to whom I am indebted for many improvements.

Florence 1972), Bologna, I, 1974, 47–73; "Logique du langage et logique de la grammaire", in *Modèles logiques et niveaux d'analyse linguistique* (Actes Colloque Metz 1974), Paris (Klincksieck) 1977, 15–33; "Vers une typologie des champs lexicaux", *CahLex* 27, 1975-II, 30–51, and the volume *Strukturelle Bedeutungslehre*, edited by Horst Geckeler, Darmstadt (Wissensch. Buchgesellschaft) 1978 (a collection of the most important articles on structural semantics).

Within Coseriu's school, Horst Geckeler, *Strukturelle Semantik des Französischen* (Romanistische Arbeitshefte, edited by G. Ineichen and Chr. Rohrer, 6), Tübingen (Niemeyer), 1973; and independent of any school Peter Schifko, *Bedeutungstheorie, Einführung in die linguistische Semantik*, Stuttgart-Bad Cannstatt (Frommann-Holzboog) 1975.

As an introduction to general semiotics: Georges Mounin, *Introduction à la sémiologie*, Paris (Les Éditions de Minuit), 1970.

Introduction

"Neither in concepts nor in language is anything isolated"

Wilhelm von Humboldt: *Über die Verschiedenheit des menschlichen Sprachbaues und ihren Einfluß auf die geistige Entwicklung des Menschengeschlechts*, Berlin, 1836, p. 205.

For several years, the study of semantics has been making progress which can be considered revolutionary. "The study of content is the order of the day", writes Nicolas Ruwet in 1964, in an excellent survey of the contemporary state of general linguistics[1]. As we know, we are indebted to the nineteenth century for historical grammar, the basis of modern linguistics, to which de Saussure and the twentieth century added the fundamental notions of synchrony and structure, linguistic geography and the sociology of language. Instead of retracing the history of linguistics, which is generally known, I should like to emphasize what I consider to be the essential result of this evolution: a series of new and fruitful distinctions:

(1) between synchrony and diachrony,
(2) between language and speech, or between system, norm and speech (Coseriu),

---

[1] Nicolas Ruwet, "La linguistique générale aujourd'hui", in *Archives européennes de Sociologie*, 5, 1964, pp. 227–310. See also Uriel Weinreich, "On the Semantic Structure of Language", in *Universals of Language*, Cambridge/Mass. (The M.I.T. Press), 1963, pp. 114–71 (the "misguided positivism" of Bloomfield is overcome, p. 153).

(3) between phonetics and phonology,
(4) between the level of expression and the level of content,
(5) between form and substance (these last two in Hjelm-
     slev's terminology),
(6) between the object language and the metalanguage, on
     different levels, – a recent important distinction.

One could add still more to those already mentioned[2]. To
make distinctions is to introduce order, but is, at the same
time, to split up an essential unity. But such is the eternal
paradox of science, to divide single units in order to make
them clear.

As a branch of science, semantics is about seventy years old,
a respectable age. She has had daughters and sons, semasiological daughters and onomasiological sons perhaps, although I
can make no guarantee as to their sex. In any case, the family
is well-behaved, and to prove it one need only glance at
Quadri's historical–bibliographical manual[3]. The large number
of studies that already exist are for the most part the fruits of
traditional lexicology derived from linguistic geography and
the school of de Saussure. The theoretical foundation, then,
dates from the years 1900 to 1920, enriched by a series of
articles by Jud, Jaberg, von Wartburg and others[4]. But theoretical considerations remained on a secondary level – linked
especially, in any case, to questions of diachrony – in spite of
Trier's insistence on the importance of lexical fields, around

---

[2]"We consider the distinction between *denotation* and *designation*
to be essential to any workable program in semantic research", U.
Weinreich, op. cit., p. 154, n. 3.

[3]Bruno Quadri, *Aufgaben und Methoden der onomasiologischen
Forschung. Eine entwicklungsgeschichtliche Darstellung*, Bern
(Francke), 1952, xviii + 271 pp.

[4]For details of this evolution see Kurt Baldinger, *La semasiología,
Ensayo de un cuadro de conjunto*, Rosario (Universidad Nacional del
Litoral, Facultad de Filosofía y Letras), 1964, 55 pp. [= *Die
Semasiologie, Versuch eines Überblicks*, Berlin (Akademie-Verlag),
1957]. Translated into Spanish by Graciela García Montaño de
Gardella (with two appendices on the most recent evolution).

1930[5]. Ullmann, in about 1950, made an inventory of this evolution in an excellent synthesis, and at the same time established a body of synchronic doctrines[6] centred on the famous *name–concept–thing* triangle, the exterior form of which goes back to Ogden and Richards[7]. I myself have followed (in an article titled "Sémasiologie et onomasiologie", *RLiR* 28, 1964, 249–272; published as an appendix to this edition) the road which Ullmann had left open. At present scholars are trying to coordinate this traditional and semi-structural semantics – as Weinrich calls it – with the revolutionary pressures exerted from all sides, especially during the last few years: from

---

[5]See, for example, Suzanne Öhmann, "Theories of the 'Linguistic Field' ", in *Word*, 9, 1953, pp. 123–34; and now, especially, Horst Geckeler, *Zur Wortfelddiskussion . . .*, München (Wilhelm Fink), 1971: (= *Semántica estructural y teoría del campo léxico*, Madrid, 1976); also E. Coseriu, "Vers une typologie des champs lexicaux", *CahLex* 27, 1975, 30–51.

[6]S. Ullmann, *The Principles of Semantics*, [1]1951; [2]1957; *Semantics. An Introduction to the Science of Meaning*, Oxford (Blackwell), 1962, 278 pp. Applied to French: S. Ullmann, *Précis de sémantique française*, Bern (Francke), [1]1952, [2]1959; translated into Spanish: S. Ullmann, *Introducción a la semántica francesa*, traducción y anotación por Eugenio de Bustos Tovar, Madrid (C. S. I. C., Instituto "Miguel de Cervantes"), 1965, xvi, 483 pp. S. Ullmann, *Language and Style*, Collected Papers, Oxford (Blackwell), 1964, ix, 270 pp. (see my review in *ZrP*, 82, 1966, pp. 597–600); S. Ullmann, *Meaning and Style*, Collected Papers, Oxford (Blackwell), 1973, x, 175 pp [see my recent review in *ZrP* 89, 1973, 609]; also, the following articles: "Stylistics and Semantics" in *Literary Style: A Symposium* (ed. S. Chatman), Oxford (University Press), 1971, pp. 133–155; "Le vocabulaire, moule et norme de la pensée", in *Problèmes de la personne,* ed. I. Meyerson (Colloque du Centre de Recherches de Psychologie comparative, Ecole Pratique des Hautes Etudes, Sorbonne, 6e Section: Sciences économiques et sociales, Congrès et Colloques XIII), Paris–The Hague (Mouton), 1973, pp. 251–269 [= Original version of *Language and Style*, Chap. 10]; "How the Vocabulary grows", *Modern Languages* 54, 1973, pp. 1–8.

[7]Ogden and Richards's triangle in *The Meaning of Meaning*

structuralism[8], from automatic translation and general linguistics, from logic[9], and from information theory[10]. All these tend-

---

([1]1923, [10]1949 – fifth impression, 1960 p. 11) is reproduced here:

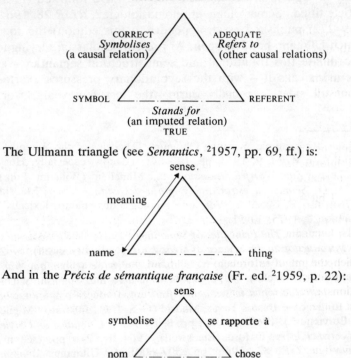

THOUGHT OR REFERENCE

CORRECT
Symbolises
(a causal relation)

ADEQUATE
Refers to
(other causal relations)

SYMBOL

REFERENT

Stands for
(an imputed relation)
TRUE

The Ullmann triangle (see *Semantics*, [2]1957, pp. 69, ff.) is:

sense

meaning

name

thing

And in the *Précis de sémantique française* (Fr. ed. [2]1959, p. 22):

sens

symbolise

se rapporte à

nom

chose

represénte
(rapport fictif)

[8]The structuralists began to be concerned with semantics in particular after the *VIIIe Cong. Int. des Linguistes*, Oslo, 1957; see below, Chapter 3, note 1.

[9]"The new approach to logic, usually called "symbolic", "mathematical", or "logistic", was essentially initiated by Gottlob Frege. Frege took as a starting point phrases instead of concepts, more precisely, a phrase structure with an empty slot in which there is a variable which can be replaced by individual objects or by classes". Franz Schmidt, *Zeichen und Wirklichkeit*, Stuttgart (Kohlhammer), 1966, p. 87.

[10]"According to information theory created by Claude E. Shannon in 1948, who based it on the calculation of probabilities and statistics – a theory which later also acquired importance in linguistics – one "bit" of information consists, in the first place, of symbols, such as letters, words, phrases, numbers. Quantitatively a "bit" of information is given when, from a quantity of symbols which are possible within the total of the signs, a selection can be made of preferred symbols, so that, based on this selection, the individual quantity of the information contributed by each symbol can be measured. This quantity, or rather size, called H, is measured by the smallest number of yes-and-no decisions enabling the receiver of the information to reconstruct it; starting with n selected symbols and s possible symbols, we arrive at the equation (according to Hartley, 1928):

$$H = n \cdot \log_2 s,$$

being the unit of measurement for the quantity of information, that is, the information content of each symbol, or the unit of counting (numerical unit) for binary decisions, equal to

$$1 \text{ bit} = 1 \log_2 2.$$

Shannon then generally calculated H for the integral value of a symbol i recurring with a determined probability. In such cases, it is always a question of a logarithmic number of binary decisions, by which the bit of information is defined mathematically, that is, of quantitative relations or proportions. The messages or communications, given their dependence on actual and potential signs, are subject to these relations. The concrete content of the information, which is all that interests the sender and receiver of the message, does not concern the information engineer at all (as in cybernetics). The qualitative determination of the message is obtained not through the content, but only by verification, that is to say, it is by mathematical determination that the message is conveyed by a fixed number of logarithmic operations. The concrete content, underlying the existing relations of magnitude, is known only by the sender and receiver of the message, since by understanding the symbols, they can treat them as signs. The logarithm on base 2 has been selected because the machines that transmit and formulate the signs (that is, signals, in the sense of cybernetics), for example, electronic digital computers, are so constructed that they concretize only two possible states, e.g. the "on" or "off" position of a relay, the switching on or off of an electric current, positive or negative magnetization, whether there is or is not a hole at a certain place on a perforated card; in this respect the

encies are connected; all (except Coseriu) are limited to the synchronic level and attempt to approach the realm of content with more precise methods, whether on the syntagmatic level or on the paradigmatic level. I shall limit myself to the paradigmatic level, the realm of "pure" lexicology, so to speak[11].

In this series of lectures, I shall attempt to follow with you my own road toward a *structural* semantics, a path which is still open and, I believe, full of promise. It is the road which goes

---

machines work in the same way as the yes-or-no decisions that must be made". Franz Schmidt, *Zeichen und Wirklichkeit, Linguistisch-semantische Untersuchungen*, Stuttgart (Kohlhammer), 1966, pp. 95 ff.

[11]H. Weinrich, in the review of a study by B. Pottier, sees the future of semantics from the syntagmatic side: "There will be a kind of semantics which will no longer be the semantics of the word, but rather the semantics of the phrase, semantics in which the determination by the context will have its full value" (*Rom. Phil.* 18, 1965, p. 458).

In the same sense Knud Togeby, "Grammaire, lexicologie et séman-tique" in *CahLex* 6, 1965, pp. 3–7: "so the lexicon must be represented as a complex of combinatory possibilities" (p. 4): "At last we come to *semantics*. In my view, this is only accessible via the behaviour of morphemes. It could be that morphemes have a sense and that this sense is the reason for the way they behave. There is a philosophical problem there with reference to which I would not dare to take up a position. All I know, and all anyone can know as a linguist, is that we have in front of us texts in which morphemes are distributed according to certain rules. *This syntactic behaviour is the only linguistic key that can open the door onto semantics*" (p. 5); "if we push these studies of combinatory possibilities as far as possible, perhaps we shall find confirmation in practice of Greimas' semantic analysis. But we cannot make this semantic analysis in a sure enough way unless we have built it on the foundations of the combinatory possibilities" (p. 7). See also, in this sense, Inger Rosengren, *Seman-tische Strukturen. Eine quantitative Distributionsanalyse einiger mittel-hochdeutscher Adjektive* (Lunder Germanist. Forschungen 38), Lund-Kopenhagen, 1966, 153 pp. We believe that both outlooks (syntagmatic and paradigmatic) are justified, and are, in fact, far from being contradictory. – See now Part II chapter 7.

from Ullmann's *triangle* to Heger's *trapezium*[12], which evolved within the framework of European scientific evolution, characterized especially by the names of Pottier[13], Greimas[14], and Coseriu[15]. I must excuse myself for speaking mainly of my

---

[12]Klaus Heger, "Die methodologischen Voraussetzungen von Onomasiologie und begrifflicher Gliederung", in *ZrP* 80, 1964, pp. 486–516 = "Les bases méthodologiques de l'onomasiologie et du classement par concepts", in *TraLiLi* (Strasbourg), III[1], 1965, pp. 7–32.

[13]B. Pottier, "Vers une sémantique moderne", in *TraLiLi*, II[1], 1964, pp. 107–37; *Recherches sur l'analyse sémantique en linguistique et en traduction méchanique*, Publications linguistiques de la Fac. des Lettres et Sciences Humaines de l'Univ. de Nancy (Série A: Linguistique appliquée et Traduction automatique, II), 1963, 38 pp. (reviewed by H. Weinrich, *Rom. Phil.* 18, 1965, pp. 456–58; Jean Bourguignon, *RLiR* 27, 1963, pp. 494–95). See also other studies by B. Pottier, especially "Du très général au trop particulier en analyse linguistique" (*TraLiLi*, I, 1963, pp. 9–16); *Introduction à l'étude des structures grammaticales fondamentales* Nancy, 1962, 48 pp. *Linguistique générale, théorie et description*, Paris (Klincksieck) 1974, 338 pp. There is now a Spanish translation of some articles published during the last fifteen years: B. Pottier, *Lingüística moderna y filología hispánica*, Spanish version by Martín Blanco Álvarez, Madrid (Gredos), 1968, 246 pp.

[14]A. J. Greimas, *Sémantique structurale, Recherche de méthode*, Paris (Larousse), 1966, 262 pp. [Ital. trans.: *La Semantica strutturale*, Milano (Rizzoli), 1968; Ger. trans.: *Strukturale Semantik*, Braunschweig (Friedr. Vieweg und Sohn), 1971]; cf. on these studies the article by Grosse, "Zur Neuorientierung der Semantik bei Greimas. Grundgedanken, Probleme und Vorschläge". *ZrP* 87, 1971, 359–393. Also from Greimas, *Modelli semiologici*, edited by P. Fabbri e G. Paioni, Urbino (Argalìa Editore), [1967]; *Du sens. Essais sémiotiques*, Paris (Ed. du Seuil), 1970; A. J. Greimas et al., *Essais de sémiotique poétique*, Paris (Larousse), 1972.

[15]E. Coseriu, *Teoría del lenguaje y lingüística general*, Madrid (Gredos), 1962, 327 pp.; "Pour une sémantique diachronique structurale", in *TraLiLi* (Strasbourg), II[1], 1964, 139–186; "Structure lexicale et enseignement du vocabulaire", in *Actes du Premier Colloque International de Linguistique appliquée* (Nancy, 26–31 octobre,

own evolution – it is the one I know best. As a result, the picture given here shows one line of the European evolution, with glances at others which, no doubt, would deserve a more complete description[16].

1964), Nancy, 1966, 175–217; "Das Phänomen der Sprache und das Daseinsverständnis des heutigen Menschen" [The phenomenon of speech and the understanding of present-day man], in *Die pädagogische Provinz* 21, 1967, 11–28; "Lexikalische Solidaritäten", in *Poetica*, I, 1967, 293–303; "Zur Vorgeschichte der strukturellen Semantik: Heyses Analyse des Wortfeldes 'Schall'," in *To Honor Roman Jakobson* (*Essays on the occasion of his seventieth birthday*), The Hague–Paris (Mouton), 1967, 489–98 [reprint 1970, see Preface].

[16]I do not discuss, for example, the theories of László Antal, *Questions of Meaning*, The Hague (Mouton), 1963, 95 pp. (see the review by G. Mounin, *La Linguistique*, II, 1, 1966, 151–52): *Content, Meaning and Understanding*, The Hague (Mouton), 1964, 63 pp. (see the critical review by G. Mounin in *La Linguistique* III, 2, 1967, pp. 151–54); nor North American semantics; see J. J. Katz and J. A. Fodor, "The Structure of a Semantic Theory", in *Language* 39, 1963, 170–210; translated into French: "Structure d'une théorie sémantique avec applications au français" (French examples were given instead of the original English ones), in *CahLex* 9, 1966, 39–72; Samuel Abraham and Ferenc Kiefer, *A Theory of Structural Semantics*, The Hague–Paris (Mouton), 1966, 98 pp. ("Our theory is based on transformational grammar"). For some more recent works see Preface to this edition.

Part I

ULLMANN'S TRIANGLE (OGDEN AND RICHARDS) REALITY – CONCEPT – WORD

1

Presentation of the Triangle

Ullmann's triangle is, I repeat, our starting point:

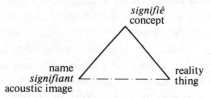

Figure 1

This triangle derives from that of Ogden and Richards (see above, Introduction note 7) and from Ferdinand de Saussure, on whose theories practically the whole modern science of language, traditional linguistics as well as structuralism, is based[1]. De Saussure, in his well-known system of oppositions,

---

[1]Of course many of de Saussure's ideas are found in earlier times; see the following recent articles: K. H. Rensch, "Ferdinand de Saussure und Georg von der Gabelentz, Übereinstimmungen und Gemeinsamkeiten dargestellt an der langue-parole Dichotomie sowie der diachronischen und synchronischen Sprachbetrachtung", in *Phonetica* (Basel/New York), 15, 1966, 32–41; K. H. Rensch, "Organismus-System-Struktur in der Sprachwissenschaft", in *Phonetica*, 16, 1967, 71–84; E. Coseriu, "L'arbitraire du signe" (see below, Ch. 2, note 2); E. Coseriu, "François Thurot [1768–1832]", in

contrasted synchrony, that is, the linguistic description of a given moment, with diachrony, which had dominated linguistics in the nineteenth century. The recognition of synchrony was accompanied by the realization that language is organized structurally. The elements of the language are not lacking in mutual relationships with neighbouring elements, but rather, they all form a connecting network, so that change in one element may involve change in another element, on each level of language, from sound (the system of the functional relations of sounds is the object of phonology), continuing on through morphology and syntax up to the lexicon. In addition, Gilliéron[2] had, independently of de Saussure, laid the foundations of linguistic geography and at the same time come to recognize structural relations. During the last seventy years, structural relations have increasingly occupied the centre of linguistic investigation; thus, Ullmann is right in saying that twentieth century linguistics differs from that of the nineteenth century primarily because of its structural orientation.

The triangle which we are discussing also leads us to the idea of structural relations. As I have already said, it is based ultimately on de Saussure, who distinguishes two parts within the word: an expression and a content, *signifiant* and *signifié* (see Fig. 2).

ZFSL 77, 1967, 30–34 [the triangle of *signifiant*, *signifié* and thing is found as far back as in the Stoics and in Augustine (*verbum*, *dicibile*, *res*), etc.]; José G. Herculano de Carvalho, "Segno e significazione in João de São Tomás" [born in 1589 in Lisbon], in *Portugiesische Forschungen der Görresgesellschaft*, Erste Reihe: *Aufsätze zur portugiesischen Kulturgeschichte*, 2. Band, Münster, 1961 152–76 ["vox → conceptus → res," p. 165]; concerning the general evolution of linguistics in the nineteenth century, see Siegfried Heinimann, "Zur Auffassung des Geschichtlichen in der Historischen Grammatik des 19. Jahrhunderts", in *Festgabe Hans von Greyerz zum sechzigsten Geburtstag*, Bern (Herbert Lang), 1967, 783–807.

[2]See Sever Pop and Rodica Doina Pop, *Jules Gilliéron, vie, enseignement, élèves, oeuvres, souvenirs* (Travaux publ. par le Centre international de Dialectologie générale près l'Université catholique de Louvain, fasc. IV), Louvain, 1959, viii + 196 pp.

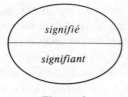

Figure 2

Signifiant is the synonym of *acoustic image*[3]; for example, the series of sounds $t + ei + b + l$. Nevertheless, this series of sounds does not become a word until it is associated with a certain representation, the *signifié*. So a word, or linguistic sign, is an acoustic image + representation (signification)[4].

---

[3]Heger (*TraLiLi*, III[1], 1965, p. 11), is right to distinguish them more precisely: "whereas the *signifié* should be understood as an exclusively psychological unit, with the *signifiant* it is difficult to decide whether it is

> an exclusively psychological unit
>   (*signifiant* = source of the stimulus),
> a psycho-physical unit
>   (*signifiant* = phonetic form)
> or an exclusively physical unit
>   (*signifiant* = acoustic image)".

In order to do justice to de Saussure, one should also read the article by R. Engler, "Rôle et place d'une sémantique dans une linguistique saussurienne", *Cahiers Ferdinand de Saussure* 28, 1973, 35–52.

[4]Here I leave to one side the difficult problem of the unity of the word (is *pomme de terre* one word?). On this, see K. Togeby, "Qu'est-ce qu'un mot", in *TCLC* 5, 1949, 97–111; F. Hiorth, "On defining 'word'," in *SL* 12, 1968, 1–26; Charles Müller, "Le mot; unité de texte et unité de lexique en statistique lexicographique", in *TraLiLi*, 1, 1963, 155–73 ("the two questions which have motivated this work are: 'Is the word a unit, a fraction of a unit, or two units?' and 'Are these two units the same word or two different words?' At the same time these two questions are included in a more general one, that of the linguistic sign, a psychological reality which is hard to

Table, in English, brings to mind the more or less schematic representation of a piece of furniture, which is, as a result, a schematic image (I prefer the term *mental object*). By virtue of this image, *table* is a word for an English speaker, but not for a German. Therefore, a word always consists of two parts: a form (= *signifiant*) and content (later we shall say: form of expression + form of content). We shall see what far-reaching repercussions this double nature of the linguistic sign, of the word, has for language and for the science of language. This double nature is irreducible. Bipolarity is a fundamental fact of language – *without bipolarity there is no natural language.*

But to these two elements, the acoustic image and the schematic representation which this image evokes, there is added yet a third, an extralinguistic phenomenon, reality itself. The acoustic image *table* only brings to mind a schematic representation of the thing. If I say, "Tomorrow I'm going to buy a table", I do not yet know which table I shall buy. *Table* evokes the category. And if I say, "Yesterday I bought a table", I know what the table is like in reality, but the person I am speaking to does not; he only has an idea of the category (see Figure 3). This may seem very elementary and obvious,

---

measure by absolutely objective procedures," p. 173; "One must admit that there is no perfect norm, because the complex and unstable character of language is never fully amenable to quantification," p. 172). See also Otto Ducháček, "Le mot et le concept", in *Sborník prací filosofické fakulty brněnské university*, XI, 1962, řada A 10, 149–53; A. Rosetti, "Autour du mot", in *Mélanges Gardette*, *TraLiLi*, 4[1], 1966, 427–28; José G. Herculano de Carvalho, *Lições de linguística*, 3[a]. ed., Coimbra, 1962–1963, 434 ff. (he distinguishes between three types of words; *cavalo*; *altifalante*; *guarda-sol*); A. Martinet, "Le mot", in *Diogène* 51, 1965, 39–53; Christian Metz, "Remarque sur le mot et sur le chiffre. A propos des conceptions sémiologiques de Luis J. Prieto", in *La Linguistique* (Presses Universitaires) 2, 1967, 41–56; Christian Rohrer, *Die Wortzusammensetzung im modernen Französischen*, Thesis, Tübingen, 1967, 4 ff.; Klaus Heger, *Monem, Wort und Satz*, Tübingen, 1971, especially pp. 61 ff; also Heger 1976 (see below II Chapter 7).

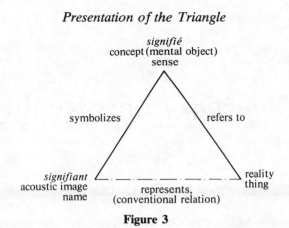

Figure 3

but it has far-reaching consequences for language and the science of language. De Saussure saw this clearly, saying: "The linguistic sign does not join a thing and a name, but rather a concept [mental object] and an acoustic image", and in the Middle Ages the scholastics expressed the same thing through the well-known formula *Vox significat mediantibus conceptibus*[5].

In its present triangular form, these relations were first set out by Ogden and Richards, *The Meaning of Meaning*, 1923 (4th. ed. 1936)[6]. I am adopting the somewhat simplified form used by S. Ullmann[7].

[5]These fundamental problems are very clearly summed up in S. Ullmann, *Précis de sémantique française*, [2]1959, pp. 19 ff.; *The Principles of Semantics*, [2]1957, pp. 69 ff.; *Semantics. An Introduction to the Science of Meaning*, Oxford (Blackwell), 1962, 278 pp.

[6]See above, Introd. note 7.

[7]The best explanation of Ullmann's triangle is in his article "The Concept of Meaning in Linguistics", in *Archivum Linguisticum* 8, 12–20.

2

Signifiant and Reality

(a) LACK OF MOTIVATION

But let us take a more detailed look at each one of these relationships. It is easy to understand that there is no direct relation between *signifiant* and reality. Otherwise, how would it be possible to designate the same thing in different languages with different acoustic images: *table, mesa, Tisch*? In other words, the *signifiant* is not motivated by reality[1]; the linguistic sign is arbitrary[2]. If this were not the case, it would not be possible for the form to change, that is, there would be no history of language. To anyone who has ever learned a second language this is obvious. Only the person who does not speak or understand any language besides his mother tongue tends to identify word and thing; like the Tyrolese peasant who, upon returning from Italy, told his neighbours about that wonderful country. He added, however, that the Italians must

---

[1] Concerning this and other related problems, see also S. Ullmann, "Descriptive Semantics and Linguistic Typology", in *Word* 9, 1953, 225–40, especially pp. 229 ff.

[2] This theory has a long tradition from Aristotle to de Saussure, on whom modern linguistics is based; see E. Coseriu, "L'arbitraire du signe. Zur Spätgeschichte eines aristotelischen Begriffes", in *ASNSL* 204, 1967, 81–112; Rudolf Engler, "Théorie et critique d'un principe saussurien: L'arbitraire du signe", in *CFS* 19, 1962, 5–66; Rudolf Engler, "Compléments à l'arbitraire du signe", in *CFS* 21, 1964, 25–32.

be very stupid, because, when referring to the animal that everyone recognizes as a *Pferd*, they insisted on calling it a *cavallo*[3]. And a Chilean colleague, Professor Echeverría, told me that his grandfather had said "I cannot believe that everyone will not understand me if only I speak very slowly"! The basis of these anecdotes is that words and reality are identified; but the humorous effect consists in the fact that, except for this Tyrolese peasant and this Chilean grandfather, everyone knows that the same object is designated in different ways in different languages; putting it in theoretical terms, there is no direct relation between the word and reality.

(b) ONOMATOPOEIC MOTIVATION

But someone might raise the objection that there do exist words which are imitative, or rather, onomatopoeic, in which the object is incorporated directly into the language, such as *ding dong* for the sound of bells. This is, in fact, the only lexical category in which there does exist a certain direct relation. But on closer observation, even these cases involve a process of abstraction. The thing itself is not incorporated into the language – only an acoustic signal[4]. For this reason onomatopoeic

---

[3]The anecdote is recounted by Martinet, *Éléments de linguistique générale*, Paris, 1960 (prologue). For other examples, see W. von Wartburg, *Problemas y métodos de la lingüística*, Madrid, 1951, pp. 290 ff.; in the second French edition of 1963, p. 187; *Problems and Methods in Linguistics*, revised ed. with the collaboration of Stephen Ullmann, translated by Joyce M. H. Reid, Oxford (Blackwell) 1969, pp. 171 ff.

[4]See especially Ruth Lehmann, *Le sémantisme des mots expressifs en Suisse romande* (= *Romanica Helvetica* 34), Bern (Francke) 1949, and the review of S. Heinimann, in *VR* 13, 144–148; see, further, the studies of Mario Wandruszka, "Poésie et sonorités und das Problem der phonetischen Motivation", in *Romanistisches Jahrbuch* 16, 1965, 34–48, and E. Coseriu, "L'arbitraire du signe", in *ASNSL* 204, 1967, 81–112, especially 105, 107, 109. José G. Herculano de Carvalho, *Lições de linguística*, 3rd ed., Coimbra, 1962–1963, pp. 181 ff., distinguishes between *pure and conventional onomatopoeias* (the latter may be lexicalized or non-lexicalized).

words can have different forms in different languages, according to the characteristic considered as typical. For example, German-speaking Swiss sometimes call a motor scooter *töff töff*, instead of *prun prun*, the more general German phrase; the dog is called *bow-wow* in English, *wauwau* in German, *guau-guau* in Spanish, *vauuau* in Portuguese, *wanwan* in Japanese, *gnaf-gnaf* in French and *hoghog* in Kaingan (Aryon Rodrigues gave me this final example); a cock's crow is represented as *cock-a-doodle-doo* in English, *kikiriki* in Spanish, *kikeriki* in German and *coquericot* in French, etc[5]. Once these onomatopoeic words become part of the language, they often evolve just as other words do; that is, through phonetic changes they can lose their onomatopoeic character. In which case they join the great mass of unmotivated words (see, for instance, the entry on PAPILIO, FEW 7, 581a).

---

[5]"People sometimes talk of so-called "expressive" words that imitate the noises of nature, onomatopoeia. But even in these cases it is agreed that languages do not use identical terms, and, therefore, nature does not dictate them. The noises of animals, of dogs and cats for example, are given different onomatopoeic terms in French and in English. The fact is that the phonological system of a language plays its rôle even in these extreme cases. The confusion between language and reality is called 'verbal magic' . . ." (Knud Togeby, "Langue, science, littérature et réalité", in *Revue Romane* 8, 1973, 298–303, especially p. 298). Compare the selection of characteristic traits in the designations of secondary motivation: "The *elephant*, for example, is called in one language 'the one who drinks twice' (because he first drinks with his trunk and then with his mouth); in another language he is called 'the one with two tusks'. Neither of these designations is false, but neither is absolutely correct, either; both are accepted, since they have to do with something distinctive about the elephant which catches our attention". Karl Löwith, "Die Sprache als Vermittler von Mensch und Welt", in *Beiträge zu Philosophie und Wissenschaft, Wilhelm Szilasi zum 70. Geburtstag,* Munich (Francke), 1960, 141–60 (especially p. 151).

(c) INDIRECT MOTIVATION AND POPULAR ETYMOLOGY

In most words, the motivation is not primary, that is, they are not motivated by reality. Nevertheless, we must quickly add that *secondary* motivations are extremely frequent. For example, the noun *fox* is not motivated, but the verb *outfox* ("to get the better of someone by cunning") is motivated. Cp. Spanish *encabritarse* and German *sich bäumen* ("to rear up", of a horse), respectively from *cabra* (goat) and *Baum* (tree). Nevertheless, here there is no direct motivation through reality, but only an indirect one through *fox*[6]. Every metaphor depends on such indirect motivations, and *outfox* is only a lexicalized metaphor. We can even go much further: all semantics is based on secondary motivations since all new shades of meaning are motivated by the existing ones. There is a characteristic discrepancy between the lack of motivation of primary words and the ever perceptible (human) need for motivation.

Evidence of this specifically human need for motivation is seen in the interpretations and modifications of popular etymology. We give one of the best known constellations the names *Great Bear* or *Great Dipper* or *the Plough* (in many languages it is called *Great Chariot*). The names *Great Dipper*, *Plough* and *Great Chariot* are self-evident: the constellation does look like a dipper with a long handle or a plough or chariot with a wagon pole. But where is the similarity with a bear? Even the most active imagination would be unable to find the slightest resemblance. Much of this was unclear in the specialized literature on the subject until Szemerényi observed that *chariot* is the original and authentic name, while *bear* is based on a misunderstanding of popular etymology.

---

[6]See W. von Wartburg, *Problèmes et méthodes de la linguistique*, Paris (Presses Universitaires), ²1963, 136–47 [= *Problems and Methods in Linguistics*, 127–137], and also E. Coseriu, "L'arbitraire du signe", in *ASNSL* 204, 1967, 99 (speaking of Christian Wolf), and 110 (speaking of de Saussure).

The image of the chariot was also used in ancient Mesopotamia; in Akkadia the same word meant "chariot" and "bear". This was misunderstood by the Greeks and translated as "bear". At this point, the name "Bear" was assured for the constellation in the future:

$$\text{"chariot"}$$
$$|$$
Akkadian *eriq(q)u* "Chariot" + "Bear"
$$|$$
$$\text{Gr. "bear"}[7].$$

The peculiar thing about this example is the fact that we are not upset by the fact that the image and the reality do not correspond to each other. Or have any of you in fact ever been surprised by the name *Great Bear*? If so, you are very observant, an honourable exception. In general, for popular etymology any hypothetical explanation is sufficient. It is enough to be aware that there is a motivation[8]. In some Ger-

---

[7]Oswald Szemerényi, "Principles of Etymological Research in the Indo-European Languages", in *Innsbrucker Beiträge zur Kulturwissenschaft* 15, 1962, p. 190. No less interesting is the popular etymology based on the false interpretation of *septentrion*: "The seven plough-oxen" for the same constellation (Lat. *trio* "ox"), an interpretation already found in Antiquity. This vision of the seven stars of the Great Bear as seven oxen also goes beyond the bounds of the imagination. Szemerényi demonstrates that *septentrio* goes back to *septemsterion* "seven stars" (ib., pp. 188 ff.). Once again, popular etymology leads us to an only apparently motivated vision, with no actual basis in reality.

[8]This tendency towards secondary motivation – even if it is not fair or logical – can bring about a change on the level of expression. In Portuguese *canapé* was changed to *camapé* because of identification with *cama* "bed" and *pé* "foot", "chair-leg", although legs are not distinctive features of a couch; pseudo-motivation is enough (the example – studied from a different point of view – is found in José G. Herculano de Carvalho, "Inovação e criação na linguagem", a special edition of the *Revista da Universidade de Coimbra* (Coimbra) 20, 1962, 18 pp., especially pp. 9 ff.).

man dialects the word *Mönch* (monk) is used for the cross-bar of a window ("Fensterkreuz"). Perhaps one could imagine a monk with his arms open, if one is looking for an explanation. In reality, the monk has nothing to do with this extension of meaning. *Mönch* ("cross-bar"), is the translation of Medieval French *moinel* ("cross-bar"), which was felt to have been derived from *moine* < MONACHUS, and translated analogously. This *moinel*, however, comes from MEDIANUS "situated in the middle"[9], whereupon no further explanation is necessary for its use as the word for "cross-bar". It would be interesting to examine the countless popular etymologies for their real force of expression (compare, for example, the ideal of the *green eyes*, which has no basis in fact)[10].

---

[9]*Fenestre à moyen* is older. See *FEW*, 6[1], 580b and 587b.

[10]See Th. Heinermann, "Die grünen Augen", in *RF* 58, 1944, 18–40; Harri Meier, "Os olhos verdes na literatura", in *Ensaios de filologia românica*, Lisbon, 1948, 191–206; E. Glässer, "Die grünen Augen im portugiesischen Mittelalter und das galizianische Schönheitsideal", in *GRM* 40 (= N. F. 9), 1959, 351–59.

3

The *Signifiant*

(a) POLYSEMY: THE SEMASIOLOGICAL FIELD

Another result of the lack of motivation of words is the fundamental fact that one word can have several meanings – *polysemy*, in other words. The same acoustic image can be the symbol for different realities; that is, it can have differing contents or significations. What, for example, does the Spanish *corona* mean? *Corona* can signify the crown of a king or a wreath of flowers. Although they are two very different things, look different and have different functions, in the Spanish Academy Dictionary they are grouped together under one meaning: "a ring of branches or flowers, natural or artificial, or of precious metal, with which the head is encircled; sometimes a mere ornament, sometimes an honorary emblem, sometimes a symbol of dignity". So this first meaning corresponds to a wide field of reality; and this first meaning is followed in the Academy Dictionary by twenty-four further

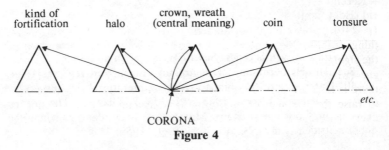

Figure 4

14

ones; thus *corona* is also used for an "old coin", or even several coins; *corona* can also mean "tonsure", "halo", "top of a hill", "the forward part of a fortification", etc. If we relate this to our triangle, this means that within one *signifiant* (acoustic image) a whole series of meanings leads to a whole series of representations or mental objects (see Fig. 4). This "fan" of significations constitutes the *field of significations*, the *semasiological field*[1]. At this point, then, we meet our first linguistic structure, the semasiological structure. It is not the only one, but it is the most obvious.

(b) THE CONTEXT

If a word can have several meanings, we can then pose immediately the next question: How does the listener work out which of these meanings is the one intended in each case? He works it out on the basis of the broader linguistic structure which we can call the *syntagmatic structure*. We do not speak with isolated words but with sentences. The isolated word is put into a broader context, and through this it is decided what is meant by the individual word; i.e. the context determines

---

[1]On these problems, see the studies by Rulon Wells, "Is a Structural Treatment of Meaning Possible?", in *Reports for the Eighth International Congress of Linguists* (Oslo, Aug. 5–9, 1957), Oslo University Press [2 vol., 347 pp. + suppl. I–II], pp. 197–209 [see *RFE.* 44, 1961, p. 207]; Louis Hjelmslev, "Dans quelle mesure les significations des mots peuvent-elles être considérées comme formant une structure?", id., pp. 268–86 [see *RFE* 44, 1961, p. 209].
– Recently Ramón Trujillo, *Elementos de semántica lingüística*, Madrid (Ed. Cátedra) 1976, has written: "Polysemy, then, does not exist" (p. 240), "polysemy is not an actual fact: it only exists if we look at things from the point of view of the *signifiant*, or rather from that of the *signifiant* on its own" (ib.). He is here confusing the level of *langue* (where there is polysemy) and that of *parole* (where normally there is not). Besides, Trujillo contradicts himself: "It is possible . . . to raise the problem of polysemy as a structural factor existing in every language . . ." (p. 242) and: "most of the difficulties arise through polysemy"! (p. 250).

the meaning within the concrete linguistic situation[2]. This determinative function of the context is so efficient that we can even use the wrong word; in general, the listener will correctly understand what is meant, and insert the right word in place of the wrong one. Even so, it can also happen that in spite of using the right word, the contextual determination remains incomplete, and the listener will not understand what the speaker is trying to say. In this way there arises what we call a misunderstanding. This occurs often with newspaper headlines, which offer only a very limited context. When I read recently the headline *Ball in Paris* in a German newspaper, I naturally thought of a dance, a *Ball*. But the article, that is, the context, revealed that *Ball* referred to the American Undersecretary of State, George Ball[3].

---

[2]In the sense of *verbal context*, and not of *idiomatic context* or *extraverbal context*. Concerning this triple differentiation, which is necessary and correct, see E. Coseriu, "Determinación y entorno," in *Teoría del lenguaje y lingüística general*, Madrid (Gredos), 1962, pp. 282–323, especially pp. 313, ff.

[3]Here is a polysemic joke told in Latin America, where *vivo* has two meanings: "alive", and "clever".

"¿Cuántos hijos tiene?"	(How many children have you got?)
"Siete"	(Seven)
"¿Todos vivos?"	(All alive?)
"No, uno trabaja"	(No, one is working)

On the bumper of a car in Bogotá I read "Baja como el peso y sube como el dólar": Get out/Go down like the peso and come in,/go up, like the dollar; a play on the double meanings of *bajar* and *subir*. See also Mauro de Almeida, *Filosofia dos párachoques* (Instituto Joaquim Nabuco de Pesquisas Sociais, Ministerio da Educação e Cultura, Recife, 1963). For example: *Entre sem bater* (usually, 'come in without knocking') "the request of a motorist who surely dislikes those who come into his car and make the whole bodywork tremble when they slam the door", p. 103; a play on two meanings of *bater* (knock, slam); etc.

[Editor's note: cp. the modern Merseyside joke, "I'm not working class, I've got a job"]

So if the word is determined primarily through the context, we must wonder how there can be dictionaries. In a dictionary, the word is isolated, presented without a context, and despite this, with all its acceptations. This is possible because the dictionary replaces the context with a "definition". In the realities of speech, the twenty-five meanings of *corona* are determined by means of twenty-five different textual relations; this is what happens in the dictionary with the help of twenty-five different definitions. The dictionary, which takes as a starting point the external form of the words, is alphabetically ordered in order to present the semasiological field of each word (acoustic image), that is, the structure of its meanings. Through these considerations we have also implicitly sketched out a first and provisional definition of *signification* or meaning (and thus, the answer to a question much discussed in linguistic science); signification associates a certain acoustic image with a particular schema of representation, that is, with a particular mental object (the concept, in Ullmann's triangle).

(c) UNITS AND LEVELS

The *signifiant* – as we saw in the preceding chapter – bears a semasiological field. The linguistic sign brings together a *signifiant* and a *signifié*. But what is a linguistic sign? We have already referred to this difficulty of defining a *word* (chapter 1, note 4). Pottier is now distinguishing *mot* (*lexie*) and lexeme[4].

---

[4]Pottier defines the *lexie* (lexeme) as "unité de comportement". He distinguishes between the *lexie simple* ("coïncide avec le mot: *chien*"), the *compound lexie* (*brise-glace*, etc.), the *complex lexie* (*pomme de terre, au fur et à mesure*, etc.), see "Présentation de la linguistique, Fondements d'une théorie," *TraLiLi*, V, 1, 1967, p. 16. Pottier distinguishes between the word (*le mot*) and the lexeme *lexie*: "The *mot* is the smallest compound unit. Every word is composed of morphemes" [= moneme in our terminology]. "There are in French two types of words: words of lexeme plus grammeme" [= morpheme in our terminology], "words of grammeme(s) . . . three classes of words: lexical words, grammatical words, substitutes" (ib., p. 15). Since

Often the word or *lexie* is made up of a combination of two meaningful units:

> "farmer" = *farm*   + *-er*

> word or *lexie*   meaningful unit + meaningful unit

> *lexeme*   + *morpheme*

In this case the word or *lexie* is made up of a *lexeme* and of a *morpheme*. Both are meaningful units. The only difference between the two is the fact that we can establish a closed set of morphemes; lexemes, on the other hand, constitute an open list (and the number of lexemes is much greater than the number of morphemes)[5]. We call the minimal meaningful unit the *moneme*:

MONEME

MORPHEME   LEXEME
(limited inventory) (unlimited inventory)

The moneme[6], whether morpheme or lexeme[7], is the smallest

---

these distinctions are not important within the framework of our study, we shall make no difference between *word* and *lexie*. (There is also now a Spanish edition, see n. 6.)

[5]*Morphemes* are often bound forms and *lexemes* are often free forms, but not always; there are *free morphemes* (French *moi*, as opposed to *je*, a bound form) and *bound lexemes* (for example, *him-* in Germ. *Himbeere*; *-di* in Fr. *Lundi, mardi*, etc.); see Klaus Heger, "La conjugaison objective en français et en espagnol," *Langages* (Didier/Larousse), 3, 1966, pp. 19–39 (especially p. 22). See also the Spanish edition, *La conjugación objectiva en castellano y en francés*, Instituto Caro y Cuervo, Bogotá, 1967, 23 pp., especially p. 4: *tele* in *teléfono, telégrafo, televisión*, etc. (special edition of *Thesaurus*, 22, 1967) reprinted in K. Heger, *Teoría semántica* II, 1974, 87–105.

[6]B. Pottier now uses a different terminology:

morphème

morphème grammatical   morphème lexical
or grammème   or *lexème*
(limited inventory)   (unlimited inventory)

unit with two facets, so to speak: it is at the same time a *form of expression* (*signifiant*) and *form of content* (*signifié*); the moneme reflects the fundamental bipolarity of language (without this bipolarity, as we have seen, there is no language).

Analyzing the moneme as *signifiant* we arrive at other units which are not meaningful, but are still distinctive units:

phoneme	*syllable, phonetic word*, etc.
minimal distinctive unit	non-minimal distinctive units

The phoneme, as a matter of fact, is not a bearer of meaning, but it plays an important distinctive rôle: thus, in English, *seed*, *siege*, *seek*, *seal*, *seem*, *seen*, *seep*, *sees*, *seat*, and *seethe* are distinguished by just one "sound", which we call a *phoneme* precisely when it serves to distinguish between two or more "words" (= monemes). To put it another way, the phoneme is a sound which serves to differentiate on the level of *language* (*langue*); individual variations of pronunciation are only phonetic variants on the level of *speech* (*parole*). Phonology studies sounds insofar as they have distinctive functions. In general, monemes and words are made up of two or more phonemes (there are, however, extreme cases where there is only one phoneme, such as the case of French *eau*, /o/, "water", in which the phoneme is at the same time the

---

See his article "Présentation de la linguistique, Fondements d'une théorie", in *TraLiLi*, V, 1, 1967, pp. 7–60 (especially pp. 14–15 and 59–60): *Lingüística moderna y filología hispánica*, 3rd ed. Madrid 1967; *Lingüística general*, Madrid, 1976.

[7]The distinction between *morpheme* and *lexeme*, however, is not absolute. See, for example, Pottier, "Sémantique du fini et sémantique du non-fini", Actes du 10th Cong. Int. des Linguistes, Bucharest, 1967, II, Bucharest 1970 385–89. Harald Weinrich, "Semantik der Metapher", *Folia Linguistica* (Acta Societatis Linguisticae Europeae), 1, 1967, pp. 3–17 [especially p. 7], argues that morphemes have a very broad meaning, because of which they lend themselves to metaphors much less than do lexemes, which have a precise and more limited meaning.

moneme and the word). As we see, the phoneme plays a rôle similar to that of the context; by means of phonemes we distinguish between different words as bearers of semasiological fields; by means of the context, we distinguish the significations of each word. Thus, phonemes (the phonological structure) make the preliminary organization of the meaningful units; the context (the syntagmatic structure) has the function of semantically specifying these meaningful units, which are still complex[8].

Both distinctive units and meaningful units can be studied at increasingly high levels:

distinctive units:
    phoneme   minimal distinctive unit
    syllable   ⎱
    phonetic word ⎰   non-minimal distinctive units
    context   level of phonology of the context
                                or syntagmatic phonology

meaningful units
    moneme   minimal meaningful unit
    (morpheme or lexeme)
    group of monemes   ⎫
    (word, compound words[9],
    idioms, etc.)   ⎬ non-minimal meaningful units
    sentence
    literary genre
    etc.   ⎭

---

[8]Concerning the analogies and differences between the different levels, see E. Coseriu, "Pour une sémantique diachronique structurale," in *TraLiLi*, II, 1964, pp. 139–86, passim; G. Mounin, *Les problèmes théoriques de la traduction*, 1963, passim; Albrecht Neubert, *Analogien zwischen Phonologie und Semantik*, *Zeichen und System der Sprache*, vol. III, Berlin (Akademie-Verlag), 1966, pp. 106–16; José Pedro Rona, "Les parties du discours, un niveau d'organisation du langage", Actes du 10th Congr. Int. des Linguistes, *Résumés des Communications*, Bucharest, 1967; Bucharest 1970 337–41, Tübingen 1977 (Tübinger Beitrage zu Linguistik, ed. by Gunter Narr, 78).

[9]Concerning compound words, see the study by Christian Rohrer,

At different levels, we can discover which paradigmatic systems the units belong to or examine their realizations within multiple contexts; that is, we can study them in their *paradigmatic* framework or in their *syntagmatic* framework. The family of words is a paradigmatic framework.

The word or *lexie*, the object of lexicology, is, as we see, a complex unit (a non-minimal meaningful unit), analyzable into smaller units which are meaningful and distinctive (except where we are dealing with borderline cases); on the other hand it is put into larger syntagmatic structures. Language consists of a complex and complicated interplay of units with different functions which combine on different levels:

```
   4        2              3           2    2   4
        ⏜          ⏜            ⏜      ⏜
...n - o - n  –  k - ə - n - f - ɔ: - m  –  i - s - t – s ...
   1  1  1    1  1  1  1  1   1  1  1  1
```

1 = phonemes (minimal distinctive unit).
2 = morphemes (minimal meaningful units in a closed set), "non-", "-ist", "-s".
3 = lexeme (minimal meaningful unit in an open list), "conform".
4 = context (syntagmatic framework).

It is interesting to note that there are considerable quantitative differences from 1 to 4, which correspond to the outline of traditional grammar: 1, Phonology; 2, Morphology; 3, Lexicology; 4, Syntax. The number of *phonemes* in each language is limited and determinable, often between 20 and 50. The number of *morphemes*, also comprising a closed list, is greater, but still delimitable; we estimate that this number might reach a few hundred. The number of *lexemes* is considerably higher, but even when one includes technical and scientific termi-

---

Die Wortzusammensetzung im modernen Französisch (Doctoral thesis), Tübingen, 1967, ii + 263 pp. (2[d] ed. 1977). Rohrer was a student of Coseriu's.

nology, the *lexies* will hardly be more than 100,000 in the dictionaries.

This rapid characterization of linguistic units and levels[10] was necessary for a better understanding of the nature of the word as a complex linguistic sign and of the *signifiant* as bearer of a semasiological field. Before discussing the equally complex problems related to concepts and their relation to reality, we shall examine the problem of homonymy and its relation to polysemy.

(d) HOMONYMY AND POLYSEMY

If words coincide phonetically in their historical development, that is, if they coincide in their phonological structure, we speak diachronically of *homonymy*:

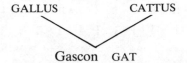

GALLUS   CATTUS

Gascon GAT

From the synchronic point of view, *gat* has two meanings: "cock" and "cat". Synchronically homonymy is a kind of polysemy, one word with two meanings[11]. On the other hand,

---

[10]See now the much more elaborate hierarchy of the different linguistic units set up by Klaus Heger, *Monem, Wort und Satz*, Tübingen 1971; *Monem, Wort, Satz und Text*, 1976.

[11]See Otto Ducháček, "L'homonymie et la polysémie", in *VR*, 21, 1962, pp. 49–56; Klaus Heger, "Homographie, Homonymie und Polysemie", in *ZRP*, 79, 1963, pp. 471–91, and "Temporale Deixis und Vorgangsquantität ("Aspekt" und "Aktionsart")", in *ZRP*, 83, 1967, pp. 512–82 (especially §1.2). On polysemy and homonymy, see also Charles Muller, "Homonymie et polysémie dans l'élaboration du lexique contemporain", *Études de linguistique appliquée*, I, 1962, pp. 49–54; G. Gougenheim, "Homonymie et polysémie", in: Conseil de l'Europe/Council of Europe (Strasbourg 16 janvier 1963), Comité de l'enseignement supérieur de la recherche, Projet 10/21 *Méthodes d'enseignement des Langues Vivantes* (Compte rendu du Colloque sur

in the linguistic consciousness of the speakers, one word with two meanings which are "very far" from each other can be felt to be two words, when no relationship between the two meanings can be established. *Gat*, "cock" and "cat", have probably come to be felt as one word, since both meanings refer to domestic animals; that is, on the plane of content there is an intimate relationship, although they are two different words from a historical point of view. Conversely, a word can evolve semantically in such different directions that the relationship between the two meanings is lost, with the result that, in the linguistic feelings of the speakers, two homonyms are born. Take, for example:

French *voler* "to fly"
French *voler* "to rob"

which both come from Latin *volare*[12].

Thus, on the level of synchrony, two words can be felt as

---

les Moyens d'Enquête sur la Connaissance et la Diffusion du Vocabulaire, Strasbourg 19–21, nov. 1962), pp. 10–20, 54–55; Johannes Klare, "Zum Problem der Differenzierung von Homonymie und Polysemie", in *Omagiu lui Alexandru Rosetti la 70 de ani*, Bucharest, 1965, pp. 445–50; Rebecca Posner, "Homonymy, Polysemy, and Semantic Change", in *Language Sciences* (Indiana University, Research Center for the Language Sciences), 27, Oct. 1973, 1–8 [of diachronic orientation]. Recently: Ekkehard Zöfgen, "Polysemie oder Homonymie? Zur Relevanz und Problematik ihrer Unterscheidung in Lexikographie und Textlinguistik", in *Lebendige Romania* (Homage H.-W. Klein), Göppingen 1976, pp. 425–464.

On the synchronic level we can define *homonymy* as two sememes (see below) which have no seme in common, but which are joined to the same moneme. See, for example, José G. Herculano de Carvalho, *Lições de linguística*, 3rd ed., Coimbra, 1962–1963, p. 145.

[12]See S. Ullmann, "Sémantique et Étymologie", in *Cahiers de l'Association Internationale des Études Françaises*, 11, 1959, pp. 322–35, especially p. 326.

being one word with two meanings, and one word with two meanings can be felt as two words. Homonymy can become polysemy and polysemy can become homonymy. We see, then, that the differentiation introduced by de Saussure between synchrony and diachrony corresponds in fact to two different perspectives for examining and interpreting the same object.

4

Reality and Mental Object

(a) THE DETERMINATION OF THE MENTAL OBJECT IN THE GENERAL LANGUAGE

One could say that *reality* itself is not an object of linguistics, since its existence lies beyond language. Language is already a transposition of reality. But precisely because of this, I can only understand this transposition of reality when I consider it in relation to reality itself. In other words, linguistics cannot overlook the *mental object/concept* (notions which we shall try to distinguish in the Second Part) which, at the same time, have a relationship to extralinguistic reality. Language is linked to reality through conceptual representation: *vox significat mediantibus conceptibus*[1]. Or, as Humboldt has already said: "When in the soul, the idea arises that language is not simply a means of exchange for mutual understanding, but a genuine *world*, which the spirit, by its own efforts, has to put between itself and objects; then the soul is well on the way to discovering more and more of that *world* and to projecting the spirit into it"[2].

---

[1]See above, Chapter 1, Notes 1 and 5.

[2]W. von Humboldt, *Über die Verschiedenheit des menschlichen Sprachbaues und ihren Einfluss auf die geistige Entwicklung des Menschengeschlechts*, Berlin, 1836, p. 205. See also Wartburg, *Einführung*, [2]1962, p. 170 [*Problems and Methods in Linguistics,* Oxford 1969, p. 162]. See also O. Ducháček, "Le mot et le concept", in *Sborník prací filosofické fakulty brněnske university*, XI, 1962, řada

As a result, we cannot ignore the much discussed question of the relation between reality and concept. Georges Mounin correctly points out:

> Semantics is the part of language where we move most noticeably from closed linguistic structures to the ever-open structures of experience; where we move from linguistics to the nonlinguistic world, to the logic of an experience of the world. Semantics is the part of linguistics where Saussure's formula is false[3], the part where the *langue* cannot be studied in itself, because it is the part where *we move continuously from the langue to the world and from the world to the langue*[4].

In linguistics a common agreement has not yet been reached as to the existence of *concepts*. Since the concept of "concept", on the other hand, is a well established term in philosophy, for the present I would prefer to speak, not of concept, but of *mental object*, that is, of a *schema of representation*. Is a schema of representation a summary, by abstraction, of a certain field of reality? Reality is of infinite variety, with no fixed borders in practice, but only imperceptible transitions. Let us take a simple example (Figure 5).

Even this schematic representation (of "house") brings us face to face with a problem[5]. Where, on the one hand, is

---

A 10, p. 151 ("The concept can bring to our mind the idea of the object in question as well as the word which names it, whereas the word can only evoke the concept, and it is by means of this latter that the idea of a concrete object can arise in our mind, for example, that of the table in our dining-room").

[3]This is the formula which closes the *Cours de linguistique général*: "Linguistics has as its sole real object the language studied in and for itself" (ed. 1916, p. 324).

[4]Georges Mounin, *Les problèmes théoriques de la traduction*, Paris (Gallimard), 1963, p. 138. See also Knud Togeby, "Langue, science, littérature et réalité", *Revue Romane* 8, 1973, pp. 298–303.

[5]See, for example, the study by G. Mounin, "Essai sur la structuration du lexique de l'habitation" [in modern French], in *CahLex*, 6, 1965, pp. 9–24 ("in sum, 146 words or meanings"!, p. 11); for

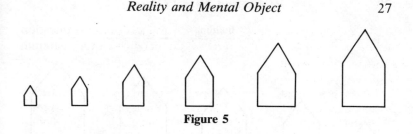

Figure 5

the limit with "hut", and on the other hand, the limit with
"mansion"? "Hut", "house", "mansion", are schemata of
representation, which seem, in each case, to sum up hierarchi-
cally a section of reality. Somewhere within reality there must
exist the limit between "hut" and "house", and between
"house" and "mansion". But this "somewhere" cannot be
determined with the precision of a line, but rather as a border
zone, or zone of transition. A border which is not a border has
something disagreeable about it for the scientist, who feels
himself to be obliged, *ex officio*, to draw lines. Would it not at
least be possible to fix the borders statistically? Take a
hundred people in front of an ordinary house, and they will all
agree that this is a "house". Statistics work here. But as soon
as we put these same people in the presence of a border-zone
of reality, there will be an argument. Some will say that it is a
"house", others that it is a "hut". The clever ones will say that
it is a "building", or a "dwelling", trying to evade the issue in
this way. They select a superior mental object, that is, a
schema of representation that includes at the same time the
mental objects 'hut', 'house', 'mansion' (a wider field of reality) (see Figure 6).

Rumanian, see Angela Bidu-Vrănceanu, "Contribution à l'analyse
structurale du lexique, Le lexique d l'habitation en Roumain", *Revue
Roumaine de Linguistique* 19, 1974, pp. 321–343 [with a matrix ("by
plotting") p. 336, ff.]; and in the same volume, the article "Modalités
d'analyse structurale de lexique, Le système des dénominations des
animaux domestiques", pp. 525–546 [see also on this subject, Lothar
Wolf, *Sprachgeographische Untersuchungen zu den Bezeichnungen
für Haustiere im Massif Central*, Tübingen, 1968].

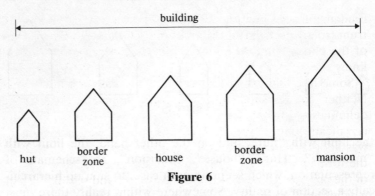

Figure 6

But the problems of delimitation are repeated on the higher level of the mental object 'building'. For example, is a construction which is only just under way already a building? Jurists give us two answers. In the German Penal Code, article 305, a construction under way is a building; in article 243, section 2, it is not! The first article refers to certified material damage, and protects things of value – here, a construction under way is already a building; the second section refers to burglary – in this case a construction which is in progress is not yet a building. That is jurists include or exclude the same reality within the mental object, depending on the purpose in each case.

A favourite example is the scale of colours. Where are the objective limits between *red* and *brown*? In German, one says, in such cases, *rotbraun* ("redbrown"). In Spanish they say *color chocolate* (chocolate coloured), *color canela* (cinnamon coloured), *color castaño* (chestnut coloured), and the colour between red and black is usually called *atezado* (tanned) or *rojinegro* (red-black). In English, we may say *reddish-brown*, copper-*coloured*, *auburn*, etc., depending on the circumstances; the colour between red and black may be called simply *dark red*. As becomes obvious to us in this example, extra-linguistic reality only knows imperceptible gradations. Language is what creates distinctions within a reality that has no boundaries. The eye can distinguish, in pure colours, a scale of 300 hues. Ordinary language, however, makes use of a few fundamental designations. The distribution of the colour spectrum (solar spectrum) is different in each of the linguistic areas of the earth. Korean, for example, has no green, so far as I know[6].

Something similar happens with the seasons of the year. Neither the division into four seasons nor the temporal delimitation of each season is given to us by nature. In Latin, *ver* means both "spring" and "summer"; *aestas*, "summer", was adopted later in Latin. This led, in the fourth century, to the forms *primum ver* and *prima ver*, properly, "the first part of the period of time which includes spring and summer", from which came the Italian and Spanish form *primavera* ("spring") while the Rumanian word *vară* preserves Old Latin *ver* in the sense of "summer". The French word *printemps*, "spring", comes from Latin *primum tempus*. Language reflects the problem and the relativity of the transformation of realities into conceptual classifications.

Where are the limits between a *mound*, a *knoll*, a *hill* and a *mountain*? What is called a mountain in flat country is only a hill to people who live in the mountains[7].

---

[6]"A single name for colours in the cool part of the spectrum – indigo, blue and blue-green – is common. Chinese has such a word which may also refer to grey or black and also carries an idea of the colour being a characteristic of something. This word, *ch'ing*, would not be applied to colours like dyes. For paper and paint there are separate words. But *ch'ing* sky is blue, *ch'ing* grass is green, *ch'ing* mountains are purple, *ch'ing* cattle are black, and *ch'ing* horses are grey". J. Ornstein and William W. Gate, *The ABC's of Languages and Linguistics*, Philadelphia and New York (Chilton Books), 1964, p. 110 [the example is from Whorf]. On the colour scale, see the recent article by Lothar Wolf, "Zur Diskussion über Terminologie und Semantik", in *Übersetzer und Dolmetscher*, edited by Volker Kapp, Heidelberg (Quelle und Meyer), 1974, p. 51 (based on Mounin); Catford, *A Linguistic Theory of Translation*, London, 1965, p. 51; A. Bidu-Vrănceanu, *Systématique des noms de couleurs*, Recherche de méthode en sémantique structurale, Bucharest 1976.

[7]See Toivi Valtavuo, *Der Wandel der Worträume in der Synonymik für "Hügel"* (Mémoires de la Soc. Néophilologique de Helsinki, XX,

Where, in reality, is the border between "light" and "dark"? In these scales, reality knows no borders. Where is the border between "young" and "old", between "well" and "ill"[8], between "fast" and "slow"[9], between "hot" and "cold"[10], between "stupid" and "clever", between "good" and "bad"[11], between "beautiful" and "ugly"[12], between "big" and

---

1), Helsinki, 1957 (especially p. 8). See also Horst Geckeler, *Zur Wortfelddiskussion, Untersuchungen zur Gliederung des Wortfeldes "alt – jung – neu" im heutigen Französisch* (International Library of General Linguistics, edited by E. Coseriu, 7), München (Wilhelm Fink), 1971, 566 pp. (cf. the reviews by M. Sandmann, *Archiv für das Studium der neueren Sprachen* 211, 1974, pp. 181–184, Alberto Zuluaga in *Thesaurus* 28, 1973; [a resumé of this book will be found in Horst Geckeler, *Strukturelle Semantik des Französischen*, Tübingen (Niemeyer), 1973, §3.2.5.]); Horst Geckeler, "Lexikalische Strukturen im Vergleich, kontrastive Skizze zur Strukturierung des Wortfeldes "alt – jung – neu" im heutigen Italienisch, Spanisch und Französisch", in *Interlinguistica* (Festschrift Wandruszka), Tübingen (Niemeyer), 1971, pp. 123–137. Horst Geckeler, *Semántica estructural y teoría del campo léxico* Madrid (Gredos) 1976, 385 pp. Also, see the important article by E. Coseriu quoted in the Introduction, n. 5.

[8]Compare in German *indisponiert/unpässlich/unwohl/kränklich/krank/schwerkrank/todkrank* (and the ironic *todsterbenskrank*); or the series *leicht verletzt/verletzt/schwerverletzt – leicht verwundet/verwundet/schwer verwundet*.

[9]Concerning the imprecise borders between German *plötzlich* and *sofort, schnell* and *sofort* see J. Blass, "Der Ausdruck der zeitlichen Unmittelbarkeit" (= *Romanica Helvetica*, 68), Bern, 1960.

[10]In German *kalt/lauwarm/warm/sehr warm/heiss/sehr heiss/glühend heiss*; Ducháček (*CahLex*, 6, 1965, p. 62) gives for French the series *glacé(gelé)/glacial/froid/frais/tiède/chaude/caniculaire (torride)/ardent (bouillant)/brûlant (incandescent)*.

[11]In the *Cartelera de cines* (List of films) published in the Madrid newspaper *ABC* films are classified as *muy buenas – buenas – discretas – mediocres – malas*.

[12]See, for ex., Otto Ducháček, *Le champ conceptual de la beauté en français moderne*, Prague, 1960; "Le champ conceptuel de la beauté en français moderne", *Vox Romanica* 18, 1960, pp. 297–323; "Joli-

"small"[13]? And nevertheless, we know very well how to distinguish between "cold" and "hot", etc. Yet the 'clarity' is not in the borders, but in the oppositions. This is seen very clearly in antonyms such as "up" and "down", "in front" and "behind", etc.

At this point, we must take a decisive step, and ask which is imprecise, the mental object or the reality? We can very well distinguish between the mental object 'house' and the mental object 'mansion'. We have no difficulty in distinguishing between the mental objects 'day' and 'night', between 'young' and 'old'. The difficulties begin when we have to apply our mental objects to realities which do not correspond exactly to our mental schema. We are not sure if it is a 'hut' or a 'house' if the real object has at the same time some characteristics of a hut and some of a house. The reality corresponds to neither of our mental objects. Our uncertainty is based, then, precisely on the fact that we have too exact an idea of what a hut and a house should be.

---

beau", *Le Français Moderne* 29, 1961, pp. 263–284, etc.; Otto Ducháček–Ružena Ostrá, "Etude comparative d'un champ conceptuel", *Etudes Romanes de Brno* 1, 1965, pp. 107–169 [which deals with the field of beauty in Latin and in the Romance Languages].

[13]Concerning the different types of antonyms, see O. Ducháček, "Sur quelques problèmes de l'antonymie", in *CahLex*, 6, 1965, pp. 55–66; L. Guilbert, "Les antonymes – Y a-t-il un système morpholexical des antonymes?", in *CahLex*, 4, 1964, pp. 29–36; J. Pohl, "Les antonymes: économie et conscience linguistique", in *Linguistic Research in Belgium*, ed. by Yvan Lebrun, Universa Wetteren (Belgium), 1966, pp. 99–111 [statistical results; 100 students answered the question "What is the antonym of . . .?" Along with well established antonyms with 100% agreement, such as *fort/faible*, *convexe/concave*, *petit/grand*, *lourd/léger*, there were other very divergent answers]; Wolfgang Müller, "Über den Gegensatz in der deutschen Sprache", in *Zeitschrift für deutsche Wortforschung*, 19, pp. 39–53; see also A. J. Greimas, "Les Topologiques: essai de définition d'une classe de lexèmes", in *CahLex*, 4, 1964, pp. 17–28. Recently: Maria Iliescu, "Oppositions sémantiques: antonymie linguistique et antonymie logique", *Folia Linguistica* X, 1977, pp. 151–168, which is excellent.

The borders of the reality which corresponds to the mental objects are not, furthermore, precise or imprecise in the same way in all areas of the vocabulary. Some clear borders, such as those that exist, for example, between the days of the week, do not come from reality, but are imposed upon it by convention, and thus constitute an exception (this is a case of nomenclature within ordinary language; it is not an accident that one speaks of the *names* of the days of the week). On the other hand, even names are drawn back by speech towards the elasticity of inexactness. The humourist James Thurber was once asked by his grandson how long a minute lasted. "That", replied Thurber, "depends on the circumstances. Normally a minute consists of sixty seconds. But when someone says, 'Just a minute, please', it means at least a quarter of an hour"[14]. In fact, this is a case of polysemy, that is, two different mental objects (one with precise but artificial borders in reality, the

---

[14]Cf. on this point, the following dialogue, taken from a humorous Mexican magazine:

A philosopher was saying to someone, "For me, a thousand years are like one minute".
"And a thousand *pesos*?"
"Like five *centavos*".
"Then, Sir, please lend me five *centavos*!"
"Just wait one minute".

The background of this is the conflict between chronologically fixed time, and the experience of time, which can be observed in the general language. Among the Ifê-Yoruba of Africa, for example, the *osse*, or week, usually has seven days. But in fact, the idea of 'week' is closely bound to the regional market cycles. The idea of 'week' can thus vary from one region to another, according to the importance and periodic holding of the *markets* . . . the *odon* designates the year; years are counted as a function of the traditional festivals celebrating the harvest of arrow-root tubers, the principal cultivated food of the Ifê-Yoruba. The *odon* involves about thirteen lunar months. It is solemnly celebrated by all the Ifê-Yoruba, and marks the start of a new period of time.
(Yao P. Assogba, "La mesure de temps chez les Ifê-Yoruba", in *Au fil des événements* [Université Laval, Québec], 23-2-1972.

other, in ordinary language, with imprecise borders in reality). The application of a word (which corresponds to a certain mental object) to a borderline reality is one of the most important causes of semantic evolution.

To sum up: language *can* follow limits given by nature (if there are any), but does not necessarily follow them, at least. In general, reality knows no borders, but only gradations without fixed borders. In such cases – and this is the normal case – the dividing lines do not exist in reality, but only in the language. Coseriu[15] correctly says:

> Meaning is the structuring of human experience. But this does not fit delimitations or dividing lines given *previous* to language. In principle, this structure could be completely different, and, as a matter of fact, different languages do show different patterns of meaning. Thus, individual languages are not to be seen so much as different names, from a purely material viewpoint, for things already given, but rather networks of signification which organize in different ways the world as experienced. Or, putting it another way, language is not the *confirmation*, but rather the *imposition*, of borders within what is experienced. Naturally, this does not mean that linguistic structuring cannot agree with an objective, physical, or natural delimitation; in fact, the pattern of meaning *can*, but does not *have to*, correspond to objective delimitations. Thus, for example, there is no imperative reason to distinguish between German *essen* ["eat", speaking of people] and *fressen* ["eat", speaking of animals], or between *essen* ["eat"] and *trinken* ["drink"] although there are, in fact, many languages which make these distinctions. A *Leiter* ["ladder"] and a *Treppe* ["staircase"] may be objectively different, but Italian [*escala*] and Spanish [*escalera*] do not establish this difference. The

---

[15]Eugenio Coseriu, "Das Phänomen der Sprache und das Daseinsverständnis des heutigen Menschen" [The Phenomenon of Language and Comprehension of Existence in Modern Man], from *Die Pädagogische Provinz*, 21, 1967, pp. 11–28. New edition in E. Coseriu, *Sprache, Strukturen und Funktionen*, XII Aufsätze (TBL 2), Tübingen, 1970, pp. 111–135; this passage is on p. 115; see also "Der Mensch und seine Sprache", ib. pp. 137–158; "Vers une typologie des champs lexicaux", *CahLex* 27, 1975 – II, pp. 30–51.

meaning "Pferd" ["horse"] may coincide with a natural species, but such meanings as *Roß* ["steed"] or *Mähre* ["nag"] do not (pp. 3–4).

Coseriu is right, and one may even doubt whether there really are borders within reality – a problem which is still being debated[16]. The result of this situation is the following postulate: the determination of the mental objects of the ordinary language cannot be based on reality, but on the language itself. The definitions of mental objects must analyse semantic oppositions, distinctive features; definitions must, in general, be intensional, not extensional[17]. Mental objects are intensionally definable, the limits of reality are not, at least not within the ordinary language[18].

(b) THE DETERMINATION OF THE MENTAL OBJECT IN SCIENTIFIC LANGUAGE

The only language which tries to follow (or create?) objective borders is scientific language. To continue quoting Eugenio

---

[16]Among linguists, Coseriu thinks there are, Heger thinks there are not, or at least he is sceptical. – As for the formation of concepts, J. E. Heyde, "Priorität des Allgemeinen" (in *Festschrift für Wilhelm Eilers*), Wiesbaden (Otto Harrassowitz), 1967, pp. 546–557, in contrast to the traditional doctrine of progressive abstraction from the particular to the general, argues for the priority of the general concept. There is no unanimity, then, even on this point.

[17]Concerning intensional definitions, see part I, chapter 5; concerning extensional definitions, part II, chapter 5, paragraph k, and part II, chapter 7.

[18]"So it is useless, in consequence, to want to interpret linguistic structures from the viewpoint of claimed structures in reality: we must begin by making clear that there are no structures *in* reality, but structures *imposed on* reality by human interpretation" E. Coseriu, "Structure lexicale et enseignement du vocabulaire", in *Actes du Premier Colloque Int. de Ling. appliquée*, Nancy, 1966, p. 187 [German version, *Einführung in die strukturelle Betrachtung des Wortschatzes*, Tübingen, 1970, p. 17].

Coseriu[19]:

But the three characteristic features of signification which we have just established make possible at one and the same time the transcending of language, i.e. its relation with the world of things themselves, even if it is with a world structured and arranged by the language. The delimitation of things through language is not an obstacle to its relationship with things; in reality, it is a way of *getting* to the things themselves. Language, as signification, makes possible speech, as affirmation, which refers to the things alluded to, and thus leads to the knowledge of the things. Knowledge only exists in relation to what is already delimited and conceived of in language, even when the knowledge makes no reference to what is linguistic, but to the extralinguistic, but given by means of language; that is, not to what is signified, but to what is designated. In this regard, there has been talk of a linguistic "between-world" (*Zwischenwelt*), an intermediate linguistic world, a second world between us and the real world. This is a striking and suggestive, but at the same time dangerous formulation, since there is really only *one* world, and the creating of form in the world through language is not a limitation of it, but on the contrary provides the very possibility of knowledge of the world as such; each language is a basis and instrument for the scientific knowledge of the world. The so-called linguistic "between-world" is a world of meanings, which has no effect on what is designated, but only makes it appear as if it were subject to some kind of order. The creation of form through language does not take place *in* the world of things, but on the level of human understanding, i.e. at the most, *in relation to* the world of things. Language, as it were, prepares things for knowledge, presenting a first and necessary delimitation of them. But this first delimitation can be overcome through knowledge, and that by virtue of language, and following that model.

The fact is that scientific knowledge moves from the "arbitrary linguistic structuring" of the world to an objectively motivated structure, which is also one of the possibilities of language. Since

---

[19]Eugenio Coseriu, "Das Phänomen der Sprache und das Daseinsverständnis des heutigen Menschen", from *Die Pädagogische Provinz*, 21, 1967, pp. 11–28; [reprinted in E. Coseriu, *Sprache, Strukturen und Funktionen*, XII Aufsätze (TBL 2), Tübingen 1970, p. 111–135].

the linguistic structure can in theory be any whatever, it can be, among other things, objectively motivated. Among the many possibilities of language, there is also the possibility of a language with an objective basis, that is to say, a language that establishes and gives value only to those delimitations which correspond to objective and objectively evaluated dividing lines. In this respect, the *language of science*, technical language, is simply one of the possibilities of language, which, let it be said in passing, is also realized in part in natural languages, representing what in these languages consists of *nomenclature* and technical terminology. Such a language can then only designate "existing" things. But the difference between the existent and the non-existent is also only made possible by means of language. The question about the existence of things, indeed, is only made possible by means of the existence of a meaning, in relation to which we ask ourselves whether such existing things, which correspond to the essence contained in the meaning can be demonstrated to be present in our experience of the world or not. The identification of meaning and existent object is a serious mistake which involves a subversion of the only possible way of proving existence. The difference between existence and non-existence is unknown to language as such. But language makes it possible to ask about existence, and hence also makes possible a conventional specialist language containing only names for existing things.

In the third place, since signification consists precisely of the possibility of designation, language can be made into a system of designation, that is to say, a system in which designation and signification coincide, and in which names are chosen beforehand for designations of individuals or of classes[20]. It is true that natural

---

[20]It is obvious here that Coseriu uses the terms *signification* (= *designatio*, referring to intensionally defined concepts) and *designation* (= *denotatio*, referring to extensionally defined concepts) differently from the way we use them (compare below, part I, chapter 7); for Coseriu's terminology, see *Actes du Premier Colloque International de Linguistique appliquée,* Nancy, 1966, p. 209, with a very clear graphic chart. In principle, each concept can be defined intensionally by distinctive features and extensionally by enumeration of real referents. Compare Holger Steen Sørensen, "The relationship between meaning and reference", 10th Congr. Int. des

language can designate what is individual, but, with the exception of proper names, only by means of reciprocal determination through universals and with the help of the context and situations (for example, "this rose", "the mayor of our city", etc.). On the other hand, natural speech can also designate classes, but linguistic classes are for the most part "inclusive", that is, certain words can designate at one and the same time a subordinate class and a more inclusive one. Thus, for example, *figli* in Italian designates "sons" as opposed to "daughters", but it can also designate the class of "sons and daughters", "children". The German word *Tag* ("day") designates the opposite of *Nacht* ("night"), but also day inclusive of night (for example, *drei Tage*, "three days" where what is meant is three days and three nights). *Steigen* (ascend) designates the opposite of *fallen, hinuntergehen* (descend), but it can also designate a motion in the opposite direction. In this sense it is said that linguistic oppositions, in contrast to logical ones, are not *exclusive*, but rather *inclusive* [as are the *complementary* oppositions of phonology]; in them, a term which is equal to Non-A may also be used for A. But specialized language, based on the language itself, can, on the one hand make certain words function exclusively as individual designations (proper names), and, on the other hand, can determine certain words as designations for exclusive classes. Specialized language, can, for example, make the purely linguistic opposition:

| day | night |

into an opposition of specialized speech:

| day | night |

This indeed happens normally in the language of science. In this sense, the language of science is no more than a specialized use

Linguistes, *Résumés des Communications*, Bucharest, 1967, p. 345 ("Identification of meaning with denotata is widespread. It is a false identification").

of natural language. But this does not mean that natural language as such is to be considered as an imperfect preliminary to science. It is true that science uses language, but it is concerned with the designated things themselves, in that it analyses these things and makes a statement about them. Language, on the other hand, does not in itself give any information about the the things referred to; it can only *represent* them. It is true that linguistic structuring is already knowledge, but only the first stage of knowledge, a merely differentiating knowledge, which simply conceives of something as identical with itself and different from other things (pp. 5–7).

What Coseriu is writing about[21] represents the *ideal* of scientific language, an ideal rarely attained. In reality, scientific language makes use of the ordinary language, and many times it cannot avoid its implications of polysemy, homonymy, etc. Many debates on terminology are the consequence of this fact. The difference between the *structured lexicon* of the language, and the *'nomenclative'* and *terminological* lexicon of science[22] is not so sharp as Coseriu would like to believe[23].

---

[21]For more details, see E. Coseriu, "Structure lexicale et enseignement du vocabulaire", in *Actes du Premier Colloque International de Linguistique appliqué* (Nancy, 26–31 Oct., 1964), Nancy, 1966, pp. 175–217 (especially pp. 181–90; "In part, terminologies are not 'structured' at all (they are mere enumerative 'nomenclatures', corresponding to delimitations within things), and, in so far as they are, their structuring does not correspond to the norms of the language but to the viewpoints and requirements of their respective sciences and techniques concerning the reality of things itself", pp. 182–83).

[22]"The important thing is to recognize that, in what is called the "vocabulary" of a language, there are broad areas which are purely "designative" and where the only possible "structuring" is enumeration [the basis of extensional definition], and others which are structured, but not from the viewpoint of the language; there is a *structured vocabulary*, which is linguistic, and a *vocabulary of nomenclature or terminology*" (ibid., p. 184).

[23]See the reservations of Mme. Hirschberg in the discussion, ibid., pp. 233–35: "We are far from the enumerative namings of M.

Coseriu"; of M. Larochette, ibid., pp. 236–37: "In the first place, ordinary language uses scientific or technical terms which, for this reason, are structured with the same right as usual terms, and can probably use them all. If they are not all structured, at least all are structurable. They cannot be considered as representations of things, as proper names are, since terms like *oesophagus*, *carburettor*, *triangle*, *sergeant-major*, can be used metaphorically. Very occasionally a new term is created with a view to designating a particular object which becomes capable of designating other objects, exactly like the neologisms of the common language. For their part, science and technology use as "technical terms" words from the common language (for example, in linguistics, *language, discourse, speech*, etc.). If someone objects that true "terms" do not exist except within a very specialized language, it is sufficient to observe that there is no science that does not use words from the common language; even scientific language is a diasystem. On the other hand, a technical or scientific term does not designate an exterior reality which merely has to be recognized, but rather a reality which has been thought up, or an aspect of this reality, with the result that the man of science must *define* the reality he is designating by means of a term, and by defining it, he creates an "object" which is not an immediate fact. Each new definition of the phoneme, for example, creates a new "object" which the word "phoneme" is capable of designating"; and of S. Ullmann, ibid., pp. 224, ff.: "The distinctions E. Coseriu proposes between *structured vocabulary, which is linguistic* and *vocabulary of nomenclature and terminology* (p. 184) is no doubt valid; it will be profitable, then, if not to exclude terminological expressions from the realm of structural lexicology, at least to leave them to one side for the moment, reserving the right, as E. Coseriu says, 'to come back to them at a second stage' (ibid.). But one might wonder whether popular nomenclature, in botany, zoology, etc., should be grouped with technical and scientific expressions. It is well-known how much linguistic folklore, how many fantastic metaphors and how many popular etymologies and idiosyncratic structuralizations there are deposited in these nomenclatures; from the structural point of view, one only has to think of examples such as distinctions in German between *Kraut* and *Unkraut*, and between *Blume* and *Blüte*, which are unknown in French; the contrast between the English morphosemantic series *strawberry, raspberry, blackberry, whortleberry*, etc., and their unequal French counterparts, *fraise, framboise, mûre, airelle, . . .*".

But there is no doubt that Coseriu's distinction does contain a nucleus of truth, at least a theoretical truth. Scientific classification does not necessarily coincide with the classification of the ordinary language. The example of the German word *Walfisch* ("whale") is well-known. The whale, in German, is called a 'fish' (*Fisch*) in the ordinary language, even though it is a mammal. A *Nachtschwalbe* (literally, a "night-swallow"; *night-jar*), is not a swallow (*Schwalbe*); *Fledermäuse* (bats) are not mice (*Mäuse*) and *Flughunde* ("flying foxes") are not dogs (*Hunde*). English has many similar examples: *sealion, pineapple*, etc.

And "the true relation between 'fruit' (Ger. *Obst*) and 'vegetables' (Ger. *Gemüse*) is such that the untrained person (= non-scientist) cannot precisely determine the limits between the two products. Thus, he usually classifies the tomato as a vegetable, although botanically it is a fruit"[24]. Scientific terminology at least *tries* to follow natural borders (if there are any) and *tries* to avoid polysemy; if there are no natural borders, it tries to *create* borders within reality (which makes it possible to give an exact definition by enumeration, that is, an extensional definition based on reality). Furthermore, the mental object of ordinary language remains unanalysed in the speaker's subconscious; the scientist, on the other hand, analyses mental objects and gives definitions of terms (which presuppose an analysis). The scientist, discovering a *new* mental object (which presupposes a previous analysis) can invent a new term and define it precisely (either intensionally or extensionally)[25].

---

[24]*Basler–National–Zeitung* of Sept. 13, 1960 (no. 427).

[25]In addition, scientific language, insofar as it speaks of linguistic facts, is a metalanguage, an important distinction (see Part II, Chapter 2, and E. Coseriu, "Structure lexicale et enseignement du vocabulaire", in *Actes du Premier Colloque Int. de Linguistique appliquée*, Nancy, 1966, pp. 190, ff. J. Dubois y L. Irigaray, studying "Les structures linguistiques de la parenté" (*CahLex*, 8, 1966, pp. 47–69), found the same difficulty in distinguishing between linguistic structures and extralinguistic social and cultural structures: "The fundamental problem posed by these structural analyses is to distinguish what is a fact of linguistic structure and what is a fact of the social-

It is interesting to examine how modern physics comes to terms with this fundamental problem of language. The physicist Werner Heisenberg indicates in his article "Speech and Reality in Modern Physics"[26], how new knowledge leads us to realities and real events confronted by which our established natural language fails us (*up*, *down*, *simultaneous*, *space*, *time*, *place*, *speed*), and it can only continue to function by means of a conscious enrichment with mathematical terms (for example, *energy*, *impulse*, in modern physics), or by means of a conscious and, so to speak, poetic rejection of exact terms, such as in the theory of relativity. Even so, "the language of classical physics" continues to be necessary and useful to help us understand each other when speaking about experiments and results (in normal space). Physics must either be satisfied with the inexact application of words corresponding to mental objects already deeply rooted, or it can escape towards a new well-defined terminology or nomenclature with no polysemy (Coseriu), or towards mathematics, that is to say, towards a non-linguistic sphere[27].

---

cultural structure formed by kinship relations between the members of a particular community. There is in practice a real risk of describing, through the language, the social structure, the structure of the objects referred to (*denotata*), rather than determining the system of the lexemes themselves. It is also necessary to carry out the linguistic analysis by distinguishing the two levels and taking as a basis the morphological rules that direct the composition of the lexical structure of the kinship terms" (p. 47).

[26]Werner Heisenberg, "Sprache und Wirklichkeit in der modernen Physik", in *Wort und Wirklichkeit*, edited by the Bayerische Akademie der Schönen Künste (Academy of Fine Arts), Oldenburg, 1960, 163 pp. (quoted from the review by Peter Hartmann in *Germanistik*, 2, 1961, p. 322).

[27]"At the XIV Nobel Prize Congress in Lindau Max Born affirmed that some ideas such as *absolute certainty* and *absolute exactness* and *absolute truth* are pure chimeras, and should not be accepted by any science. Each affirmation of probability is true or false from the viewpoint of the theory that serves as a basis for this affirmation. This mobility of thought is presented as 'the greatest blessing conferred by present day science'" (*Rhein–Neckar–Zeitung*, 26-6-1964).

(c) LEGAL LANGUAGE

The best example of a scientific language to be found between ordinary language and nomenclature is, in my opinion, legal language. This language makes use of ordinary language to a great extent. Ordinary language functions very well with mental objects to which stretches of reality without fixed borders correspond. But as soon as we try to draw precise borders in reality by means of language, we run into enormous difficulties. This is why we should pity jurists, who, making use of ordinary language, have to draw precise borders. From the viewpoint of language theory, this is impossible; yet, juridically, punishment, and even the alternative *guilty–innocent* depends on such a limiting of reality. It is worth looking at the records of court proceedings. Not long ago, a German court had to draw the line separating *light* and *dark*, because a motorist, driving without lights, had caused an accident just as it was getting dark. How dark does it need to be for a driver to feel obliged to turn on the lights? The limits between *day* and *night* are as imprecise as those between *light* and *dark*:

dawn,	day	dusk,	night
morning twilight		evening twilight	

Language wisely helps us with mental objects to name these transitions, but the borders between *dawn* and *day*, *day* and *dusk*, *dusk* and *night* are still imprecise. The oppositions are clear, the limits are vague.

One would at least think that we know what a man (= person) is. The ordinary language distinguishes man from God and from the animals. But as soon as we ask for the borders in reality, "When does a man become a man?" we face the same problem. Does a man come into existence when he is conceived or at the moment of birth? Jurists, characteristically, give us two different answers. In the German Civil Code, we are told, in article 10, "The juridical capacity of a man begins at the moment of his birth". But in the Penal Code, article

217, which has to do with drawing a precise limit between abortion and infanticide, he becomes a man *before* birth, that is, *when labour pains begin.* Infanticide, then, is punishable during and after birth. In the Civil Code, a man becomes a man later than in the Penal Code[28]!

This is why definitions play such an important rôle in jurisprudence. For jurists, the borders of meanings are more decisive than the centre of meanings, while in ordinary language, the centre is more important than the edges. Jurists would need definitions based on limits which exist in reality (if there are any), or imposed on reality, which is usually impossible in the ordinary language (see the next chapter, concerning definitions).

The humorist always profits most from this situation. Northcliffe, the Press Lord (also called the "Napoleon of the dailies"), was once asked what *news* was, to which he replied, "If a dog bites a man, that is not news, but if a man bites a dog, then that is news". And the elderly Chancellor Adenauer, on one occasion, said that he did not think *being young* had

---

[28]See Karl Engisch, *Einführung in das juristische Denken*, Stuttgart ³1964, pp. 108–9 (in a Spanish translation *Introducción al pensamiento jurídico*, Madrid, 1967, p. 140). Another example is the border between *life* and *death*, which has become very problematic for modern medicine (see the article by Kurt Rudzinski, "Verwischte Grenzen zwischen Leben und Tod – Der Einbruch der modernen Forschung in die Rechtssphäre" [The Blurred Boundaries between Life and Death – The Invasion of Modern Research into the Sphere of Law], in *Frankfurter Allgemeine Zeitung*, 2-7-1966, n. 150; or between *living matter* and *dead matter*: "Viruses have been identified as agents of many infectious diseases, such as smallpox, poliomyelitis, measles, mumps, head-cold, flu, and also verrucas and rabies. They seem to be bisexual animals at the borders between living and inanimate material. When they manage to penetrate into the body of some human being or animal, they seek out hospitable cells and force them to produce millions of new viruses of the same kind. But they can also be found in the state of being able to survive in the form of inanimate crystals outside a cell with life, without, however, being able to multiply", in *Spiegel*, no. 7 (Feb. 10, 1965, p. 80).

anything to do with age[29]. But in reality, these are not definitions that will satisfy the jurist. His dilemma consists of converting words from the ordinary language into 'terms', often leading to attempts at exhaustive definition, which become terribly complicated. I give here a few examples. Every German has an "income", and furthermore, he thinks he knows what "income" means, since he lives on it. But, just what is "income" in the legal definition? Let us take a look at the *German Manual of Fiscal Law:*

Income (Einkommen) can be defined as the surplus left to the individual from the totality of net earnings and profits (if not in currency its value will have to be calculated in currency), which, in a period to be determined, comes in from permanent sources, and which permit the achievement of the means necessary to satisfy needs, after the deduction from the total sum (which, if not in currency, will have to be calculated in currency), of the expenses incurred during the same period as the said sources of income were exploited, (as the net profit is calculated after the deduction of general expenses); and furthermore of dividends from specified stock shares, paid periodically and thus are repeated periodically to defray payments in kind, which, therefore, can be consumed without diminishing the monetary value of the capital disposable at the beginning of the period, but which, if

---

[29]It is no less difficult to define words which are in fashion, such as, for example, *ídolo* in Portuguese (in Brazil): "Young men today dream of becoming an 'ídolo'. Under this vague noun, here put in inverted commas to distinguish it from the other sense, also figurative, given to the word, an infinity of definitions are hidden. The *"ídolo"* is the person who attracts the admiration of adolescents, not on his own account for his personal qualities, sometimes dubious, but for the position he occupies. To be an *ídolo* means to be surrounded by girls, have one's photograph in papers and magazines, and, also, posters over the walls of the city, and above all to own the latest car, even if he cannot drive it, being under age. *Ídolo* is any young man (he must be young) who stands out from the rest. He can be the famous singer, well known sportsman, or even the bandit in the news. The definition, as can be seen, varies with time and place."

not consumed can be added to the said capital, which is for this reason increased.

I am perfectly happy if you understand none of that, because I cannot understand it in German either.

After this, the definition of *initial endowment* [German *Erstausstattung*] is almost naïve:

> Initial endowment is the endowment of a new apparatus, of a new mechanical plant, of a new installation, of a new ship, or of a new establishment, with the means and equipment required to exploit the same. The first endowment is financed and activated without consideration of the duration and the value of the means of investment[30].

What is the difference between a *workman* [German *Arbeiter*] and an *employee* [*Angestellter*]? Both fall into the more general category of *worker* or *wage earner* [German *Arbeitnehmer*]. A court in Frankfurt had to decide this question, and, after a long discussion, came to the conclusion that what is characteristic of an employee is *being seated*. More exactly, an

---

[30]From the Decree regulating traffic, etc., *Bulletin* of Jan. 25, 1957, part 2.

Another example is the following definition of *Railway*: "Device directed toward the repeated transport of persons or things over appreciable distances upon a metal base which, by its consistency, disposition and gloss, is designed to make possible the transport of great weights or the obtaining of relatively large velocity in the movement of transport and which, by virtue of this quality, in relation to the forces of nature used, furthermore, for the production of movement of transport (steam, electricity, animal or human muscular activity, on an inclined plane of the road also to the weight itself of the recipients of transport and their load, etc.), is capable of producing in the functioning of the device a relatively intense effect upon the said base, according to the circumstances, useful only in the way intended and also potentially destructive of human life and harmful to the health of men," in *Entscheidungen des Reichsgerichtes in Civilsachen*, vol. I, 1888, p. 252.

employee is one who does office work while being seated. The judge had to make this decision in a case in which was in dispute the obligation to pay insurance to employees (social security), since there was no *clear description of the legal concept "employee"*, not even in the corresponding law which deals with insurance for employees. In this law, the concept 'employee' *is supposed to be known by everyone.* "A logical determination of the concept is not possible because into the concept 'employee' a typical and real social evaluation is condensed", comments the labour court of Frankfurt. The insurance law enumerates only marginally a series of activities which imply the insurance obligations for employees: "Office employees, as long as they are not occupied exclusively as messengers or in cleaning and similar jobs; also office apprentices and typists" (II Labour court 313/56; Kurier, 2-1-1957).

To take an example from the field of economics, what is an *original container*? This question had to be decided by the First Bench of Criminal Affairs of the Federal Court in a trial about wines. A wine dealer had mixed two different vintages from his own vineyard which, although pure and cultivated by him, showed a marked difference in quality, and had sold them under the label "original container". The amount was some 700 litres. The Federal Court saw in this an infringement of paragraph 7, article 2 of the wine law. The legal prohibition there expressed, on calling mixed wine a "vintage", refers to other denominations with the same sense, such as, for example, "original container". Among the legal reasons justifying the denomination "vintage", must be added, dealing with "original container", the fact that the treatment and packaging must be carried out in the wine grower's own cellar. The judgement refers only to mixing wines of different quality. On the other hand, it expressly leaves undecided whether a mixture of wines of the same value and from the same grower fall within the said paragraph and article of the wine law or whether, on the contrary, such a mixture can be sold under the label "original container". Not even the Supreme Court could arrive at a valid definition, once and for all, of what is meant by "original container".

The question of the original container and of the quality of wine is naturally very important in tourism. But what is *tourism* itself, in the legal sense? As was brought to light not long ago[31], there is no generally accepted definition of tourism. A magazine of tourism exists without defining it. This is a typical situation in linguistics: We all know what tourism is, but a definition acceptable to jurists does not exist.

Definitions can also have highly political implications. Concerning the famous "Spiegel" scandal, in Germany, which resulted in the arrest of several editors of the Hamburg weekly, the question was vividly posed as to what *treason against the nation* is. Articles 99 and 100 of the German Penal Code affirm that treason consists of revealing state secrets. By "state secrets" is meant "facts, objects and information, and in particular documents, pictures, models and formulas or information about them, the secrecy of which must be kept from a foreign power for the good of the German Federal Republic or any of its constituent States". According to this, a person commits treason "who deliberately causes a state secret to fall into the hands of a person not authorized to know it, or makes it public, thus placing in danger the German Federal Republic or any of its States [*Länder*]". "According to the German Decree, a secret becomes a state secret when it is important for the good of the state" (*Rhein-Neckar-Zeitung*, Oct. 31, 1962). It is clear that the problem has not been solved by this, but only postponed. Now, we could pose the question as to what is the *good of the state*. And who decides on the good of the state? We are in a vicious circle. The solution of one question leads us to the next.

For some years, now, the concept of the *Policy directors of Europe* has played a major rôle in European diplomacy. The meeting of Chambers of Industry and Commerce, in Bonn, on

---

[31]"The question of what tourism is has not yet found a satisfactory answer", Victor Münster, in *Der österreichische Betriebswirt*, no. 11, 1961, p. 237, referring to K. Krapf, "La notion du tourisme", in *Zeitschrift für Fremdenverkehr*, 9, 1954, fasc. 2 pp. 50, ff.

Jan. 15, 1959, faced the difficult problem of how to define this concept.

> The top policy directors [*Führungskräfte*] of Europe are those persons of both sexes who are especially qualified from the economic, scientific, political, technical or administrative point of view, and who, given their personality, and a combination of knowledge, linguistic and otherwise, as well as their experience abroad, are prepared to act
>
>   (a) as officers or employees with German nationality in national or European institutions,
>
>   (b) as members or experts on German delegations in European or international negotiations,
>
>   (c) as German representatives on all types of European commissions, or
>
>   (d) as experts or editorial advisers on European questions in German organizations, associations, institutions or firms. These definitions are, of course, considered provisional[32].

One could suppose that at least the concept of a public institution such as the *postal and telecommunications service* would be defined with more precision. Not long ago, in connection with a second television programme in Germany, there arose a problem of competition between the federal government and the regional governments.

> In general terms, what is being discussed is whether radio and television can be divided into a technical part, a cultural part, and an organizational part, in which case the technical part would fall under federal legislation, and the other parts under the cultural sovereignty of the States [*Länder*], or whether, on the other hand, radio, given the present state of legislation in Germany and its legislative traditions, belongs entirely under federal jurisdiction. Related law-suits brought before the Constitutional Tribunal raise many juridical administrative problems, because the

---

[32]Meeting of the German Chambers of Industry and Commerce in Bonn. Rundschreiben an die Industrie- und Handleskammern betr. Europäische und internationale Fragen Nr. 4/59.

concept of postal and telecommunications service has to be clarified, since this service, according to article 73, number 7 of the fundamental law [*Grundgesetz*], falls within federal jurisdiction (*Rhein-Neckar-Zeitung*, 25-11-1960).

Let us go to what seems, at first sight, to be a quite harmless realm, geography. One would certainly expect that at least here we would find clear delimitations. Nevertheless, in Switzerland, there has been a debate for a number of years as to the concept of *Eastern Switzerland*. As a term in the ordinary language, there would be no problem at all: it can easily be defined as "the eastern part of Switzerland". But as a scientific term (juridical, political and economic, with legal consequences) this definition proves to be insufficient. An effort was made to find an extensional definition (describing in reality everything that forms part of Eastern Switzerland) in an Assembly convened expressly for this purpose, which turned out to be a very risky enterprise. A Swiss newspaper published the following about the session, and Dr. Hans Munz's report:

Eastern Switzerland, as a geographical concept, is not of interest to this purpose. In order to have political effectiveness this concept would have to cover a region which at least in some respects represented a common destiny, or, at least, was felt as such. If in Thurgau such a question were asked of a group of people from different parts of the canton, we would certainly get very different answers. For the inhabitants of the Northern part of this canton, it may be reasonable for the region of Eastern Switzerland to have as its border, in addition to their own canton, St. Gallen and Appenzell. For those who live in the lower part of the valley, on the other hand, it is natural to include Zürich as well. For the region of Untersee and Rhein, Eastern Switzerland cannot be conceived of without Schaffhausen. A sure definition has not yet been found. But if one had been found, there would have been no choice but to make the reservation that this was not entirely appropriate for Thurgau. There is hardly any sense in speaking of a community feeling which is supposed to be valid for the whole canton of Thurgau in relation to other territories of Eastern Switzerland. The result, then, is that, given present circumstances, it is very difficult to obtain a consensus in Thurgau concerning the territories that come under the name "Eastern Switzerland". It has never been attempted in Thurgau circles, according to the report, to give greater importance to Eastern Switzerland. At least here the opinion is expressed that the efforts to give a political structure to Eastern Switzerland have come almost exclusively from St. Gallen. The idea is very widespread that a stronger union of Eastern Switzerland in a strict sense, with the intention of underlining in this way certain common aims, would lead almost automatically to an oganization of other similar structures in other parts of German Switzerland, in a spirit of competition. As Dr. Munz sees things, then, it is impossible to forge a concept of Eastern Switzerland with general political value. Only if this fusion can be limited to specified requirements can such an endeavour be successful. Someone would have to take the initiative and, as a result, St. Gallen appears to be the most appropriate, given its size, population and importance. Here, however, we run into our first psychological obstacle. In the same way that an individual does not usually appreciate being placed under tutelage, independent political communities are not inclined to subordinate themselves to another without specific need. In any case, a great deal of tact is required (*National-Zeitung* of Basel 24-10-1960)[33].

All these examples illustrate the difference between ordinary language and scientific language. Ordinary language functions with mental objects which have not been analysed, but which can be analysed by oppositions (intensional definitions). Scientific language would need terms whose application to reality does not prove to be problematical, a nomenclature

---

[33]A similar case: In the newspaper Le Devoir [Québec] of July 24, 1972, Claude Morisset complains of the way "America" and "USA" are taken to mean the same thing: "If the inhabitants of the USA call themselves 'Americans' and call their country 'America', should the Canadians, Québecois, Mexicans, Chileans and other Americans accept this US imperialism? . . . Latin Americans are more and more using *estadounidense* to refer to one from the US; let us have the same concern for accuracy and pride as they do, in always using the term *étatsuniens*".

with borders fixed in reality. For this reason juridical language (including political-juridical or economic-juridical) is in a particularly difficult situation. Making use of words from common speech, the jurist has to analyse them as if they were terms with borders fixed in reality.

One of the most famous examples among jurists is the concept of *aggression*.

A determination of the concept of 'aggression' of general value is still lacking, since up to now, all attempts by the UN to establish a legal definition of 'aggression' have failed.

Since the definition of war as 'continuation of politics by other means' lost its validity, and the rejection of violence, with the prohibition of annexation by force, related to it, became a generally recognized principle, both in International Law and in the actual practice of States there have been repeated attempts to define the concept of 'aggression' as a central and decisive concept of international Law for the peaceful coexistence of peoples[34]. From that time, too, dates the dispute concerning the possibilities of determining the concept of 'aggression'. While some consider such an exact definition of 'aggression' impossible, and even undesirable, preferring a more elastic conceptual

---

[34]Since the creation of the League of Nations in Geneva, above all, the discussion about "aggression" and the related concepts of outlawing war has not quietened down; see, for example, Clyde Eagleton, "The Attempt to Define War", in *International Conciliation*, n. 291; Heinrich Kipp, article "Annexion", in *Wörterbuch des Völkerrechts* (= *WVR*), founded by Karl Strupp, publ. by Hans-Jürgen Schlochauer, Berlin (de Gruyter), 2nd ed., 1960, vol. 1, pp. 63–68, 66–67; Royal Institute of International Affairs, *International Sanctions*, New York, 1938, pp. 177–87; Louis B. Sohn, *Cases and Materials on World Law*, Brooklyn (Foundation Press), 1950; Louis B. Sohn, *Cases on United Nations Law*, Brooklyn (Foundation Press), 1956, pp. 845–58; Quincy Wright, "The Concept of Aggression in International Law", in *American Journal of International Law* (*AJIL*), vol. 29, 1935, pp. 368, ff.

determination, others feel that a juridically exact definition would be very helpful in avoiding war[35].

The usefulness of an elastic conceptual determination rests on the idea that the 'aggressor' can only be proven 'on the basis of a free appreciation of all the circumstances in each particular case'. This opinion originates in criticism of a 'rigid' conceptual determination, which requires precisely described circumstances. Such circumstances do not contain the elements that constitute aggression, but rather are formed on the basis of enumeration of those actions by states that represent an aggression [extensional definition]. For this purpose it is explained that the concept of 'aggression' is a concept 'per se', an 'original' concept, which is not susceptible to any supplementary determination. Those who oppose this conception allege that acts of aggression could not be enumerated exhaustively; thus, an enumeration would give a pretext to those who had decided to perpetrate an 'aggression'. Above all, the 'rigid' conceptual determination would not take into account that the state who takes the first step in any kind of violence (which, according to a 'rigid' definition, would have to be classified as aggression) could consider that he was engaging in a defensive war.

In view of these difficulties, the United Nations Charter, in spite of the various debates at the San Francisco conference, has not attempted any definition of the concept of 'aggression'. Article 39 of the UN Charter employs the concept of 'aggression', but leaves it to the Security Council to determine what must be considered as 'aggression'. Thus the Charter follows the arguments of those who favour an elastic conceptual determination[36].

---

[35]The arguments within the UN which have been set forth for and against the type of definition – general, enumerative or combined – are compiled in the report of 2-12-1954 on the discussion in the sixth committee of the General Assembly of 14-10 to 10-11-1954. *General Assembly Official Records (GAOR)*, IX. Annexes, Agenda Item 51, 8-12, reproduced in Sohn, *Cases*, pp. 852–58.

[36]Friedrich Klein, "Der Begriff des 'Angriffs' in der UN–Satzung" ["The Concept of 'Aggression' in the UN Charter"], *Festschrift für Hermann Jahrreiss*, Köln–Berlin–Bonn–München (Carl Heymanns Verlag), 1964, pp. 163–88 (my gratitude to my colleague Hans

One should remember the well-chosen words of Sir Austen Chamberlain in the House of Commons, concerning the efforts of the League of Nations to define the concept of 'aggression' used in Kellogg–Briand Pact:

> I therefore remain opposed to this attempt to define the aggressor, because I believe that it will be a trap for the innocent and a signpost for the guilty (24-11-1927)[37].

We see that not only linguists but also jurists have lost the certainty that it is always possible to delimit concepts in reality[38]. Let us continue with a quotation from the well-known German legal philosopher, Karl Engisch[39].

> There was a time when people had no difficulty in believing in the possibility of obtaining absolute clarity and juridical certainty

---

Schneider, of the School of Law of the University of Heidelberg, for pointing out this work). Now, also see Stephan Verosta, "Zum Begriff des Angriffskrieges 1790–1815" in *Anzeiger* (Österr. Akad. der Wiss., Phil. Hist. Kl.) 110, 1973, 77–79.

[37]See Carl Schmitt, *Der Nomos der Erde*, Köln, 1950, pp. 248–55 (my gratitude to my colleague Hans Schneider for this reference).

[38]See also the article by Wilhelm Gallas, "Gründe und Grenzen der Strafbarkeit – Gedanken zum Begriff des Verbrechens", in *Heidelberger Jahrbücher*, 9, 1965, pp. 1, ff. Gallas shows the impossibility of defining the notion of *crime* in an absolute way (the notion is related to the needs of society). In another article ("Der Schutz der Persönlichkeit im Entwurf eines Strafgesetzbuches – E 1962", in *Zeitschrift für die gesamte Strafrechtswissenschaft*, 75, pp. 16–42), Gallas discusses notions which are no less problematical, such as *private sphere of the individual, insult*, etc.

[39]Karl Engisch, *Einführung in das juristische Denken*, Stuttgart (Kohlhammer), [3]1964, pp. 106, ff.; the English is based on the Spanish translation: Karl Engisch, *Introducción al pensamiento jurídico* (translation by Ernesto Garzón Valdés), Madrid (Ediciones Guadarrama), 1967, xviii + 272 pp. (quotes from pp. 137, ff.), as revised by L. Molina and myself; there also exists a Portuguese translation: Karl Engisch, *Introdução ao pensamento jurídico*. Tradução e prefácio de J. Baptista Machado, Lisbon (Fundacão Calouste Gulbenkian)[3] 1972.

by means of norms exactly conceived, and above all, in the possibility of guaranteeing absolute lack of ambiguity in all the decisions and acts of the judges and administrative authorities. This era was the Enlightenment. . . . . This concept of the relation between the judge and the law loses ground throughout the nineteenth century. Not only was it considered that the requirement of a binding relationship between the judge and the law was unattainable, because it is not possible to conceive laws so exactly and bring about their interpretation in official commentaries in such a precise and exhaustive way as to eliminate all doubts concerning their application, but it was also thought that that requirement of submission to the law, was in the long run no longer an ideal (pp. 137, ff.).

The situation today is very different, and more complicated:

The principle of the legality of justice and of the executive remains intact in itself. One may cite article 20, paragraph 3, of our Fundamental Law [= Grundgesetz], which determines that executive power and the administration of justice are subject to the Law. But the laws themselves are structured in such a way in all branches of Law that the judge and the administrative officials can not only arrive at their decisions on the basis of fixed juridical concepts, whose content can be discovered by their interpretation, but they are called upon to formulate variations independently, and in this way, to decide or act as if they were legislators. This same thing will happen in the future, since it always has to do with a more or less binding relationship to the law. Let us consider therefore more closely the formation of juridical thought in those cases where the relationship to the law is loose, where in *this* sense we meet the so-called "equitable law" (*ius aequum*), in opposition to the "strict law" (*ius strictum*).

The starting point for our next consideration must be the methodology of legislation itself, starting from the supposition that there is now a loosening of the bonds between the courts, the administrative authorities and the law. Today we find various forms of legal expression, which have as a consequence that whoever applies the law acquires more independence relative to it. We distinguish as forms of this type: *indeterminate juridical*

concepts, normative concepts, concepts of free interpretation [=
Ermessensbegriffe] and the so called *general clauses*[40] (pp. 138,
f.).

Engisch distinguishes between:
(1) absolutely determinate concepts/indeterminate concepts:

By *indeterminate concept* we understand a concept whose content and extension[41] are to a large degree uncertain. In the Law,
absolutely determinate concepts are very infrequent. Nevertheless,
one must include among these the numerical concepts used also
in Law (especially those which are related to the concepts of
measurement, time, and money: 50 kilometres, a twenty-four
hour period, 100 marks). Most juridical concepts are at least par-
tially indeterminate. This is true, for example, of *natural concepts*
adopted by Law, such as 'darkness', 'nocturnal repose', 'noise',
'danger', 'thing'. And it is true to an even greater extent of juridical concepts proper, such as 'murder', 'illegality', 'crime',
'administrative act', 'legal business', etc. According to Philipp
Heck[42] it is possible, with respect to indeterminate concepts, to
distinguish between a *'conceptual nucleus'* [Begriffskern] and a
'conceptual periphery[43]'. When we have a clear knowledge of the
content and the extension of the concepts, we are dealing with
'conceptual nuclei'. Where doubt arises, the 'conceptual
periphery' begins.

[this, in fact, is a case of the application of the concept to
borderline realities].

---

[40]It appears that Engisch uses *concept* (Begriff) to mean linguistic
sign (unity of *signifiant* and *signifié*), which is common in many non-
linguistic sciences.
[41]The German word here is *Umfang*. It appears that *content* and
extension correspond to what we call *intensional* and *extensional* definition.
[42]Ph. Heck, *Gesetzauslegung und Interessenjurisprudenz*, 1919, p.
173; *Begriffsbildung und Interessenjurisprudenz*, 1932, pp. 52 and 60.
[43]The German word is *Begriffshof*, which refers to an area around
the nucleus, but excludes the nucleus itself.

It is obvious that on a moonless night, at twelve o'clock, in the open country with no lights, there is darkness; but doubt arises, for example, in the twilight hours. There is no confusion as to the fact that pieces of land, furniture, and food are 'objects'. The situation is different, however, when we are dealing with electricity or a trail of smoke (aerial publicity) in the sky . . . (pp. 139 f.)

(2) normative concepts/descriptive concepts:

Many indeterminate concepts are also, in a sense which we shall have to elucidate more closely, '*normative concepts*'. These concepts are set up in opposition to '*descriptive concepts*', that is, to those concepts that make a 'descriptive' reference to real or seemingly real objects, objects that are fundamentally perceptible or in some other way open to experience: 'man', 'death', 'cohabitation', 'darkness', 'red', 'velocity', 'intention'. As can be seen, among these descriptive concepts there are also indeterminate concepts. This does not mean that all indeterminate concepts are at the same time 'normative'. Normative concepts are often to a great extent indeterminate, and offer, as a result, many significant examples of indeterminacy and also of the uncertainty and relative freedom that exists in the application of the law. What are we to understand, then, by 'normative' concepts? Unfortunately, the idea of 'normative concept' is not in itself without ambiguity. If one assumes that each juridical concept is a constitutive element of a juridical norm and that through this it receives meaning and content, then one would really have to consider every juridical concept as 'normative' (and within the 'legal assumptions of fact' every element of those assumed facts), which, as a matter of fact, has already happened (Erik Wolf). But in this case, the 'descriptive' concepts to which we referred previously would also be 'normative' concepts, since the concepts of 'person', 'death', 'darkness', have, as juridical concepts, a particular meaning, which can be perfectly distinguished from the meaning of the corresponding biological, theological or physical concepts. But when one speaks of normative juridical concepts, as distinct from descriptive concepts, one obviously means something specific, something other than mere belonging to the system of juridical norms, or to the legal assumptions of fact. (Belonging to this system is an attribute of every juridical concept. It produces what we could call an 'evaluative relation'

(Wertbezogenheit), that is, the relation of the content and of the extension of each juridical concept to the specific evaluative ideas of a juridical nature). Nevertheless, opinions are divided as to where to look for normative juridical concepts in the strict sense (as distinct from descriptive juridical concepts), since here we are dealing to a certain extent with questions of terminological preference. We want to emphasize two different concepts of what is 'normative' in a strict sense, in order to give preference, finally, to one of them. On the one hand we can understand by 'normative' juridical concepts those which, in contrast to descriptive concepts, point to data that are not immediately perceptible or open to experience, but only come to be imagined and understood in connection with the world of the norms. I can imagine the descriptive concepts of 'person', 'death', and 'darkness' as simple concepts of experience, even when they include a reference to value; that is, even when their content and extension are determined by juridical norms. On the other hand, for something to be 'another's', and therefore a possible object of theft or unjustified appropriation or material damage means that it 'belongs' to some person other than the malefactor. In this way, a sense of property, as expressed in the Civil Code, is logically presupposed as a normative complex. I cannot imagine a thing being 'another's' without at the same time thinking of the norms of property. There is also a sense of normative content (and not only of evaluative relation) in juridical concepts such as 'matrimony', 'relationship by marriage', 'official' [Beamter], 'under age', 'indecent', 'without a police record', 'dishonest', 'unjust', and other similar ones, all of which base their meaning content on some norm. By this we do not mean to say that normative juridical concepts thus defined have to be completely indeterminate. Concepts such as 'matrimony' and 'under age' are relatively determinate, since the conditions presupposed for their application are fairly exactly described. There also exists the possibility of *defining* these conditions by means of descriptive characteristics, for example, declaring an 'under-aged' person to be one who is not yet twenty-one years old. Because of this reducibility to descriptive characteristics, it may seem to some people that the sense of "normative" just given is not sufficiently specific. The true meaning of what is 'normative', which is also the second and preferable meaning of normative in the strict sense, can only be found in the fact that an *evaluation* is always necessary in order to apply a normative concept to a particular case. Whether someone is married or under age can be established by means of descriptive criteria. Whether on the other hand certain behaviour is 'dishonest', a motive is 'unjust', a piece of writing is 'indecent', or a theatrical performance is 'blasphemous' – compare in this last connection the famous painting by George Grosz showing Christ on the cross wearing a gas mask and soldier's boots – can only be decided on the basis of value-judgement. . . . Normative concepts of this type are called concepts which 'require evaluative content' (wertausfüllungs-bedürftig). By this dreadful word is meant that the normative part of these concepts has to be filled with value-judgements in each case. For the present the question can remain open as to whether the value-judgement is a matter of subjective and personal evaluation by whoever is applying the law, or whether we have to look for some connection with previously given ideas of the general public or of a 'ruling class'. For the moment, the term 'evaluation' will have to indicate to us both evaluations by individuals and the subsequent carrying-out [Nachvollzug] of the evaluations of others. In one way or another the evaluation in all rules is generally subject to an indeterminacy which makes normative concepts seem to be a special kind of indeterminate concepts (pp. 141–43).

(3) Concepts of free appreciation [Ermessensbegriffe] (free appreciation/union to the objective norm of what is just):

The independence [Eigenständigkeit] of the personal evaluation about which we have just spoken seems at first glance to be the characteristic of a special class of concepts which also serve for the 'loosening' of legal binding relationships, that is to say, the *concepts of free appreciation* [Ermessensbegriffe], so widely discussed at the present time. What do "free juridical criteria" and "free administrative criteria" mean other than the personal evaluation of the judge or the government official? But the concept of free appreciation [Ermessen] is among the most ambiguous and difficult in legal theory. The difficulties become more acute and acquire special importance due to the fact that the theory of free appreciation [Ermessen] has become at the same time the key-stone of trial law. The important question here is whether free appreciation decisions by the administrative authorities can be examined and corrected by courts of justice,

and whether free appreciation decisions of the courts can be modified by higher courts . . . (pp. 143, f.).

It is obvious that the concept of "free appreciation" which we
have just expounded is of a special character. In this concept it is
not a matter simply of indeterminacy and evaluation, but of *personal* evaluation. The opinion arrived at by the official entrusted
with the decision, perhaps after internal conflicts, is of a binding
nature, and – within certain limits – the criterion of what is juridically just. The pure concepts of free appreciation, then, constitute a special category *alongside* indeterminate and normative
concepts, or at least *within* indeterminate and normative concepts.
. . . Some distinguish between indeterminate concepts and concepts of free appreciation; others classify these last concepts
within the first. The same happens with the relationship between
normative concepts and those of free appreciation. . . . The field
of free appreciation is small and is limited principally to the
administration. So-called judicial free appreciation is in large
measure not free. Here it is rather a matter, most of the time, of
normative concepts which do indeed require an evaluation, but
not a personal evaluation, rather an objectively valid and unambiguous evaluation. But those concepts which point to an
authentically free evaluation are inevitably at the same time
(within certain limits) indeterminate and normative concepts . . .
(pp. 148–49).

It will always be a problem to know where and when free
appreciation can be accepted in the sense we have just described
(p. 151).

(4) General clause and casuistic method [cp. intensional
definition and extensional definition (by enumeration)].

The 'casuistic' method is a variety of the 'legal assumption of
fact' (understood as a collection of assumptions which conditions
the legal organization of legal consistency) which groups together
special cases in their specific peculiarity. A 'casuistic' assumption
is, for example, that of article 224 of the German Penal Code: If
a premeditated bodily wound has 'as a consequence that the
injured person loses an important limb, the sight of one or both
eyes, the hearing, speech or the capacity of reproduction, or is
left considerably affected for the rest of his life, or contracts a
fatal disease or disability or mental illness', the offender will be
sentenced to imprisonment for up to five years and not less than

one year [= enumerative method]. On the other hand we have to classify as a *'general clause'* the first part of article 260 of the 1930 plan: 'if the injured person is seriously harmed in body or in health . . .' By "general clause" we have to understand a way of expressing assumptions of fact that covers in very general terms a whole area of cases and prescribes for them their appropriate treatment in law. . . .

The difference between the casuistic method and the general clause method is admittedly only relative. Within article 224 of the Penal Code, already quoted, the first part of the assumption of fact ('an important limb of the body') stands out in contrast to the other elements of the assumption of fact as if it were a general clause, in spite of the fact that the total assumption of fact of article 224, in comparison with article 260 of the 1930 plan, is casuistic. On the other hand even the general clause of article 260 of the 1930 plan is comparatively casuistic, if we place it side by side with a decree made by the governing council of Munich in the spring of 1919: 'Any crime against revolutionary principles will be punished. The type of punishment is left to the free discretion [freies Ermessen] of the judge'. Penal clauses of such a general character are not regarded with favour in states subject to the rule of Law. They are incompatible with the general principle *nullum crimen sine lege*, which makes a certain 'casuistic' approach indispensable. . . .

A truly commendable combination of the casuistic method and the general clause method is the so-called *'exemplifying method'*. . . .

We must now ask ourselves what the relationship is between 'general clauses' and indeterminate concepts, normative concepts and concepts of free appreciation. Does it have any special significance? One has to admit that this is the case only under certain conditions. . . . Nevertheless, in practice, almost only those general clauses come into consideration which are at least at the same time indeterminate and normative, whereas it cannot be said that general clauses are usually at the same time clauses of free appreciation. . . . Must we not at least allow general clauses to be included in indeterminate normative concepts, or occasionally also in concepts of free appreciation? In fact, general clauses, from the point of view of methodology, possess no peculiar structure (pp. 152–56).

. . . The application of the Law is part of the life of the Law itself. It is not possible to rationalize completely what is alive (p. 168).

And this conclusion coincides with what Bachof says:

> According to Bachof, the previous alternative of distributing indeterminate concepts between on the one hand powers of appreciation which are theoretically not subject to fundamental revision (except where there is a typical error in appreciation), and on the other hand juridical concepts completely subject to revision, appears to be outdated. Rather, it is necessary to distinguish between:
>
> (1) more or less determinate juridical concepts, the application of which to concrete circumstances is juridically revisable;
>
> (2) indeterminate juridical concepts, the application of which requires subjective appreciation which lies within a certain latitude of forming judgement [Beurteilungsspielraum], and which, when it falls within this latitude, is not juridically revisable;
>
> (3) powers of appreciation which grant to the authority a margin of freedom of decision within which it can make decisions and implement them according to its own criteria and, not least important, from the point of view of what is appropriate in each case [This last paragraph is found in note 155].

Therefore, jurists have clearly recognized that really only a very small proportion of the concepts that come into play juridically correspond to well defined or definable borders in reality. Even these borders are artificially established most of the time, and not preexistent (e.g. 24 hours, 40 kilometres, 100 marks). In these cases we have to deal with a terminology or nomenclature (Coseriu), as in the sciences. If such borders do not exist (in concepts such as 'honorable', 'bad', 'danger', 'noise', etc.), then we must resort to concepts such as 'norm' and 'appreciation', concepts the application of which to each juridical case proves in reality to be elastic. The inevitable application of concepts to borderline cases in reality continues to be the dilemma of legal practice. We shall be better able to explain this difficulty of applying intensionally defined concepts, when we have examined in detail the essence of intensional definition.

5

The Definition of Mental Objects

(a) POTTIER'S ANALYSIS

In Chapter 4 we showed that often language does not follow borders given by, or imposed on, nature. Language is not the confirmation (Feststellung) but rather the establishing (Festsetzung) of borders within experience (Coseriu). This situation should lead us to fundamental methodological conclusions. A definition based on borders within reality proves in general to be impossible[1]. *Definition* means, etymologically, *delimitation*; this delimitation, however, is not there in reality, but is rather a *creation* of the definition. The mental object is an abstraction from many realities which are related to each other, but the list of these realities remains in general open, precluding any complete enumeration (and, thus, any extensional definition). Nevertheless, I can identify (= relate with the mental object) a table as 'table' even though I am seeing it for the first time. How can I do this? What are the constituent features of the mental object? How can we find the *distinctive features* which distinguish one mental object from the others?

Bernard Pottier blazed the trail with his study *Recherches sur l'analyse sémantique en linguistique et en traduction*

---

[1]See below for extensional definitions.

mécanique[2]. Since this work seems to me to be of fundamental importance, I shall go through the crucial passages in detail (concerning the mental object "chair"):

1. LEXICAL SELECTION

If precision is carried to the extreme, it is possible to affirm that there are no two "chairs" that are identical. Nevertheless, faced with 1,000 different objects, a person may have the same reaction and choose the term *chair* 1,000 times to designate them. If 1,000 persons are shown these 1,000 chairs, we can elicit the term *chair* a million times.

In linguistics, this coincidence of subjectivity is what is called *objectivity*. Extreme scepticism would be the negation itself of scientific experiment.

If, in the presence of a series of objects $(x^1, x^2, \ldots x^n)$, the answer is regularly $/x/$, it will be said that $/x/$ is the *lexical unit* (*lexie*)[3] which designates these objects.

(Visual tests are obviously the simplest; one can also imagine rigidly enforced contextual tests.)

Just as there are no two objects that are exactly identical, neither do two people exist who have exactly the same experience, that is, the same lexical inventory with the same content. Here, too, it is necessary to generalize, normalize (that is, to convert into a norm) and apply the experiments to a relatively homogeneous group of subjects. This is what scientific procedure involves.

2. THE DETERMINATION OF THE SEMEME

Let us take each one of the objects designated by the lexical unit *chair*, and let us describe each of these chairs as completely

---

[2]*Publications Linguistiques de la Faculté de Lettres et Sciences Humaines de l'Université de Nancy*, 1963, 38 pp. (quotes pp. 11–19). English examples have been added where possible.

[3]"*Lexie* (= lexical unit of the language); *pierre, bateaumouche, chemin de fer*, etc."; cf. B. Pottier; *Introduction à l'étude des structures grammaticales fondamentales*, Nancy, 1962 ([2]1964); in English e.g. *rock, grandmother, brother-in-law*, etc. See now B. Pottier *Linguistique générale, Théorie et description*, Paris 1974, index; *Lingüística general*, Madrid, 1976.

Table 1

	chair 1	chair 2	chair 3	... ...	chair n
q^1 = back	+	+	+		+
q^2 = velvet	+	−	−		(+)−
q^3 = 4 legs	+	−	+		+(−)
q^4 = wooden	−	+	−		−(+)
q^5 = to sit in	+	+	+		+
... ...					
q^n = ...					

as possible. Let us make a list of the characteristics found (q) and mark next to each individual object whether it possesses that characteristic or not (+ or −). (See Table 1.)

There are some complex questions which will have to be thoroughly unravelled, such as the question of the number of legs.

When the answer *no* is given to the question of whether the chair has four legs, the questions concerning three legs, two legs and one leg have the possibility of being answered by *yes*. In fact, the number of legs is a variable; what is constant is the notion of *leg*.

It will be noticed immediately that certain characteristics are always answered by *yes*, while others are answered by *yes* or *no*.

It will be said, then, that in a series of *n* objects, trait *q* is pertinent if it occurs *nq* times.

Table 2

	chair 1	chair 2	chair 3	... ...	chair n	Σ
1^1 = back	+	+	+	(+)	+	$n\,q^1$
1^2 = velvet	+	−	−	(+/−)	+	$(n-m)\,q^2$
1^3 = on at least one leg	+	+	+	(+)	+	$n\,q^3$
1^4 = wooden	−	+	−	(+/−)	−	$(n-m)\,q^4$
1^5 = to sit in	+	+	+	(+)	+	$n\,q^5$
1^6 = for 1 person	+	+	+	(+)	+	$n\,q^6$
1^7 = red	+	−	−	(+/−)	−	$(n-m)\,q^7$
.. ..						

Let us return to the preceding table once more, completing it, as in Table 2.

Column Σ reveals a certain number of characteristics q present n times: q^1, q^3, q^5, q^6. These collectively constitute the *sememe* of /chair/.

The lexical unit /chair/ (a formalization) has, then, a *sememe* (semantic substance), the elements, or *semes*, of which are:

$$s^1 = \text{with a back}$$
$$s^2 = \text{on a leg or legs}$$
$$s^3 = \text{for 1 person}$$
$$s^4 = \text{to sit in}$$

or even $\boxed{S_a^{\ 1} \text{ (chair)} = (s^1, s^2, s^3, s^4)}$

Here we are dealing with an *absolute sememe*, in which nothing matters except the lexical unit *chair* itself.

If we do the experiment with the lexical unit *armchair* the result will be the absolute sememe $\boxed{S_a^{\ 2} \text{ (armchair)} = (s^1, s^2, s^3, s^4, s^5)}$ where s^5 is the seme "with arms" And so on.

3. DETERMINATION OF GROUPS OF OBJECTS

The comparison of two objects.

Since the sememe is a group of semes, the comparison of two sememes involves a comparison of two such groups. If we compare *chair* and *armchair* we see that they have in common four semes and that *armchair* has as its own the seme s^5 "with arms":

$$S^1 = (s^1, s^2, s^3, s^4)$$
$$S^2 = (s^1, s^2, s^3, s^4, s^5)$$

If we apply *chair* and *armchair* to the same group of objects we can characterize "S^1 (chair)" as being without seme s^5, that is, as the possessor of a negative answer s^5 (which does not possess seme s^5).

The sememe of *chair*, then, becomes a *relative sememe* (relative to a given group), in this form:

$$\boxed{S_r^1 \text{ (chair)} = (s^1, s^2, s^3, s^4, \bar{s}^5)}$$

Here is a test to show that s[5] is the pertinent semantic trait which allows us to differentiate *chair* from *armchair*.

Leaving the English to consider the original French example, if we ask subjects to complete the sentence beginning "je voudrais m'asseoir *sur* . . ." [I should like to sit *on* . . .], we get answers with *chaise* [chair] and answers with *fauteuil* [armchair]; it is the seme s[4] which comes mainly into play in this case. If the beginning of the sentence is "je voudrais m'asseoir *dans* . . ." [I should like to sit *in* . . .], *fauteuil* is very frequent and *chaise* is practically nonexistent (tests carried out in Nancy and Poitiers). The result, then, is the following:

> *sur* combined with *fauteuil/chaise*
> *dans* combined with *fauteuil*

The motivation for the opposition *"sur/dans"* [*on/in*] is of the type "not-inside/inside". Thus, the "inside" idea suggested by *dans* rejects (unconsciously, in the subject) the combination with *chaise* which does not have seme s[5] "with arms." This, then, is a practical, indirect test[1].

We can also ask for completion of sentences like "If I were to put arms on this *chaise* the result would be . . ." or "If I were to take the arms off this *fauteuil* the result would be . . .". The coincidence of the answers shows the well-foundedness of the selection of the pertinent semes.

The set of objects for comparison.

If there existed a method for grouping objects according to well-defined and objective criteria, the problem of "fields" (semantic, associative . . .) would need no further solution. Unfortunately, nothing of this kind exists. The tests, such as "je voudrais m'asseoir *sur* . . .", provide some indications; but responses include not only *chaise*, *fauteuil*, *tabouret* (stool), but *genoux* and *herbe* as well (knees, grass).

Theoretically, we have to search through a large number of sememes, for intersections referring to an important number of semes. Then we would have a distribution of this type, as in Table 3.

Table 3

	s^1	s^2	s^3	s^4	s^5	s^m	s^n
chaise/chair	+	+	+	+	−		
fauteuil/armchair	+	+	+	+	+		
tabouret/stool	−	+	+	+	−		
genoux/knees						+	
herbe/grass							+

The intersection based on the answers expressed allows us to group together *chaise, fauteuil, tabouret.*

From this point on, we shall work with the following set of objects: *chaise, fauteuil, tabouret, canapé* (sofa), *pouf.*

4. THE ARCHISEMEME AND ITS POSSIBLE FORMALIZATION

Once a set is defined, one must ask what is the archisememe which dominates it, and which would be defined by the intersection of the sememes in question.

Table 4

	s^1	s^2	s^3	s^4	s^5	s^6	
chaise/chair	+	+	+	+	−	+	$= S^1$
fauteuil/armchair	+	+	+	+	+	+	$= S^2$
tabouret/stool	−	+	+	+	−	+	$= S^3$
canapé/sofa	+	+	−	+	+	+	$= S^4$
pouf/pouffe	−	+	+	+	−	−	$= S^5$

s^1 = with a back
s^2 = raised above the ground
s^3 = for one person
s^4 = to sit in or on
s^5 = with arms
s^6 = with solid material

The pertinent semes of the five objects under consideration are listed in Table 4.

Let us abstract the intersection of these relative groups:

$$S^1 \cap S^2 \cap S^3 \cap S^4 \cap S^5 \cap S^6 \cap = (s^2, s^4)$$

The question to be posed is the following: does there exist a formalization (a lexical unit) the sememe of which is precisely the group (s^2, s^4)? In Modern English the answer is yes; *seat* (compare French *siège*, Spanish *asiento*). A *seat* is an object on which a person may sit (primary function) and which is raised above the ground (s^2) (a carpet is not a seat, etc.).

It often happens that an archisememe isolated by analysis has no lexical expression. Thus, for example, for the "object on which a person climbs" (obtained from the grouping of *ladder*, *footstool*, *platform*, *footboard* . . .), English has no archilexeme (cover-word, superordinate).

Intuitively it would be tempting to continue the generalization and say that seats themselves can be classified under a still more comprehensive archilexeme, such as *furniture*. But suppose that to be considered as "furniture" an object must be solid or rigid. In this case, a *pouffe* could not be said to be "furniture", because it lacks seme[6]. If a member of the set under consideration cannot be included in a higher set, the primary set remains outside the higher set.

Archilexemes are continually being created to answer the need for cover terms – e.g. *educators*, *ancestors*, *acids*, *the arts*, *sports*, *fuel*, etc.

5. THE GENERALIZING PROCESS – SUMMARY

(1) *Graphic illustration*

Let us classify the five elements of the group *seat* according to the closeness with which they coincide (only one pertinent seme differentiates two lexical units) (see also Figure 7):

$$\left.\begin{array}{l} \text{pouffe – stool: } s^6 \\ \text{stool – chair: } s^1 \\ \text{chair – sofa: } s^5 \\ \text{armchair – sofa: } s^3 \end{array}\right\} \quad \begin{array}{l} (s^2, s^4) \text{ are the common base} = \\ A^1 [= \text{archisememe}]. \end{array}$$

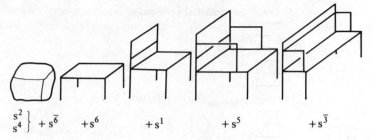

$$\begin{matrix} s^2 \\ s^4 \end{matrix} \Big\} +s^{\bar{6}} \qquad +s^6 \qquad +s^1 \qquad +s^5 \qquad +s^{\bar{3}}$$

Figure 7 Possible schematic representation of these objects

(2) The relationship between *seme – sememe – archisememe*.

The *seme* is one element of the aggregate *sememe*. The *archisememe* is the grouping of the intersection of several *sememes*.

$$\boxed{\text{seme} \in \text{sememe}}$$

Example:

$$\left. \begin{matrix} s^1 \in S^1 \\ s^2 \in S^1 \\ s^3 \in S^1 \\ s^4 \in S^1 \\ s^5 \in S^1 \end{matrix} \right\} \quad S_a^1 = (s^1, s^2, s^3, s^4, s^5)$$

$$\boxed{\text{archisememe} \subset \text{sememe}}$$

Example:

$$\left. \begin{matrix} A^1 \subset S^1 \\ A^1 \subset S^2 \\ A^1 \subset S^3 \\ A^1 \subset S^4 \\ A^1 \subset S^5 \end{matrix} \right\} \quad A^1 = S^1 \cap S^2 \cap S^3 \cap S^4 \cap S^5$$

Pottier introduces in this study the term *seme* (= *distinctive feature*). The *definition* is the sum of the semes and at the same

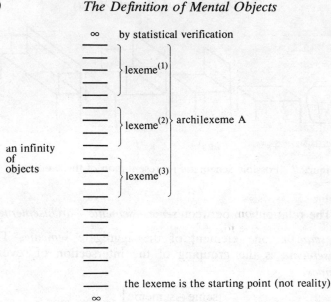

∞   by statistical verification

} lexeme⁽¹⁾

} lexeme⁽²⁾ } archilexeme A

an infinity
of
objects

} lexeme⁽³⁾

the lexeme is the starting point (not reality)

∞

Figure 8

time the sum of the distinctive features[4] (Heger speaks later of
the *differentiae specificae*[5]). Pottier's method is semasiological:
he analyzes the content of the word *chaise* in its normal or
central meaning, applying this word to an open series of
objects called *chaise*. (See Figure 8.)

---

[4]In the same sense, A. J. Greimas: "So each *lexeme* can be
described as a particular arrangement of *semes*", *CahLex*, 4, 1964, p.
21. — See also G. Mounin: "The analysis of the definition of a lexical unit (as given by a dictionary) allows us to take apart and put
together again the *signifié* of a *signifiant* on the basis of units of meaning smaller than the *signifiant*. French *paillotte* (straw hut) contains six
of these units: /building/, /for living in/, /rudimentary/, /small/, /of
straw/, /in hot countries/. These units have in the past been given
different names by different writers: *sème* (Buyssens, etc), *sémème*
(Hattori, etc), *sémième* (Guiraud, etc)," [semantic] "*distinctive features* (Bloomfield), *figures de contenu* (Hjelmslev), *traits pertinents* of
the *signifié* (Prieto). If we choose to call them distinctive features, we
seem by definition to be postulating an isomorphism between

The semes are the features common to all the objects called *chaise*; these semes constitute and define the mental object 'chaise' and are at the same time the features that distinguish it from other mental objects.[6]

The relation between an *archilexeme* or *archilexie* (= lexicalization of an *archisememe*)[7] and a *lexeme* or *lexie* (lexicalization of a sememe)[8] can be presented as a relation of implication, as in Figure 9.

---

phonological analysis and semantic analysis; if we choose other terms, we leave the question of this isomorphism open".... "Once this analysis has been done for all the *signifiants* of a lexicon, it allows us in addition to adjust the empirical delimitations of our starting-point, by arranging the structures *not on the basis of the signifiant, but on the basis of the presence of one or more semes or features given in its definition*" (*CahLex* 6, 1965, p. 20); "we see that we can reduce all the lexical units of a lexicon to bundles of semantically distinctive features or semes" (ib. p. 21). G. Mounin presents and discusses the evolution of the idea of minimal semantic units in three chapters of his excellent book *Les problèmes théoriques de la traduction*, Paris (Gallimard), 1963: Chap. VII, "La recherche des unités sémantiques minima: Luis J. Prieto" [in relation to Hjelmslev and Martinet], pp. 95–112; Chap. VIII, "La recherche des unités sémantiques minima: Jean-Claude Gardin" [including Sørensen], pp. 113–24; Chap. IX, "La recherche des unités sémantiques minima: définitions, terminologies, terminologies normalisées," pp. 125–43. For Prieto, see his most recent publication, *Principes de noologie*, The Hague/London/Paris (Mouton), 1964, 130 pp. Prieto uses the term *noemes* to refer to the units of which senses [*signifiés*] are composed, pp. 90, ff.

[5]"The sememe, or grouping of the distinctive semes, corresponds in part to the 'specific differences' of Mr. P. Imbs" (Pottier, *TraLiLi*, III, 1, 33).

[6]The *seme* is a distinctive feature within the same conceptual system (*siège* ↔ *chaise*); the *archisememe* is common to all the sememes of the conceptual system, but is a distinctive feature in relation to other conceptual systems.

[7]*Siège* (archilexeme) contains the archisememe [s_1 ("to sit on") + s_2 ("raised")].

[8]*Chaise* (lexeme) contains the sememe [s_1 ("to sit on") + s_2 ("raised") + s_3 ("with a back") + s_4 ("for one person")].

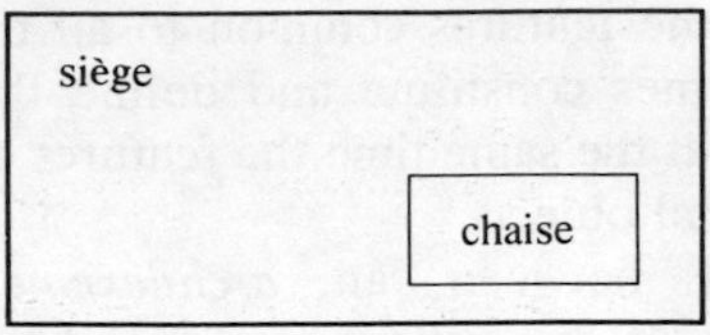

Figure 9

In this, Pottier, in a more recent work[9], follows Coseriu.[10] The mental object 'chaise' is more specific than 'siège' and therefore contains more semes or distinctive features (the consequence, in general, is a longer and more complicated definition).

A distinction must be made between the conceptual level and the level of formalization within a language. The archisememe of the French archilexeme *mesurer*, for example, can be specialized differently in different languages. Fr. *mesurer à la toise* = Liège *twèzer* (to measure height), *mesurer à la règle* = *rûler* (to rule), *mesurer* (le bois) *à la corde* = *cwèd'ler* (of wood), *mesurer au fil à plomb* = *ploumer* (with a plumb line) (see Jean Haust, *Le dialecte wallon de Liège*, 3: *Dictionnaire française-liégeois*, 1948, s. v. mesurer).

In French the formalization is made by juxtaposition of the archilexeme + differentiating lexemes; in the Liège dialect the formalization is created by special lexicalizations (compare Fr. *aller à pied*, *aller à cheval* with English *walk*, *ride*, Ger. *gehen*, *reiten*, etc.)[11]

---

[9]B. Pottier, "Vers une sémantique moderne," in *TraLiLi* II, 1, 1964, pp. 107–37 (especially p. 123).

[10]E. Coseriu, "Pour une sémantique diachronique structurale", in *TraLiLi* II, 1, 1964, pp. 139–86 (especially pp. 151, 161, 176, 178).

[11]In addition what is an archilexeme in one language may correspond to several lexemes in another (in this case the second linguistic community has a greater need to differentiate):

"What do you mean, 'snow'?" asks the Eskimo. "Falling snow snow on the ground, snow in blocks for building igloos, or what? You can't use one word for all those different things" (Jacob Ornstein

conceptual level:	archisememe + differentiating seme(s)
lexical level:	Fr. archilexeme + differentiating lexeme

Liège lexeme

Starting from the other end, that of the formalization in a given language, the conceptual analysis and, as a result, the *definition* depends on the starting point:

> Middle French (Chastellain, fifteenth century):
> *desmesurer* "dépasser les limites ordinaires d'une chose" (the definition given in the glossary: go beyond the usual boundaries of something)

But the context (*rendirent pleurs et cris lamentables . . . desmesurèrent leurs voix*) allows the definition:

> *desmesurer sa voix* "parler et pleurer plus fort que d'habitude"
> (to speak and to cry louder than usual)

The lexicographer must decide each time whether he wants to define the lexeme or the syntagm, the general sememe or the specific sememe. The use of a non-specific lexeme in a specific situation, which is quite normal, gives rise to many changes of sense (see below, the diachronic appendix).

Pottier, in his analysis, has started from the specific to arrive at more comprehensive units[12]. In the second part of the same

---

and William W. Gage, *The ABC's of Languages and Linguistics*, Philadelphia and New York (Chilton Books), 1964, p. 108).

See also our example, Part I, Chapter 6, n.3.

[12]Pottier says: "From the millions of objects that exist in reality, we have gone on to the thousands of lexemes, reduced to some extent to the archilexemes" (*Recherches* [cf. above n. 2], p. 19).

In fact, Pottier started from the word *chaise*, applying it to the objects called *chaise*. It was after this that he analyzed the relevant features of all these chosen objects, and thus arrived at the sememe.

study, 1963, Pottier completes this procedure with an analysis in the opposite direction, starting, this time, from the most general in order to find the smallest classificatory units ("Le processus inverse, qui, partant de l'Univers-unité – par exemple, la catégorie du substantif – se dirige vers des classes particularisantes" ib.). Since this part is no less important than the first, we shall also reproduce the argument here in its entirety.

CLASSEMES

We call *classemes* those distribution classes (obviously semantically motivated) determined by numerous combinatory criteria, and giving homogeneous results.

(1) If we ask the question "Have you seen the . . .?", the list of nouns which follows *the* is not significant. On the other hand, in French, there is a vey clear difference of distribution between the answers corresponding to the two following questions:

"Voulez-vous l'*amener* votre . . ." (bring):

$$\begin{cases} \text{things:} & \text{n answers.} \\ \text{animals:} & \text{n answers.} \\ \text{persons:} & \text{n answers.} \end{cases}$$

"Voulez-vous l'*apporter* votre . . ." (bring):

$$\begin{cases} \text{things:} & \text{n answers.} \\ \text{animals:} & \text{0 answers.} \\ \text{persons:} & \text{0 answers.} \end{cases}$$

We can see that *apporter* selects a grammatical object which is not normally a member of the objective set of animals or persons.

Thus we can say that

apporter + set A of nouns (things)
    − set B of nouns (persons + animals)
amener + set A or B of nouns.

Another test. Let us take the following phrase to be completed: "Qu'est-ce qu'elle rumine, ma . . .?" (What is my . . . ruminating about?). All the nouns form part of series B (32 "persons," 3 "animals"). This is also the case of "Il est enrhumé,

Table 5

TEST		all nouns set A	set B
amener X	… … …	+	+
apporter X	… … …	+	−
X rumine	… … …	−	+
X est enrhumé	… … …	−	+
X est grippé	… … …	+	+
X se baigne	… … …	−	+
X baigne	… … …	+	−
X marche bien	… … …	1 sense	2 senses

votre . . ." (Your . . . has a cold), in which all the answers are of series B. But in "Il est grippé, votre . . .,"[13] we find series A as well as series B (*fils, moteur* . . .). Only nouns of series B "se baignent dans l'eau"; those of series A "baignent dans l'eau". In English, *they bathe in the water*, speaking of persons or animals; *they soak in the water*, speaking of things.

In French, if an element of series A "marche," (goes; marches; works, runs [of machines]), the meaning is not ambiguous: "cette horloge marche", "this watch is working." If we are speaking of an element from series B, there is possible ambiguity: "Charles marche bien maintenant":

    (1) he is walking well now
    (2) he is working (getting along) well (e.g. in school).

A primary distinction gives, then, a distribution like that in Table 5, found in "normal" (not metaphorical) language:

Set A is made up of what we can call "inanimate objects"; set B the "animate objects"[14]. If a person dies, his corpse functions as an inanimate: il *baigne* dans l'eau, et on peut l'*apporter*.

(2) Within the set of "animate objects," two subsets can be distinguished, as shown by combinatory behaviour.

---

[13]For people, this means "he has 'flu"; for engines, it means, "it won't start".

[14]Robert Martin, "La catégorie de l'animé et d l'inanimé en grammaire française", *TraLiLi* IX, 1, 1969, 245–265, has studied in detail the importance of this opposition of classemes in French.

Table 6

TEST	animates		inanimates
	persons	animals	
mettre à la porte X	sense I	sense I/II	sense II
X fait une niche	2 senses	1 sense	∅

In French, if one "mettre à la porte X," where X is a person, the expression means to "expel", the primary sense; if X is a thing (for example, a sign), the expression has a second sense, "to place in front of the door." If X is an animal, the expression is ambiguous, since the animal may be considered as a person or as a thing.

Another clearer example: "X a fait une niche". X belongs to the series of animate objects. But if we are speaking of a person, there is ambiguity [Pierre a fait une niche au chien = (a) he has played a trick on the dog; (b) he has built a kennel for it]; if we are talking about aɪ. animal, there is no ambiguity.

From these examples, we see the distinctions in Table 6.

(3) Within the series of "inanimates" we can distinguish between two subsets, as shown by combinatory behaviour.

"Open X." If X refers to a material object, we have the ordinary sense I: open a sack, a box, an abscess, If X refers to an object which is not material, *open* has meaning II, (traditionally called "figurative"), that of "opening a session." Here, we have a typical case of ambiguity: if *shop* is seen as a material object, we have "open a shop" (with the aid of a key); if *shop* is seen as a non-material object, we have "open a shop" (start a business).

"Prendre X dans un certain sens." As before, with a material object we have "*sens =* direction" (*prendre un jouet/un tissu dans un certain sens*, take a toy, cloth in a certain direction). And with a non-material object "sens = meaning" (*prendre une phrase, une intervention dans un certain sens*, take a remark in a certain way). If the lexical unit can belong to both subsets, ambiguity results "prendre une *règle* dans un certain sens" [*règle* as a *ruler* or as a *rule* = norm].

"Rendre X." With material objects we have the sense of "restore" (give back). With non-material objects we generally have lexical units (*rendre la justice, rendre raison*, provide justice, satisfaction). With a term such as *honneurs* (honours) there is an

Table 7

TEST	ANIMATES	INANIMATES	
		material objects	non-mat. obj.
Open X ...	sense 1	sense 1	sense 2
prendre X dans un certain sens	sense 1	sense 1	sense 2
rendre X ...	sense 1	sense 1	sense 2

ambiguity: "rendre les honneurs" = (a) a military term; (b) give back certain cards to play (material object).

From these examples we derive the distinctions shown in Table 7.

(4) If we combine the three preceding tables, we find the classes in Table 8.

A first series of particularized classes, then, may be presented in the following way:

$$
1 \begin{cases} \text{animate} \begin{cases} \text{person} & = classeme\ 1 \\ \text{animal} & = classeme\ 2 \end{cases} \\ \text{inanimate} \begin{cases} \text{material object} & = classeme\ 3 \\ \text{non-material object} & = classeme\ 4 \end{cases} \end{cases}
$$

We may designate as *classeme* 5 all animate objects (1 + 2)
We may designate as *classeme* 6 all inanimate objects (3 + 4)

Table 8

apporter X	animate	//	inanimate	
X fait une niche	person//animal	//		
ouvrir X			material//non-material object	object
	class 1	class 2	class 3	class 4

The idealists – and some mathematicians – would be tempted
to continue dichotomisation so as to arrive at the archilexemes
discovered by the first part of the analysis. Actually, in our
opinion these two processes cannot be reconciled: they are
complementary, and every lexeme can be characterized by
indices belonging to both sememe and classeme:

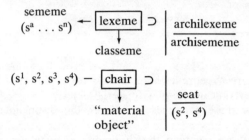

(5) However, there is a borderline case, in which the archilexeme occupies the place of a classeme. This is the case of
terms like *un truc*, *un machin*, *une chose*, ('Thingamabob') which
correspond to classeme 3 (and often 4), and of *Truc*, *Machin*,
Chose ('What's-his-name'), which correspond to classeme 1 (and
sometimes 2).

Similarly, in "Je ne vois rien", *rien* occupies the place of the
archilexeme of classemes 1/2/3/4/, while *personne* refers only to
classeme 1. In this way the language has managed to generalize
archilexical expression to the maximum.

(6) Several modern lexical studies, especially those concerning
mechanical translation, utilise semantic categories which could be
interpreted as subclassemes: convex object, edible object, peaceful animal, etc. Of course, ideally one would like to be able to
classify each lexical unit by means of a finite series of features of
this type. Thus one could predict that a "liquid" cannot be eaten
or cut. And yet we say that an engine "eats up petrol". (The
solution to this has to be sought at the phrase level.)

The trouble with these definitions is that we then find ourselves confronted with potentialities, with the *virtual*. A chair, on
one hand, has a back, is raised above ground, is designed for one
person, is intended to serve as a place to sit and, on the other
hand, it is a material object; but it has an unlimited number of
potentialities: it can be broken (water cannot), it can be bought
(like silence, but not like refraction), etc.

Thus, there are three fundamental zones of meaning for every lexeme:

(semes) archisememe	???	classeme
zone I	zone II	zone III
definition by	potentialities	membership
pertinent features	[French *virtualités*]	
infinitely		infinitely
small ⟵		⟶ big

Zones I and III are stable and are normally found in semantic characterizations that are very likely.

Zone II is unstable and represents only a possibility that depends to a great extent on context, situation, intention. . . .

For our purposes, these zones must be properly delimited for any semantic study, whether concerned with the problem of mechanical translation or not.

Zone I is, according to Pottier, the zone of the semes, of the analysis of significations, the zone of definitions. We shall analyze this zone in more detail when we speak of Heger's trapezium. Zone III is the zone of large categories, classes (*animate/inanimate*, etc.), it plays a very important rôle in grammatical analysis. Zone II, '*virtualités*' is the area of the great question-marks. I believe that this zone is amenable to a more exact analysis: see E. Coseriu's recent fundamental article on this topic[15].

---

[15]E. Coseriu, "Lexikalische Solidaritäten" [lexical solidarities], in *Poetica* (Wilhelm Fink Verlag, München), 1, 1967, pp. 103–303. This article is very important, too, for the relationship between classemes and (archi)lexemes. Between Spanish *perro* (dog) and *ladrar* (bark), for instance, there exists a 'solidarity'; Coseriu distinguishes three types of solidarities:

(1) *solidarity by affinity*: e.g. the classeme of Latin *miles*, "soldier" ("human being"), constitutes a distinctive feature for *senex* ("old, speaking of human beings").

(2) *solidarity by selection* (e.g. German *Schiff-fahren* "navigate"): the archilexeme of the determinant lexeme (the archilexeme of *Schiff*

In a 1965 article, Pottier deals especially with definition[16]. The result is a summary of the previous works:

SEMANTIC DEFINITION IN DICTIONARIES

In his article entitled *Au seuil de la lexicographie* [On the Threshold of Lexicography] P. Imbs has accurately characterized the content of the majority of definitions given by dictionaries: "A category necessarily represents a *genus proximum*, of more abstract and more general extent than the word to be defined, and does not become the equivalent of this word until the *specific difference* is indicated. A definition, then, necessarily, and as a minimum requirement, is composed of two terms"[17].

We ourselves have analysed the semantic content of a "word" distinguishing between four types of definer: sememe, classeme, archisememe, virtueme[18].

The *sememe*, or combination of distinctive semes [French *ensemble des termes distinctifs*], corresponds, in part, to the *differentiae specificae* of P. Imbs. The *classeme*, or combination of the general conceptual classes, too seldom appears in definitions. The *archisememe*, or subcombination [French *sous-ensemble*] common to a combination of sememes is the *genus proximum* of P. Imbs[19].

"ship") functions as a distinctive feature for the determined lexeme (*fahren* "drive").

(3) *solidarity by implication*: the determinant lexeme determines the content of the lexeme determined (e.g. French *aquilin*, "hooked", is only used for noses).

These solidarities have important stylistic implications; in addition, they are important for the study of metaphors.

[16]B. Pottier, "La définition sémantique dans les dictionnaires", en *TraLiLi* III, 1, 1965, 33–39 (quote on p. 33).

[17]Paul Imbs, "Au seuil de la lexicographie," in *CahLex*, 2, 1960, pp. 3–17; cf. p. 12.

[18]*TraLiLi* II, 1, 1964, pp. 107–37; cf. p. 125.

[19]Pottier says "We have likewise introduced the virtueme or combination of non-distinctive semes associated with the particular knowledge of an individual, of a group, of a series of experiences. Its determination is very difficult. The virtueme appears from time to time in definitions. For example, *trunk* 'any of various large, re-

Every *lexeme* (minimum *signifiant* of designation) will have meaning as follows:

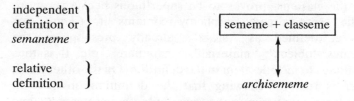

independent
definition or   } $\boxed{\text{sememe + classeme}}$
semanteme

relative
definition   }   *archisememe*

Thus, the lexeme *chair*:

$$
\begin{array}{llll}
chair & \begin{array}{l}\text{sememe}\\ S^m\end{array} & \left\{\begin{array}{l}\text{to sit in}\\ \text{raised}\\ \text{for one person}\\ \text{with back}\\ \text{no arms}\end{array}\right\} + \left\{\begin{array}{l}\text{discontinuous}\\ \text{inanimate}\\ \text{intransitive}\\ \text{material}\\ \dots\dots\dots\end{array}\right\} & \begin{array}{l}\text{Classeme}\\ C^m\end{array}\\[4em]
\begin{array}{l}seat\ \text{sememe}\\ \qquad S^n\\ \text{archilexeme}\end{array} & & \left\{\begin{array}{l}\text{to sit in}\\ \text{raised}\end{array}\right\} + \left\{\begin{array}{l}\text{discontinuous}\\ \text{inanimate}\\ \text{intransitive}\\ \text{material}\end{array}\right\} & \begin{array}{l}\text{Classeme}\\ C^n\end{array}
\end{array}
$$

In this diagram, Pottier includes classemes in the definition (semanteme). This change is very significant and important. In reality, classemes are also semes, more comprehensive semes[20]. A seme can be very specific or very general, but there

---

inforced boxes or chests for carrying clothing and personal effects, as for a vacation' (*Webster's New World Dictionary of the American Language*). The content of 'for carrying clothing and personal effects,' and especially 'as for a vacation' belong to the virtueme; this is *very often* the case, but it is not distinctive: the object would not *have to* be used for taking clothes on a holiday to be called a *trunk*." (*TraLiLi* III, 1, 1965, p. 33 note 3).

[20]We do not deny, however, the usefulness of distinguishing between *semes* (sememes, archisememes) and *classemes*. E. Coseriu, "Lexikalische Solidaritäten," in *Poetica*, 1, 1967, pp. 294, ff., shows more explicitly than Pottier the necessity for the distinction (Coseriu speaks of the distinction between *(archi)lexeme* and *classeme*, but this is a case of units of content).

is no difference in principle (see Heger's theory, below). For this reason the classeme can enter into the definition. But often the classeme proves to be superfluous because a more specific seme already implicitly contains it. *Chaise*, for example, defined as "siège", already presupposes the classemes "object", "material", "inanimate", etc. It is thus superfluous to include them in the defintion. On the other hand, Pottier is right in showing that the definition, in general, starts from more comprehensive units (archisememes) and adds more specific semes:

siège		for one person	with a back	no arms
seme 1	seme 2	seme 3	seme 4	seme 5
"for sitting"	"raised"			

(i.e. "a *chair* is a *seat* for one person with a back but no arms").

The reverse method does not turn out to be satisfactory:

chaise = tabouret				with a back
seme 1	seme 2	seme 3	seme 4	seme 5
"for sitting"	"raised"	"for 1 person"	"with no arms"	

(i.e. "a *chair* is a *stool* with a back")

because in the definition of *tabouret* is tacitly included the negation of seme 5: a *tabouret* cannot be thought of as having a back. The 'ascending' definition, as a result, would have to incorporate contradictions. But, on the other hand, it is also unacceptable, to say *tabouret = chaise sans dossier*, because a chair without a back does not exist ('with a back' is a seme of chair)[21]. We have no choice, then, but to resort to the archilexeme *seat*[22]

---

[21]Josette Rey-Debove, *CahLex*, 8, 1966, p. 77.
[22]Josette Rey-Debove, *TraLiLi*, V, 1, 1967, p. 147, present it thus

(*cavalier*, "homme à cheval": a horseman is a "man on a horse"):

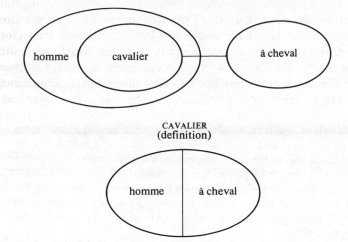

CAVALIER
(definition)

Homme is an archilexeme, *à cheval* the specific difference. Or for *saharienne* "veste de toile à manches courtes" (short sleeved jacket):

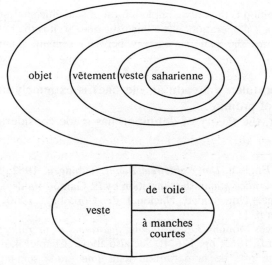

There is an advantage in making use of the immediately superior archilexeme (*veste*), and not of *objet*, of much more general semantic value (ib. 148).

(b) ALAIN AND JOSETTE REY

«Definition is knowledge of the essence», wrote the philosopher of law, Karl Engisch in 1952.[23] The importance of the *definition* for semantic analysis is a fact which has only been recognized for a few years. As recently as 1963, Georges Mounin, in his excellent book on the theoretical problems of translation, said:

> Nowhere, neither in semantics nor in lexicology, has there appeared this idea that the *definitions* of the *signifiés* can or should be the material for a scientific linguistic analysis. Now the natural approach of Hjelmslev and Prieto, the empirical techno-logical approach of Gardin, the logical approach of Sørensen, are all tending to propose that the *analysis of the definition of SIGNIFIÉS* ought officially to be seen as a task suitable for linguistics[24].

And Mounin adds:

> Definition is the only complete form of semantic analysis. Now it is a logical operation, not a linguistic one. So it is the definition that forms the real passageway between semantics and logic (p. 134).

This postulate (already an old one) is extremely important and full of promise.

In fact, the theory of definition has made considerable pro-

---

[23]Karl Engisch, *Der rechtsfreie Raum*, Tübingen, 1952; *El ámbito de lo no jurídico* (Spanish translation by E. Garzón Valdés), Córdoba (Argentina, Universidad Nacional de Córdoba), 1960, 135 pp. (quote on p. 11).

[24]Georges Mounin, *Les problèmes théoriques de la traduction*, Paris (Gallimard), 1963, pp. 126, ff. See also above, Chapter 4, n. 4, and J. Noël, "Le rôle de la définition dans une étude sémantique pré-paratoire à l'indexation mécanisée," in *Linguistic Research in Belgium*, ed. by Ivan Lebrun, Universa Wetteren (Belgium), 1966, pp. 87–97.

gress during the past few years, since the article by Imbs[25] mentioned by Pottier, thanks especially to Pottier himself, Alain Rey and Josette Rey-Debove[26]. As editors of the Robert dictionary, these last two combine theory with many years' practical experience. Josette Rey[27], in an excellent article –

---

[25]Paul Imbs, "Au seuil de la lexicographie," in *CahLex*, 2, 1960, pp. 3–17 (an illuminating exposition of the problems). We shall not speak here of studies which deal with syntagmatic level. See especially the studies by Jean Dubois, among them the article "Représentation de systèmes paradigmatiques formalisés dans un dictionnaire structural," in *CahLex*, 5, 1964, pp. 4–15, which comes closer to my views (on the series *matin/matinée, soir/soirée, jour/journée, an/année*; it has to do, then, with larger structures, see also Pottier, *TraLiLi* V, 1, 1967, p. 45).

[26]Alain Rey, "A propos de la définition lexicographique," in *CahLex*, 6, 1965, pp. 67–80; and the very full article by the same author "Les dictionnaires: forme et contenu," in *CahLex*, 6, 1965, pp. 65–102. More recent studies by Alain Rey: *La lexicologie* (Initiation à la linguistique, Série A, Lectures, 2), Paris (Klincksieck), 1970, 323 pp.; *Théories du signe et du sens* (Initiation à la linguistique, Série A, Lectures, 5), Paris (Klincksieck), 1973, 299 pp. *La sémantique* (éd.), in Langue française 4, Paris (Larousse), 1969 [on this, A. Rey himself: *Remarques sémantiques*, pp. 5–29]; "Hall et la linguistique américaine", *ZrP* 86, 1970, 205–218; "Typologie génétique des dictionnaires", in *Langages* (Didier/Larousse) 19, 1970, 48–68; "Analyzing a Semantic Analysis" [= B. Berlin, "Tzeltal Numeral Classifiers: A Study in Ethnographic Semantics", 1968], in *Semiotica* (Mouton) III, 1971, 140–154; "La conscience du poète: Les langages de Paul Valéry", in *Litterature* [revue trimestrielle] (Larousse) 4, 1971, 116–128; etc.

[27]Josette Rey-Debove, "La définition lexicographique: recherches sur l'équation sémique", in *CahLex* 8, 1966, pp. 71–94. More recent studies by Josette Rey-Debove: *Étude linguistique et sémiotique des dictionnaires français contemporains* (Approaches to Semiotics ed. Th. A. Sebeok assisted by Jos. Rey-Debove, 13), The Hague–Paris (Mouton), 1971, 329 pp. [chap. 6 of the 3rd part is concerned with the problem of definition, pp. 180–257]; see concerning this book, the article by S. Ullmann, "Lexicography: Its Principles and Methods", in *Semiotica* VIII, 1973, 276–286; Josette Rey-Debove,

perhaps the best ever written on the subject – describes the process of definition in the following manner:

> It must be remembered that what is defined is arbitrarily taken out of context[28] and presented as an unknown. Also the word is submitted to a subjective analysis, which is important in border-line cases. Once this is understood, one starts from the lexical unit to be defined. This *signifiant* to be defined is linked to a concept; this is in turn analyzed into less complex concepts. Then these concepts are named by means of several *signifiants* (defin-ers). For a defined element D there is: *signifiant* D → Concept of D → Concept which analyzes the concept of D → Regrouping of these concepts, named by means of definers A + B + C. The first part of the process is semasiological; the second, ono-masiological. This analysis is presented as an equivalence,

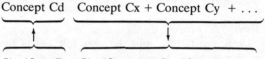

$$\text{Concept Cd} \quad \text{Concept Cx} + \text{Concept Cy} + \ldots$$

$$\textit{Signifiant} \text{ D} = \textit{Signifiant} \text{ A} + \textit{Signifiant} \text{ B} + \ldots$$

"Le domaine du dictionnaire" *Langages* (Didier/Larousse) 19, 1970, 3–34; "La sémantique européenne au Colloque de Mayence" [1967], *ZrP* 86, 1970, 190–204 [on pp. 201–204 she discusses our chapter II.5 below]; "Notes sur une interprétation autonymique de la littéra-ture; Le mode du "comme je dis" ", in *Littérature* (revue trimestri-elle) 4, 1971, 90–95; "Limites des applications de la linguistique à la lexicographie" (Dictionnaires de langue monolingues), in *Application of Linguistics*, Selected papers of the Second Int. Congress of Applied Linguistics, (Cambridge, 1969), Cambridge (Univ. Press), 1971, 369–375; "L'orgie langagière, Le sonnet à princesse Uranie", in *Poétique* (revue de théorie et d'analyse littéraires) 12, 1972, 572–583; "La métalangue comme système de référence au signe", *Le Français Moderne* 40, 1972, 232–241; etc.

[28]"Nevertheless, the definer can define only by remembering the occurrences of the word within his personal experience, that is, by going back to context. The most frequent circumstances in his mem-ory will be utilized to formulate a meaning which will serve as a basis for his work. But this 'average' meaning will not correspond to any meaning actually realized in a statement; the very principle of the definition, then, is not linguistic" [a note by Josette Rey, ib.].

and the definition is *valid*, that is, it works within one's experience of the world, if this equivalence is shown to be true, if it is correct. It is a question, then, given an element defined D with sememe Sd[29], of finding two or more words to match it, whose sememes collectively add up to Sd (*CahLex*, 8, 1966, pp. 71–72).

Josette Rey evokes the time-honoured formula: "All of the word to be defined, and nothing but the word to be defined" and then proceeds to analyze the different aspects of the defining process. She distinguishes three possibilities:

(1) Positive analysis (by *genus proximum* and *differentia specifica*: see Pottier's analysis by semes, above).

(2) Analysis by negation (definition by antonyms: *laisser = ne pas prendre*, "leave" = "not to take"; in this case there are no archilexemes).

(3) Definition by synonym (this is not an analysis)[30]. Josette Rey goes deeper into the first two possibilities in a second, more recent, article[31], adding analysis by transformation, relational definition: *timide* "qui manque d'audace"; *idéel* "de l'idée" (*timid* "lacking courage", *ideal* "belonging to ideas").

Definition is the most important task of the lexicographer. Josette Rey is right in saying: "The lexicographer is really attempting a semantic analysis; and when the results are disappointing, we should blame the lexicographer and not lexicography" (*TraLiLi* V, 1, 1967, 142). What the lexicographer does, or should do, is nothing less than an analysis of the sememes of the entire vocabulary (or at least a great part of the vocabulary) of a language. This analysis starts from a

---

[29]Sememe: combination of the elements of sense of a word or of a lexeme.

[30]We shall see later that the synonym can be an exact equivalence insofar as it concerns a symbolic sememe (with the omission of other sememes = symbolic or symptomatic factors). – See also the chapter "Définitions synonymiques", in Bernard Quemada, *Les Dictionnaires du français moderne* (1539–1863), Paris (Didier), 1967, pp. 445–449.

[31]Josette Rey-Debove, "La définition lexicographique; bases d'une typologie formelle," in *TraLiLi* V, 1, 1967, pp. 141–59.

given linguistic sign (*not* from reality) and consequently works in a semasiological direction. Such definitions (= analysis of the sememes or significations) are intensional (not extensional)[32].

Only now can we return to the problem of the application to reality of intensionally defined concepts (see above, Chapter 4, note 15). Let us take the example of the concepts 'house' and 'hut,' our original starting point (Chapter 4). A definition of these concepts will show each concept as a sememe (= sum of semes or distinctive features):

$$S_1 \text{ (house)} = (s_1^1 + s_2^1 + s_3^1)$$

$$S_2 \text{ (hut)} = (s_1^2 + s_2^2 + s_3^2)$$

If we confront an average or normal *house* or an average or normal *hut* with these concepts we can easily match sememe and reality, but if the object itself is on the borderline between 'house' and 'hut', the match is less easy: we will have, for example, a sememe $s_1^1 + s_2^1 + s_3^2$, which corresponds neither to concept S_1 'house' nor to concept S_2 'hut'. We shall be uncertain of which meaning (sememe) to apply, and, consequently, whether to use 'house' or 'hut'. We will be unsure for the very reason that the concepts (sememes) are too precise (compare above, Chapter 3b), which prevents or complicates identification, the matching of reality and concept. The speaker is forced to choose between two inexact designations, both of which include inappropriate semes. If the semes are of the same distinctive relevance, he will prefer, in the case of $s_1^1 + s_2^1 + s_3^2$, the designation *house* (S_1); in the case of $s_1^1 + s_2^2 + s_3^2$, the designation *hut* (S_2); but relevance includes subjective appreciations, so speakers will not always make the same decisions (that is why, in law, appeal to higher courts makes sense). Ordinary language often helps itself by lexicalizing concepts corresponding to intermediate realities such as,

---

[32]There are, in special cases, extensional definitions, see below. Extensional definitions are enumerative, and therefore start from reality.

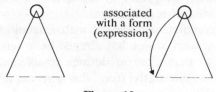

Figure 10

for example, *twilight* (S_3) between *day* (S_1) and *night* (S_2), but *twilight* presents the same difficulties of application to border-line realities, and conceptualization and lexicalization could continue, theoretically, to infinity. Intensionally defined concepts are determined (not defined) at the same time extensionally (= all the realities to which the sum of the semes determined by the definition correspond); difficulties begin when reality does not correspond to one (or more) of the semes united in the sememe[33].

(c) MEANING (SEMEME)

The much debated definition of what a 'meaning' is now proves to be very easy. 'Meaning' is what is described by the definition, that is, the sememe associated with a form (form on the level of expression, see below)[34] or, to put it another way, the mental object associated with a *signifiant*. In Ullmann's triangle the apex has the two functions shown in Figure 10.

Either I can consider the mental object as such (without thinking of its formalization in *one* given language), or I can consider it, on the other hand, as the content of a form in a given language, that is, as 'meaning' (signification). Meaning

---

[33]Another reason for the "lack of precision" in ordinary language is the fact of polysemy or homonymy (according to the preferred terminology), that is, the complexity of many *signifiés*.

[34]Here we are speaking only of symbolic features. We shall come back to this later (Part II, Chapter 5f).

(signification), then, is the relationship between a concept and a form (Ullmann); we prefer to define it as a sememe (mental object) associated with a *signifiant*.

We are in complete agreement with Eugenio Coseriu, who says in a recent work which has already been referred to[35] (we must remember that Coseriu defines *signification* (meaning) and *designation* differently from the way we do, see above, Chapter 4, n.18):

> Actually and primarily, signification does not structure exterior 'things', but only interior ones: objects of experience insofar as they are contained in the consciousness (Aristotle says that words are σύμβολα τῶν ἐν τῇ ψυχῇ παθημάτων." ("symbols of things experienced in the soul"). "The cause of the experience can be exterior, for example the sensory perception of a tree; yet the word *tree* does not signify this sensory perception, but signifies rather the tree as something apprehended by man, as something contained in his consciousness. Language as such knows no difference between exterior 'things' and interior ones; the creations of the imagination are conceived of by language in exactly the same way as objects of sensory perception, with the result that the existence of the name is no proof at all of the exterior existence of the 'thing' named. On the other hand, signification is, in the primary and absolute imposing of names, in a certain sense 'subjective'; it is the objectivization of something subjective contained in a consciousness; complete objectivity of signification is attained only be means of inter-subjectivity, that is, by means of the essential historicity of language.
>
> Signification as such does not refer to things insofar as they exist, but to the *essence of the things*, that is, to what is universal in individual experience, or, putting it another way, to the experience as its own infinite possibility. The word *tree*, for example, signifies the essence of tree, that is, the infinite

---

[35]Eugenio Coseriu, "Das Phänomen der Sprache und das Daseinsverständnis des heutigen Menschen" [The Phenomenon of Language and the Comprehension of Existence in Modern Man], from *Die Pädagogische Provinz*, no. 21, 1967, pp. 11–28, reprinted in E. Coseriu, *Sprache, Strukturen und Funktionen*, XII Aufsätze (TBL 2), Tübingen 1970, 111–135.

possibilities of the entity tree. Thus, the word *tree* can designate not only trees that exist, but also trees that no longer exist, trees that do not yet exist, and trees that have no existence at all except in the imagination. For this reason, designation of 'things' by language is also something secondary and conditioned, a possibility which is only opened up by means of signification. This latter, then, can be defined as the possibility or potentiality of designation. That is to say, the word can also designate something individual, but only by means of a general signification and an individualization, through an operation of determination. The demonstrative and personal pronouns also are universal as to their signification and only become individual designations through the situation when speaking: in themselves, 'this' and 'I' do not signify any individual object at all, but only 'this-ness' and 'I-ness.' And proper names are a secondary phenomenon in language, in the sense that they involve a process of individualization, which is historical, not accidental. Signification and designation, then, are completely different linguistic functions: signification is conceptual, designation, on the other hand, objective. Identification of the meaning with the object designated is an error from which even positivist logic, which has expressed this opinion, has been freed in more recent times (in *Die Pädagog. Provinz* 21, 1967, pp. 14–15; in the ed. of 1970 pp. 115–116).

And elsewhere Coseriu continues:

Signification is λόγος in the etymological sense, that is, selection and, thereby, representation of being, but not a confirmation of being. For this reason, language as such, as Aristotle long ago pointed out, is neither true nor false, since it involves neither a breaking up nor a reconstruction, neither διαίρεσις nor σύνθεσις, of the essence of things: language simply *stands for* the essence of things as conceived by man[36]. Words are intuitive delimitations, but not definitions motivated by and from the things themselves. Even in the case of derived and compound

---

[36]See also Harald Weinrich, *Linguistik der Lüge* [Linguistics of the Lie], Heidelberg (Verlag Lambert Schneider), 1966, 80 pp.

words, which, as Wolff recognized, correspond to a 'definition', that is, to an assertion, language cannot be accepted simply as the exposition of the "truth of things". Thus, an *Eichhörnchen* (squirrel) is not *das kleine Horn einer Eiche* (the little horn of an oak) and *Walfische* (whales) are not *Fische* (fishes)[37] in the scientific sense (p. 17).

---

[37]See more examples above, Chapter 4b.

6

Language Divides up
the World

(a) HUMBOLDT–WEISBERGER–WHORF

Language splits up the world and converts the infinite diversity of reality into a manageable and divisible network. Language orders and articulates the infinity of concrete things, and spiritual reality as well[1]. We look at the world through this network formed by language. This is no other than the "inner world" of concepts, the language image of the world envisaged by Wilhelm von Humboldt[2]. That language splits up the world

---

[1]For *contexts* and the *universe of discourse*, see Eugenio Coseriu, "Determinación y entorno," in *Teoría del lenguaje y lingüística general,* Madrid (Gredos, 1962, pp. 282–323 (reprinted from *Rom. Jahrb.* 7, 1955–1956).

[2]"To some extent, language is the exterior manifestation of the spirit of peoples; their language is their spirit and their spirit is their language; one cannot insist too much on the high degree of identity there is between the two. Just how they manage to proceed from the same original source, which is inaccessible to our understanding, is something which remains inexplicably mysterious" (W. von Humboldt, *Über die Verschiedenheit des menschlichen Sprachbaues . . .* Berlin, 1836, p. 37). "Man lives above all – almost exclusively, since his way of feeling and acting depends on his ideas – with things such as they are brought to him by language" (ib., p. 58). "The difference in languages is not a difference between sounds and signs, but rather

a difference which implies a different conception of the world" (*Über
das vergleichende Sprachstudium in Beziehung auf die verschiedenen
Epochen der Sprachentwicklung* (1820), in *Gesammelte Schriften*, ed.
by A. Leitzmann (Preuss. Ak. der Wiss.), vol. IV, Berlin, 1905, p.
27). Modern Linguistics begins with the ideas of Humboldt: "Language is the expression of the form in which the individual carries the
world within him", W. von Wartburg, *Problems and Methods in Linguistics*, revised ed. with the collaboration of S. Ullmann, Oxford
(Blackwell), 1969, p. 162 (concerning the dependence on Humboldt
see also p. 9); in the 2nd. German ed. of 1962, pp. 162 and 10, in the
2nd. French ed., *Problèmes et méthodes de la linguistique*, Paris
(Presses Univers.), 1963, pp. 175 and 10; "Possession of the name
and possession of the concept are thus very closely inter-related. *It is
they* that condition the power of abstraction. . . . Words are the land-
marks which enable man to orientate himself amid the multitude of
phenomena. In their totality, their composition and their reciprocal
relations they constitute, in the words of Humboldt, 'a veritable
world which the mind, by using its inherent powers, must interpose
between itself and objective reality'". (*Problems and Methods . . .*,
1969, p. 169; Fr. ed., pp. 183, ff.; 2nd. Ger. ed., pp. 169, ff.; Span.
ed., pp. 286, ff.; W. von Humboldt, *Über die Verschiedenl eit des
menschlichen Sprachbaues . . .*, p. 205). For a historical introduction
see the excellent work of Hans Helmut Christmann, *Beiträge zur Ges-
chichte der These vom Weltbild der Sprache*, Akademie der Wissenschaften und der Literatur, Abh. der geistes- und sozialwiss. Klasse,
1966, Mainz, 1967, pp. 441–69; also, E. Coseriu, "Über die Sprach-
typologie Wilhelm von Humboldts, Ein Beitrag zur Kritik der
sprachwissenschaftlichen Überlieferung", in *Beiträge zur vergleichen-
den Literaturgeschichte* (Festschrift Kurt Wais), Tübingen (Niemeyer)
1972, 107–135.

Benjamin Lee Whorf expresses the same idea: "The background
linguistic system (in other words, the grammar) of each language is
not merely a reproducing instrument for voicing ideas but rather is
itself the shaper of ideas, the program and guide for the individual's
mental activity, for his analysis of impressions, for his synthesis of his
mental stock in trade. Formulation of ideas is not an independent
process, strictly rational in the old sense, but is part of a particular
grammar, and differs, from slightly to greatly, between different
grammars. We dissect nature along lines laid down by our native
languages. The categories and types that we isolate from the world
of phenomena we do not find there because they stare every observer

and that we acquire this image of the world with our mother tongue is a fact of which we are not usually conscious, because even polyglots operate primarily within the same family of languages, such as within the Romance languages, or more broadly within the Indo-European family of languages, which share a common tradition. Beyond this, there are some natural distinctions, which include, for example, *day* and *night, eat* and *sleep, birth* and *death*, found in all languages. But many areas – and even these last[3] – are split up differently according to language groups or in a specific language, to such an extent that we can say: we see the world through the spectacles provided by our language, that is, to express it more scientifically, by means of concepts, of mental objects, of the schemata of representation of our mother tongue.

Spanish distinguishes, for example, between *el tren trae retraso* and *el tren lleva retraso*, "the train is late," depending on whether the train has not yet arrived or not yet left, a distinction not made in French, German or English[4]. French and Spanish, for example, do not make the German distinction

---

in the face; on the contrary, the world is presented in a kaleidoscopic flux of impressions which has to be organized by our minds – and this means largely by the linguistic systems in our minds" (*Language, Thought and Reality, Selected Writings of Benjamin Lee Whorf,* edited by John B. Carroll, Cambridge, Mass., 1964, pp. 212–13); see also G. Mounin, "A propos de Language, Thought and Reality de B. L. Whorf," in *Bull. Soc. Ling.,* Paris, 56, 1961, pp. 122–38.

[3] I noted, for example, in Bolivia, the following expressions for "eat" in Aymara: *mancam* [mánχam] (eat, speaking of adults), *ojochasim* [oχotšasim] (speaking of children), *hatum* (eat a bone), *thurum* (something toasted), *chichːm* [tšitšim] (meat), *hacum* (flour), *allpim* [alpim] (cream etc.), *papim* (mashed potatoes). – For "lift" I noted: *aptam* (general word), *ekctam* [ekχtam] (cloth, rug), *astam* (plate), *ichtam* [iɣtam] (lift a child), *irtam* (small ball or die), *itam* (big heavy thing).

[4] W. von Wartburg, *Einführung in Problematik und Methodik der Sprachwissenschaft,* ²1962, p. 168; in the French translation, ²1963, p. 182; *Problems and Methods in Linguistics,* revised ed. with the collaboration of S. Ullmann, Oxford (Blackwell) 1969, p. 168.

between *Haut* and *Fell*, "skin" and "hide". Both words correspond to French *peau* and Spanish *piel*. On the other hand,
French distinguishes between *poil* (hair on the body) and
cheveu (hair on the head), while English uses *hair*, and German, *Haar*, for both. Spanish occupies an intermediate position, it distinguishes between *cabello* and *pelo*, but *pelo* refers
to both human and animal hair[5]. Another illustrative example:
In German there is a difference between *das gleiche* [i.e.,
same, of the same type] and *das selbe* [i.e., same, total identity
= of the same type and 'material' identity], while Eng. *the
same*, Fr. *le même*, Span. *el mismo* are used for both meanings.
Thus, for example, a sentence such as "Today I ate the same
steak as yesterday" can be translated into German only as:
"Heute habe ich das *gleiche* Beefsteak wie gestern gegessen";
das selbe would produce here digestive complications!

In Germany, for several years Leo Weisgerber has been
concerned with the problem of the transformation of the world
in language (he created a new word to characterize this process: *to wordify the world* "Das Worten der Welt")[6]. It would

---

[5]See Wartburg, *Problems and Methods in Linguistics*, 1969, p. 165;
in the 2nd. German edition [2]1962, p. 166; Fr. ed., *Problèmes et
méthodes de la linguistique*, Paris, [2]1963, p. 180; Spanish ed. 1951, p.
278, with a note by Dámaso Alonso.

[6]Leo Weisgerber, *Von Weltbild der deutschen Sprache*, 2 vols., Düsseldorf, [2]1953–1954; "Das Worten der Welt als sprachliche Aufgabe
der Menschheit", in *Sprachforum*, 1, 1955, pp. 10–19 ("Verwandlung
von Sein in bewusstes Sein für Menschen", p. 16; "Sprache als Pro-
zess solcher Anverwandlung der Welt", p. 17); "Die Erforschung der
Sprachzugriffe I", in *Wirkendes Wort*, 7, 1956, pp. 65–73 [again in
Wirkendes Wort, Sammelband I Sprachwissenschaft, Düsseldorf,
1962, pp. 175–83]; "Die Gerichtetheit der Sprachzugriffe", in *Kon-
krete Vernunft – Festschrift für Rothacker*, Bonn, 1958, pp. 281–87;
"Sprache und geistige Gestaltung der Welt", in *Zeitschrift für
Pädagogik*, 2. Beiheft: Didaktik in der Lehrerausbildung, 1960, pp.
5–16; "Die vier Schauplätze des Wortens der Welt", in *Erkenntnis
und Verantwortung – Festschrift to Theodor Litt*, Düsseldorf, 1963,
pp. 11–24; "Die tragenden Pfeiler der Spracherkenntnis" in
Wirkendes Wort, Sammelband I Sprachwissenschaft, Düsseldorf

be dangerous, however, to abstract from the history of a language when considering the conceptual fragmentation of that language. If, in the above example, German distinguishes between *Haut* and *Fell*, and French says *peau* in both cases, this does not mean that a Frenchman cannot distinguish between "Haut" and "Fell". The reason is historical-linguistic. Latin distinguished between *cutis* and *pellis*. *Cutis* disappeared during the post-classical period for phonetic, and perhaps historical and cultural, reasons, and *pellis* took over its meaning. The loss of a "conceptual" difference may be due to historical-linguistic causes. Therefore it is dangerous to make inferences as to the capacity of a speech community to make distinctions from a "synchronic-linguistic vision of the world".

However, the formation of a new concept can, in fact, be the expression of new knowledge. Thus, in contrast with the

(Schwann), 1962, pp. 9–20 [ibid. other articles by Weisgerber]; "Die vier Stufen in der Erforschung der Sprachen," in *Sprache und Gemeinschaft,* Grundlegung, vol. II, Düsseldorf, 1963, 303 pp.; *Grundformen sprachlicher Weltgestaltung,* Köln und Opladen (Westdeutscher Verlag), 1963, 56 pp. [with discussion, (pp. 39–56); Weisgerber uses the term "sprachliche Weltgestaltung" instead of "sprachliche Anverwandlung der Welt," pp. 40–41]; see also his work of synthesis *Von den Kräften der deutschen Sprache*, 4 vols., Düsseldorf, 1957–1962.

Concerning Weisgerber's theories, see Helmut Gipper, "Inhaltbezogene Sprachforschung in Deutschland," Vuosikirja II/*Arsbok* II, 1961 – Förbundet För Lärarna i Moderna Sprak i Finland, 1961, pp. 27–41, and especially Helmut Gipper/Hans Schwarz, *Bibliographisches Handbuch zye Sprachinhaltsforschung,* Teil I, *Schrifttum zur Sprachinhaltsforschung in alphabetischer Folge nach Verfassern mit Besprechungen und Inhaltshinweisen,* Band I Buchstaben A–G, Köln und Opladen, 1962–1966, ccvii + 773 pp. [it has an introduction to the method of Weisgerber's school, of more than 100 pp.]; Peter Hartmann, *Wesen und Wirkung der Sprache im Spiegel der Theorie Leo Weisgerbers,* Heidelberg, 1958, 168 pp.; Paul Valentin, "Une linguistique sémantique," in *Études Germaniques,* Paris, (Didier), 19, 1964, pp. 255–61; *Sprache-Schlüssel zur Welt.* Festschrift to Leo Weisgerber, Düsseldorf, 1959.

Greeks, the Romans had no expression for "plant" (*planta* meant "the sole of the foot"). They distinguished between trees (*arbores*) and *herbae*, but neither Pliny nor the other Roman authors knew any broader concept to contrast vegetable with animal life. Albertus Magnus, a scientist, first uses *planta* in the Medieval Latin of the thirteenth century, in the title, for example, of his treatise *De vegetabilibus et plantis*. But it was only in the sixteenth century, that this scientific knowledge, expressed in the concept "plant" and linguistically in the designation *plant*, was borrowed from the Latin of the botanists into the different European languages, as a result of the popularization of botanical knowledge. *Plant* today forms part of everyday language[7]. In this way the formation of con-

---

[7]See the article *planta* in the *Franz. Etym. Wörterbuch* (9, 19) and W. von Wartburg, "Organisation et état actuel des travaux relatifs au Französisches Etymologisches Wörterbuch", in *Essais de philologie moderne* (Biblioth. de la Fac. de Phil. et Lettres de l'Univ. de Liège, fasc. CXXIX), Paris, 1953, pp. 97–114, especially pp. 102, ff.

See also the interesting work by Fritz Gschnitzer, *Studien zur griechischen Terminologie der Sklaverei* (Akademie der Wissenschaften und der Literatur in Mainz, Abhandlungen der geistesund sozial-wissenschaftlichen Klasse, Jg. 1963, no. 13), Mainz, 1964, pp. 1283–1310: "The Greek language, at least up to the beginning of the Hellenistic period, did not yet have a general linguistic term to express the concept of slave, as we understand it. ... The Greek language managed to get by with several other partial terms, but none of them even approximately covered the concept. How is one to explain this fact from a historical point of view? It would be erroneous to draw the conclusion that the absence of the expression indicates the absence of the concept. We have no doubt that the classical period in fact knew this concept, as well as the corresponding object. If the linguistic expression (for the concept in its entirety) is nonexistent, if the available terms refer only to particular elements of the concept, it could be explained as the effect of the external circumstances of an earlier period, which, no doubt, had grasped and given a name to the individual elements of the concept which later became 'slave', but had not yet learned to think of them as a unit, since in fact, these elements, in other times, had not yet been found together in life, or perhaps only in rare exceptions" (p. 1307).

cepts in a language can inform us about the way in which the world is split up by a particular linguistic community; and if we interpret the evidence with caution, it can also tell us about the state of the knowledge of that community.

(b) HEGER: CONCEPTS NOT DEPENDENT ON A GIVEN LANGUAGE

But the theories of Weisgerber and Whorf present another more serious problem. Is the concept bound to the structure of each individual language, as Weisgerber and Whorf maintain?[8] In this case, there would be no 'concepts', only 'meanings'. Onomasiology would lose its raison d'être, since it starts from the concept to arrive at a series of designations. Such a study would be superfluous, and Weinrich and other eminent linguists would be right, as would Bröcker, a philosopher at the University of Kiel, who, after a lecture, accused me of having talked for an hour about something that does not exist. Indeed, Weisgerber and his school deny the usefulness of both onomasiology and semasiology. For Weisgerber, there would be no concepts independent of a given language. Is the concept, on the other hand, an extralinguistic unit, presupposing the possibility of separating language from thought? An affirmative answer would lead us to platonic ideas, and we would get bogged down in problems which have been debated for centuries. To be sure, languages order reality according to their own individual methods, as Weisgerber and Whorf maintain. On the other hand, if onomasiology is to be more than a chimera, a solution to the problem of the concept has to be found which overcomes the two obstacles just mentioned. Klaus Heger has attempted such a solution in his article on the methodological bases of onomasiology and of classification by means of concepts[9], where he says, that the concepts we need

---

[8]Whorf, at least, admits common concepts for different languages with a common tradition (Standard Average European).

[9]Klaus Heger, "Die methodologischen Voraussetzungen von Onomasiologie und begrifflicher Gliederung," in *ZRP*, 80, 1964, pp.

for onomasiology "not only need to be ascertained in an un-ambiguous manner; it is also necessary to prove in one way or another their independence with respect to the structure of a given language. Since the concept 'is practically impossible to grasp except with the help of a *signifiant*' . . . this independence cannot be proved for an isolated concept, but only if we start from the relationships which link several concepts to each other. If the system of these relations reflects a coherent structure which assigns to each concept a place which is exclusively its own in this system, the required proof of independence is achieved, since by means of such a structure the concept is ascertained by something which does not depend on the data of the language by means of whose *signifiants* the concept is grasped" (*TraLiLi* III[1], 1965, 19)[10].

If we accept, with Heger, that the concept [cp. the *noeme* in

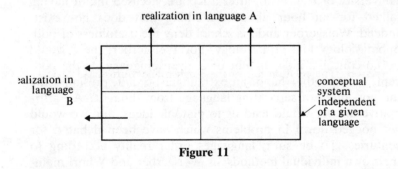

Figure 11

436–516 [= "Les bases méthodologiques de l'onomasiologie et du classement par concepts," in *TraLiLi* (Strasbourg) III, 1, 1965, pp. 7–32]. See also his book *Die Bezeichnung temporaldeiktischer Begriffs-kategorien im französischen und spanischen Konjugationssystem* (Beihefte zur *Zeitschrift für Romanische Philologie*, 104), Tübingen, 1963, viii + 244 pp. This book provoked a whole series of critical discussions in specialized periodicals. Heger answers all of them in his article "Temporale Deixis und Vorgangsquantität ('Aspekt' und 'Aktionsart')", in *ZRP*, 83, 1967, pp. 512–82.

[10]See below (II chap. 3) my analysis of the concept "remember" according to Heger's trapezium.

chap. II.7] is part of a coherent system which does not depend on a given language, we do not thereby deny that the designative systems which different languages possess to realize such concepts have their own special structures which differ between themselves (see Figure 11).

(c) CATFORD'S EXAMPLE

If, to use the examples cited recently by Catford[11], English distinguishes between *yes* and *no*, French between *oui, si,* and *non*, the very comparison presupposes a *tertium comparationis* which is formed by a conceptual framework (see the example below). Even if the elements are equal in number, the *distribution* (that is, the significations of those elements) may be different (English *brother* and *sister* are distributed in a different way from Burushaski *cho* and *yas*):

... The situational elements which are, so to speak, encapsulated in the contextual meaning of *brother* might be roughly characterized as *male* and *sibling*: those which are encapsulated in the contextual meaning of *cho* are *sibling* and *of same sex as speaker*. The relationship of the English and Burushaski lexical items to elements in the situation can be tabulated [as in Table 9].

Table 9

English	Situation		Burushaski[12]
	Speaker	Sibling	
brother	+	+	cho
	−	+	yas
sister	+	−	
	−	−	cho

(in this table + means *male*, − means *female*)

---

[11]J. C. Catford, *A Linguistic Theory of Translation. An Essay in Applied Linguistics* (Language and Language Learning, no. 8), London, 1965, viii + 103 pp. (especially pp. 40, ff.).

Klaus Heger has given me the more complete diagram (Table 10), in which nine languages are taken into account. As a result, we have three different 'sectionings' of the conceptual system.

Table 10
Noemic system for siblings

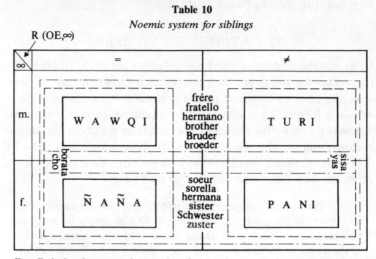

R = Relation between the speaker (or another person) and the designated sibling
OE = Speaker
S = Sex of the designated sibling
= of the same sex
≠ of different sex

Languages: – · – · English   *brother/sister*,   German *Bruder/Schwester*,   French   *frère/soeur*,   Spanish *hermanto/hermana*, Italian *fratello/sorella*, Dutch *broeder/zuster*.
– – – Burushaski *cho/yas*, Neomelanesian *borata/sisa*
—— Quechua *wawqi/turi/ñaña/pani*

---

[12]It is very interesting and instructive to note that Neomelanesian (a Creole language based on English) has exactly the same system as Burushaski:

   bǫrata (< Eng. *brother*) corresponds to *cho* ('same sex')
   sǫsa (< Eng. *sister*) corresponds to *yas* ('opposite sex')

in spite of the fact that both are English loan words (see R. A. Hall, Jr., *Pidgin and Creole Languages*, Ithaca, N.Y., 1966, p. 92).

Thus, a conceptual system which is independent of a given language (noematic system, cf. Part II, chap. 7) allows the comparison of languages, as well as the recognition of the 'sectioning' of 'reality' which each one of them realizes.

Catford continues:

> By a curious coincidence we can diagrammatize the contextual meaning of terms in the (grammatical) closed system of 'acceptance-rejection' items (yes-no) in exactly the same way. In English, selection of *yes* or *no* in response to a question (or statement) depends on what we may call 'the polarity of the situation': situation positive, answer 'yes'; situation negative, answer 'no' (irrespective of the polarity of the preceding utterance). In many other languages (e.g. at least some Slavonic languages, Arabic, Japanese, at least some Bantu languages), selection of the appropriate response depends on the polarity-relationship between question (or statement) and situation: *same polarity –* answer X, *different polarity –* answer Y. Some languages (e.g. French, with *oui*, *si*, *non*, and Norwegian and Swedish, with *ja*, *jo*, *nej*) have a three-term system here. We illustrate with English, Japanese and French (in Table 11).

The idea that a conceptual system independent of a given language is realized by particular "ways of dividing", which

Table 11

		Question	Situation	Engl.	Jap.	Fr.
e.g.	Did you? I did	+	+	yes	hai	oui
	Didn't you? I did	−	+	yes	iie	si
	Did you? I didn't	+	−	no	iie	non
	Didn't you? I didn't	−	−	no	hai	non

are proper to each language, becomes more and more obvious: "Basically, it is a matter of marking the boundaries of a neutral scale, independent of the particular divisions operated by each language within the mass of the content, with reference to which can be situated the meanings of the different signs" (Ruwet, art. referred to, p. 308; he gives, in addition, an interesting example with reference to the personal pronouns in Hanunoo, pp. 306, ff.)[13].

(d) THE GRAPHIC REPRESENTATION OF CONCEPTUAL SYSTEMS

In a recent article[14] E. Coseriu compares the different graphic representations of conceptual systems, starting from an analysis of the conceptual system "Schall" by K. W. L. Heyse in 1856[15]. Coseriu speaks of 'Wortfeld' (word field), but his own diagrams, which we shall reproduce here, show that it is really a conceptual system: the German words characterize the sememes and it would not be difficult to replace them with formulae. The fact that the system contains 'empty' positions

---

[13]We are so used to such divisions, which coincide, in many cases, in Romance and Germanic Languages, that we do not realise how many noematic oppositions we leave unexpressed, either lexically or morphologically: thus, we usually speak of *we* as being the plural of *I*, although *we* does not equal *I + I + I*; on the contrary, *we* can mean *I + you* as well as *I + he* or *I + you + he* (*they*), which makes it ambiguous (cf. the article by M. Durand on S. Ullmann, "Le vocabulaire moule et norme la pensée", in *Problèmes de la personne*, ed. I. Meyerson, Paris–The Hague (Mouton) 1973 [A conference which took place in Royaumont in 1960!], 251–269, especially p. 265.

[14]Eugenio Coseriu, "Zur Vorgeschichte der strukturellen Semantik: Heyses Analyse des Wortfeldes 'Schall' ", in *To Honor Roman Jakobson* (*Essays on the occasion of his seventieth birthday*). The Hague–Paris (Mouton), 1967, pp. 489–98: reprinted in E. Coseriu, *Sprache, Strukturen und Funktionen*, XII Aufsätze (TBL 2), Tübingen 1970, pp. 181–92.

[15]K. W. L. Heyse [† 1855], *System der Sprachwissenschaft*, edit. by H. Steinthal, Berlin, 1856, pp. 31–32.

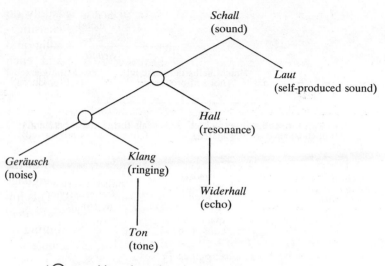

(◯ = position where there is no lexicalization in German)

Figure 12

(points where there are no lexicalizations in German) confirms that this is a conceptual system – with the slots filled by the German lexicalizations.

The analysis by Heyse gave the system illustrated by Figure 12 (as interpreted by E. Coseriu) (the English is only approximate).

This chart is very similar to the graphic method of A. Greimas shown in Figure 13[16].

Here we see better than in the previous diagram that a conceptual system is in question: the positions are defined. The German lexicalizations could be removed without destroying the conceptual system; instead of using German words, one could fill the system with lexicalizations from another language. The conceptual system is situated at the level of the

---

[16]A. Greimas, *Sémantique structurale,* Paris, 1966, p. 33.

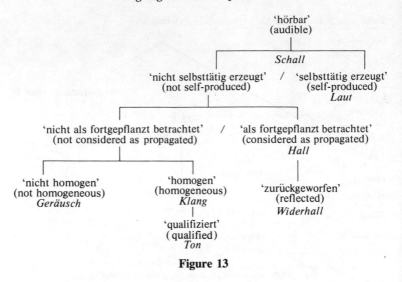

Figure 13

second metalanguage; the application of the system to a given language is made on the level of the first metalanguage[17].

Coseriu presents the same conceptual system applied to German with Pottier's graphic method (see Table 12). This diagram lets us define the (conceptual) sememe of each of the German words as shown in Table 13.

Schall is the German archilexeme for the entire system, *Hall* is the archilexeme for *Widerhall*, *Klang* the archilexeme for

---

[17]Coseriu is right in affirming (p. 493, n. 3) that this analysis does not correspond to the method of analysis of Katz and Fodor, "The Structure of a Semantic Theory," *Language,* 39, 1963, pp. 186 and 190 (see also J. J. Katz and P. M. Postal, *An Integrated Theory of Linguistic Descriptions* [Cambridge, Mass.], 1964, p. 14). The analysis of Katz and Fodor starts with the *signifiant*, not with the concepts. Nevertheless, Coseriu goes too far in saying that the analysis by Katz and Fodor has nothing to do with structural semantics. Katz and Fodor are trying to establish a semasiological structure which also has its theoretical justification (whether or not they attain this goal is another problem).

Table 12

Merkmale (features) / Lexeme	Hörbar (audible)	Selbsttätig erzeugt (self-produced)	Fortgepflanzt (propagated)	Zurückgeworfen (reflected)	Homogen (homogeneous)	Qualifiziert (qualified)
Schall	+	0	0	0	0	0
Laut	+	+	0	0	0	0
Hall	+	−	+	0	0	0
Widerhall	+	−	+	+	0	0
Klang	+	−	−	0	+	0
Geräusch	+	−	−	0	−	0
Ton	+	−	−	0	+	+
	a (s_1)	b (s_2)	c (s_3)	d (s_4)	e (s_5)	f (s_6)

+ = positives Merkmal (positive feature).
0 = gleichgültiges Merkmal (indeterminate feature)[18].
− = negatives Merkmal (negative feature).

Ton; there are no archilexemes in German to realize $(s_1 + \bar{s}_2)$ and $(s_1 + \bar{s}_2 + \bar{s}_3)$; in other words, if we remain on the conceptual level, (S_1) is the archisememe for the entire conceptual

---

[18]'Indeterminate' features are those which, for a certain content, may be pertinent for the contents subordinated to that content, as the features which correspond to other branches are likewise indeterminate for a determined semantic branch. Thus, for example, the feature 'qualified' for the content "Klang" (ringing) or the feature 'propagated' for the content "Laut." Such features may or may not appear in the texts and do not belong to the form of the content, that is, to the functional differences of the language (Coseriu, ib., p. 494, n. 4 [new edition, p. 188, n. 4]). – Cf. also the difference between *presentation in a diagram* (by mapping) and *presentation in a matrix* (by plotting) in Horst Geckeler, *Strukturelle Semantik des Französischen*, Tübingen (Niemeyer), 1973, pp. 50–51.

Table 13

Schall (sound)	(a)	$S_1 = (s_1)$
Laut (self-produced sound)	(a + b)	$S_2 = (s_1 + s_2)$
Hall (resonance)	(a − b + c)	$S_3 = (s_1 + \bar{s}_2 + s_3)$
Widerhall (echo)	(a − b + c + d)	$S_4 = (s_1 + \bar{s}_2 + s_3 + s_4)$
Klang (ringing)	(a − b − c + e)	$S_5 = (s_1 + \bar{s}_2 + \bar{s}_3 + s_5)$
Geräusch (noise)	(a − b − c − e)	$S_6 = (s_1 + \bar{s}_2 + \bar{s}_3 + \bar{s}_5)$
Ton (tone)	(a − b − c + e + f)	$S_7 + (s_1 + \bar{s}_2 + \bar{s}_3 + s_5 + s_6)$

system S_3 [$= (s_1 + s_2 + s_3)$] is the archisememe for $\acute{S}_4$; S_5 is the archisememe for S_7.

Coseriu himself prefers a graphic diagram in terms of inclusion and exclusion (Figure 14).

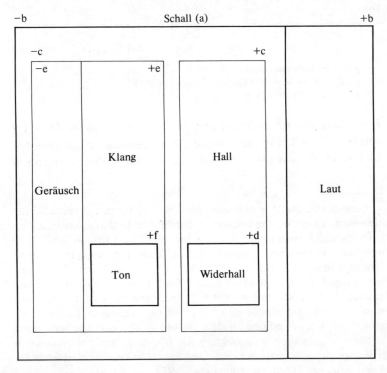

Figure 14

The analysis of some language other than German might show that this conceptual system needs to be expanded, with more conceptual positions, but, because the conceptual system does not depend on a given language, it cannot be negated by further language data (see below, Chapter 9,f).

7

Onomasiology: the Field of Designations

In an earlier chapter (3a), we dealt with the field of meanings (significations). The same form (*signifiant*) can cover a series of different contents. Each of these contents is a signification or sememe (mental object). These can be depicted in the shape of a fan linked to a form (see above, 3a). Semasiology starts from a form (*signifiant*, signifier) in order to arrive at a series of different mental objects. The combination of all the mental objects connected with one *signifiant* constitutes the *signifié* of de Saussure. In this case we start from a form (*signifiant*), and examine the whole range of its contents. But we can also choose the opposite route, onomasiology; starting from a mental object to examine all the forms or *signifiants* (designations) that express it. In Ullmann's pattern, signification proceeds from a *signifiant* (form) to a concept (mental object), and designation proceeds from a concept towards a *signifiant* (Figure 15).[1]

---

[1]Remember that our use of *signification* and *designation* does not coincide with the terminology of Coseriu; see above (I 4 note 18) and Klaus Heger "Temporale Deixis und Vorgangsquantität ('Aspekt' und 'Aktionsart')," in *ZRP*, 83, 1967 §0.2; our opposition of *signification/designation* remains within 'designatum' and does not correspond to the opposition *designatum/denotatum*.

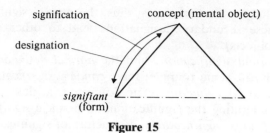

Figure 15

Semasiology and onomasiology, then, are complementary points of view. This bidirectional approach corresponds to the dual nature of the linguistic sign as form and content (form of expression + form of content, see Part II).

The significations form a field of significations. The designations form a field of designations. Thus, the concept (mental object) "head" can be expressed by a whole series of *signifiants* (forms) (Figure 16).

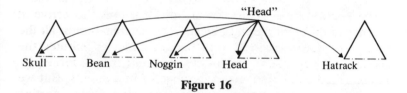

Figure 16

Head is the normal word; here is the common element in the triangle of the mental object "head". All the others are secondary designations with affective value[2]. All the designations

---

[2]As an illustration we quote this poem by Mascha Kaleko, in German:

    Apropos: Krach
Wenn zwei sich zanken,
– Mit oder ohne Grund –
Gleich istihr Mund
Voll kalter Worte,
Ihr Kopf voll böser Gedanken.

are situated in other triangles; thus, the normal significations of all these secondary designations lead to other concepts (mental objects).

The *normal significations* and the *normal designations* are situated in the same triangle; the *secondary significations* and the *secondary designations* relate different triangles.

By enumerating the significations of a single *signifiant*, we obtain a *field of significations*, a structure of significations. By looking for the designations of concept (mental object), we obtain a *field of designations*, a structure of designations. These structures are *microstructures*, since it is always a question of *one* mental object or *one signifiant*. But since there are many forms and many contents in the language, we must also ask ourselves if, at a higher level than the microstructures, there are not other broader structures, *macrostructures*, that is, whether in their turn concepts and *signifiants* are not also ordered in structures.

Wenn zwei sich zanken,
Heissen die Schlanken:
"*Magere Knochen*,"
"*Verfettet*" – die Runden,
"*Derb*" die Gesunden,
Die Grossen: "*Lang!*"

Streitsucht kennt keine Schranken.
Zank ist Gefecht.
Man kann sich zanken
Über Schiller, Liebe oder Kaffeeflecke.
– Feindlich sitzt jeder in seiner Ecke
Und hat recht . . .

(*Rhein-Neckar-Zeitung*, Heidelberg, 26/27-5-1962).
Later (II 5) we shall examine the differentiating factors in synonymy.

8

The Formal
Macrostructure

If we leave meaning out of account, *doll* and *dollar* are much closer to each other than are, for example, *dollar* and *fish*, which do not have a single phoneme in common. Phonological proximity can even become phonological coincidence, that is, homonymy (in the diachronic sense). Acoustic images (*signifiants*) can then be closer or further apart. It is on this formal basis that the alphabetical dictionary classifies words; it does so, however, according to spelling, and not according to pronunciation (it presents a graphemic rather than a phonemic structure). The alphabetical dictionary, then, presents the vocabulary in a *formal macrostructure*; the words are classified according to their graphemic proximity. But it must not be forgotten that the alphabet gives only *one* formal macrostructure (and certainly not the most interesting), since the alphabet itself is no more than an arbitrarily fixed succession of letters[1]. Other formal macrostructures are conceivable, such as the phonological series *beat, bit, bet, bat, bought, boat, boot*, etc., words which are not next to each other in the alphabetical dictionary.

In respect to our triangle the formal (form of expression, see

---

[1]See our article "Alphabetisches oder begrifflich gegliedertes Wörterbuch?", in *ZRP*, 76, 1960, pp. 521–36.

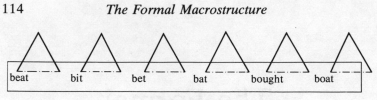

Figure 17

below) macrostructure is that shown in Figure 17. This represents only one of the different possible formal macro-structures.

9

The Conceptual
Macrostructure

(a) THE HALLIG/VON WARTBURG CONCEPTUAL SYSTEM

Immediately the question arises as to whether concepts (mental objects) form one macrostructure or several macrostructures. Since concepts embrace a portion of reality like a prism (millions of different houses are included in the same mental object "house"), the infiniteness of reality is subsumed in something finite, a relatively manageable number of concepts (mental objects). By this process language realizes the paradoxical conjuring trick of encompassing the un-encompassable with encompassable means, of limiting the limitless with limited means[1]. Languages divide up the concrete and abstract world (see I, 6), but – by their very essence – they do not make the distinctions following borders given by reality, as if on graph-paper, with mathematical precision[2], but

---

[1]Our conclusions, which are based entirely on linguistic considerations, agree completely with those of the natural sciences; see the most interesting article by Michael Koch and Dietrich Dörner, "Sprachfunktion aus neurophysiologischer Sicht" [The Function of Language from the Neurophysiological Viewpoint], published in *ZRP*, 84, 1968, pp. 521–57.

[2]Jost Trier, *Der deutsche Wortschatz im Sinnbezirk des Verstandes, Von den Anfängen bis zum Beginn des 13. Jahrhunderts*, 1931; 2nd

by means of sememes which are definable by semes and oppositions (see Part I, Chapters 4 and 5). There are mental objects
which we can order horizontally (*hut, house, mansion*), others
vertically (*house* → *building* → . . . *thing; canoe* → *boat* → . . .
thing; tree → *plant* → . . . *thing*). In this second case we move
from sememe to archisememe and arrive at a classeme. Thus,
we also have macro-structures on the conceptual plane:

> "hut"   "house"   "mansion"

Some parts of the language are clearly ordered (for example, the names of the days of the week, the names of the
months, the names of family relationships, the parts of the
body, etc.), others are hardly ordered at all. Nevertheless, in
1952 Hallig and Wartburg[3] ventured to establish a universally
valid, that is, supranational, system of concepts, in other
words, a conceptual division of the world into three great

---

ed. Heidelberg (Carl Winter), 1973, 347 pp. [see also *Aufsätze und
Vorträge zur Wortfeldtheorie von Jost Trier*, edited by Anthony van
der Lee and Oskar Reichmann, The Hague–Paris (Mouton), 1973,
216 pp.] saw, in his theory of fields, borders which are too precise.
Even in the intellectual domain, investigated by Trier, such precise
borders are still controversial. See W. von Wartburg, *Problems and
Methods in Linguistics*, revised ed. with the collaboration of S.
Ullmann, Oxford 1969, p. 163, ff., *Problemas y métodos de la
lingüística*, Madrid, 1951, pp. 263, ff., especially p. 276; in the
second German edition, [2]1962, pp. 157, ff., especially p. 165; in the
second French edition, [2]1963, pp. 169, ff., especially p. 178.

[3]Rudolf Hallig and Walther von Wartburg, *Begriffssystem als
Grundlage für die Lexikographie. Versuch eines Ordnungsschemas*,
Berlin (Akademie-Verlag), 1952, xxxv + 140 pp. In 1963 a new revised
and enlarged edition appeared, with 316 pages (with introductions in
German and French). See Kurt Baldinger, "Die Gestaltung des
wissenschaftlichen Wörterbuchs. Historische Betrachtungen zum
neuen Begriffssystem als Grundlage für die Lexikographie von Hallig
und Wartburg", in *Romanistisches Jahrbuch* (Hamburg), 5, 1952,
pp. 65–94. For Spanish, see Julio Casares, *Diccionario ideológico
de la lengua española*, Barcelona (ed. Gustavo Gili), [2]1959.

categories: A, Universe; B, Man; C, Relations between universe and man[4]. Nevertheless, the general validity and the obligatory character of such a system of concepts are very much disputed. In the prologue the authors themselves recognize the limitations. The system of concepts is not to be taken as a strait-jacket, but as an aid to be modified according to the needs of each case. Thus understood, it undoubtedly renders a valuable service. But there can be no doubt that, theoretically speaking, there does not exist a pyramid of all the concepts of a language or of all possible concepts. Heger's criticism is fully justified[5]. Heger, however, does not deny the practical usefulness of the *Begriffssystem*. But even the practical application is not without problems, as the following paragraphs will show.

(b) THE CONCEPTUAL HIERARCHY

We have referred to the conceptual hierarchy.

It is easy to find specific cases of hierarchical conceptual division (in a vertical line). No one will doubt the hierarchical ordering of *trout* → *fish* → → *animal* (archilexeme → → class). But if we try to arrange the whole language in such a hierarchical order, we shall come up against great difficulties. Neither in reality nor in language is there an absolute hierarchical division: thus, there can be no objective conceptual system which is generally and absolutely valid[6]. This is related – not only in theory (Heger), but in practical application as well

---

[4]Julio Casares, *Diccionario ideológico de la lengua española*, [2]1959, divides the vocabulary into 38 major classes, with subdivisions into some 2,000 groups, affirming that "there is no classification which is not to a great extent artificial and transitory" (p. xiv).

[5]Klaus Heger, in his previously mentioned work on the methodological bases of onomasiology and the classification by concepts (*TraLiLi* III[1], 1965, pp. 7–32 = *ZRP*, 80, 1964, pp. 486–516). See also S. Ullmann, "Orientations nouvelles en sémantique", in *Journal de Psychologie*, 1958, pp. 333–57, especially p. 356, and the criticism by Finngeir Hiorth, "Zur Ordnung des Wortschatzes", in *SL*, 14, 1960, pp. 65–84.

[6]See Heger, *TraLiLi* III[1], 1965, pp. 15–20.

– to the fact that concepts are not interrelated unilaterally, but multilaterally. The conceptual system – in practice – can be divided only unilaterally. Let us take the concept *illness*. Men, animals, even plants can be ill. But in the conceptual system of Hallig/Wartburg, plants are classified under A III, animals under A IV, and man under B. Therefore, the concept of illness has to be split up in the conceptual system, because the system of Hallig/Wartburg is conceived of from the Universe-Man opposition[7]. A conceptual system which is accurate in its evaluation of the multilateral nature of conceptual relations can never be established[8]. But to renounce conceptual classifications for this reason would be foolish. This is not the only compromise which we find essential in linguistics.

(c) "LOGICAL" OR "ASSOCIATIVE" CLASSIFICATION

Hallig/Wartburg call their principle of classification "logical," in spite of the fact that it has nothing to do with logic: "The classification of the concepts realized within this framework thus obtained is the result of a *strict logical procedure*" *(Introduction* [1]1952, p. xiv; [2]1963, p. 64)

> but frequently, during the work on the catalogue, another principle, that of *association*, attempted to replace the *logical* one, and at times, the pressure was so strong that it became very difficult to remain faithful to the 'logical' principle. There are cases, how-

---

[7]This is already found in Wilheml von Humboldt: *"Man* is opposed to the *world*, but always in *unity"* (*Über die Verschiedenheit des menschlichen Sprachbaues und ihren Einfluss auf die geistige Entwicklung des Menschengeschlechts*, Berlin, 1836, p. 207).

[8]See for this problem Werner Runkewitz, "Kritische Betrachtungen zum Begriffssystem von Hallig/Wartburg im Zusammenhang mit den Arbeiten am Altgaskognischen Wörterbuch," in *Forschungen und Fortschritte,* 33, 1959, pp. 19–24 (also in the Monatsberichte der Deutschen Akademie der Wissenschaften zu Berlin 1, 1959, pp. 73–79, with an introduction by Kurt Baldinger).

ever, in which preference was consciously given to association instead of to the conceptual connection, which was always the case when the associative connection was felt to be more natural (*Introduction* [1]1952, p. xxi; [2]1963, p. 74).

What they call *logical* classification is in fact *naïve realism* ("naiver Realismus," *Introduction* [1]1952, p. xiv; [2]1963, p. 64), that is, more or less a kind of man-in-the-street ontology (Ontologie des Durchschnittsmenschen). Thus, for example, the (French) *tabatière* ("snuff-box"), in a material sense and based on this 'naïve realism', is a little box; its conceptual place would be next to *récipient, boîte, caisse, coffre*, etc. (1st. ed., p. 22, cf. 2nd. ed. p. 181). But Hallig/Wartburg in this case prefer the 'association' with *tobacco: B* I L'homme, être physique, *k* Les besoins de l'être humain, *l* L'alimentation, *dd* Le tabac (1st. ed. p. 22; 2nd. ed. p. 142), where we also find *fumer, fumeur, pipe, allumer, briquet, blague, étui à cigarettes, fume-cigare, fume-cigarette, cendrier* – all 'by association'! – (and the 2nd. ed. adds three more: *primer, chiquer, nicotine*, also 'by association'). In this whole paragraph, only *tabac* itself (which is also found under: *A* L'Univers, III, Les plantes, *g* Les plantes d'importance industrielle) and *cigare, cigarette* belong (more or less) to the classification which Hallig/Wartburg call logical. It is true that the authors admit the existence of exceptions; but there are many more of these than one might expect. Without 'association' there would be no *corpse* at a *burial*, etc. *Shore*, in a material sense, and according to the naïve realism claimed, is a stretch of land, and not a stretch of water, but it is classified 'by association' in the paragraph La mer (A II 2), along with *côte, plage, falaise, dune*, etc., all classified 'by association.' *Rive* is found in the paragraph 'interior waters.' *Flocon* ("snow-flake") is classified with *neige* ("snow"); *ouvrir* ("to open") and *fermer* ("to shut") with *porte* ("door"), etc. This all demonstrates the difficulty of macrostructural classification, whether based on the ill-defined "naïve realism" of Hallig/Wartburg, or on some other principle. Conceptual relations are multilateral and, theoretically, a complete pyramid of all concepts is impossible. Conceptual classifications of the vocabulary are useful – we certainly do not wish to deny that –, but there are many possible classifications ("Each classification is subjective", admit Hallig and Wartburg, *Introduction*, p. xxii, 2nd. ed., p. 75), and each attempt to establish a conceptual macrostructure is open to criticism[9].

(d) GENERAL LANGUAGE AND SPECIALIZED LANGUAGE

Another difficulty, tied to each conceptual classification of the vocabulary, consists in the multiple stratification of language (even if one disregards geographical differentiation).[10] This linguistic stratification is both vertical and horizontal. It is *vertical* with respect to social levels starting from slang, continuing on up through vulgar speech, popular and familiar language and general usage, to cultivated and poetic language. It is well-known how social stratification and social environment affect the history of the word. The limits between these levels are very imprecise. The stratification is *horizontal* from the viewpoint of professions, since all around the general language, there are a great number of special languages, or rather, special terminologies; we have to remember, however, that specialization in language is linked to the social aspects of language, since the specialized language of doctors is distinguished from that of

---

[9]"The complete lexicon of a language does not form the 'mosaic' dreamt of by Jost Trier, where the lexical surface would perfectly cover the conceptual surface expressed by a language" (Georges Mounin, "Essai sur la structuration du lexique de l'habitation," in *CahLex*, 6, 1965, pp. 9–24, especially p. 20).

[10]Eugenio Coseriu distinguishes between "differences in geographical space, *diatopic* differences; differences between the social-cultural strata of the linguistic community, *diastratic* differences; and differences between the kinds of expressive mode, *diaphasic* differences" (the first two terms come from L. Flydal) ("Structure lexicale et enseignement du vocabulaire," in *Actes 1er Coll. Int. Ling. Appl.*, Nancy, 1966, p. 199) (ib., 221 my reservations about the "diaphasic" differences).

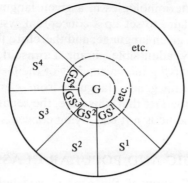

G = General language.
GS = That part of the specialized language which also belongs to general language.
S = Specialized language.

Figure 18

bricklayers socially as well as linguistically. Since at the same time part of each specialized language is also known by the layman (for example, *car, steering-wheel, motor* etc.), there is also a zone of transition in this case (see Figure 18).

Specialized terminologies are quantitatively very important. All in all, they are larger than the general vocabulary. The general vocabulary would disappear among the specialized terminologies, if the conceptual system did not distinguish the one from the other. This problem is solved by Hallig and Wartburg in the following way: they put specialized terminology in a place of its own, under C II *La science et la technique*; that part of specialized language which is known in the general language, on the other hand, is found under sections A and B.

There is no doubt that this separation of general language and scientific nomenclature is justified when one is classifying the vocabulary of a given language. One must add, however, that it is awkward to transfer these sociological differences to the level of a conceptual system which no longer depends on a given language. This system, on the contrary, should give the neutral picture which serves as a starting point. Only with its help can we assess the relationship between general language and specialized terminologies in a given language. But Hallig and Wartburg claim to set up a conceptual system which does not depend on a given language, and therefore the separation is not theoretically admissible. Franz Dornseiff, on the other hand, while classifying the vocabulary of the German language, does not separate the general language from scientific terminologies, in spite of the fact that, this time, the separation would be justified (because he is not classifying concepts but words).[11]

(e) SCIENTIFIC AND POPULAR CLASSIFICATION

Thus the classification of the general vocabulary of a given language is closely related, in a strict sense, to scientific classification. Scientific classification does not always coincide entirely with the popular conception, that is, with the classification of the general language. On the contrary, scientific language tries to *follow* recognized borders within reality (if there are any), while general language *imposes* its concepts upon reality (see the theory of Coseriu, above, Chapter 4a). This has already been demonstrated by the German word for *whale*, which considers it a fish (*Walfisch*), while zoologically it belongs to the mammals (see above, Chapter 4b). And as we have previously pointed out, the tomato is considered a vegetable in the general language, even though it is a fruit from a botanical viewpoint. Nevertheless, when we classify the vocabulary of a given language, the classification of the general language should follow the popular conception – since we are dealing with the popular linguistic division of the world, and not with scientific knowledge. If we proceeded otherwise, we would introduce the concept of the exterior scientific environment into the general language (see the last diagram) and thus we would mix two completely different spheres: general language and scientific terminologies or nomenclatures.

But as we noted in the preceding paragraph, it must be added

---

[11] I am thus modifying what I said in the previously mentioned article in *Romanist. Jahrbuch* 5, 1952, pp. 90, ff.

immediately that this has nothing to do with the conceptual system which does not depend on a given language. We quote what Heger says in this regard:

> The situation is quite different on the level of the second meta-language, where we are no longer dealing with models of the language but of linguistics. So it should be beyond question that on this second level, only scientific concepts (in our case, consequently, only a scientific concept of the "concept"[12]) can be allowed. The admission of other "concepts" into a model dealing with linguistics would end up by depriving linguistics of its scientific status. This observation corresponds to the not very original requirement that the non-scientific character of language should not be misunderstood or wrongly used as a pretext for justifying non-scientific linguistics. When, for methodological reasons, as in the case of the *Begriffssystem*, there is a need for concepts to be "extralinguistic", or rather that they should be independent of the structure of a given language, it is obvious that this cannot be

---

[12]"In principle, the requirement of a scientific concept of the "concept" has nothing to do with the question of whether the concepts one wants to classify, or which serve as a starting point for onomasiological studies, ought to be borrowed from their respective sciences. It is best to emphasize the mutual independence of the two problems, to avoid a misunderstanding that could be produced by the discussion, started by de Tollenaere, on the place occupied by the *whale* in the *Begriffssystem*. As regards the argument presented here, it is of no consequence whether the whale is classified amongst mammals or fish or elsewhere – perhaps with olives and petroleum amongst the raw materials for the production of oils. What is important is instead to classify it each time in such a way that the concept of /whale/ as so defined satisfies the requirements of the scientific concept of the "concept". Even so, in practice I agree with the view of de Tollenaere, ("La lexicologie alphabétique ou idéologique," *CahLex,* 2, 1960, pp. 21–22; Dutch edition = Alfabetische of ideologische lexicografie, Leiden, 1960, p. 10), and disagree with the view put forward in the Preface to the second edition of the *Begriffssystem* (pp. 34–5), believing that it will often be useful and advisable to follow the definitions of concepts that have been worked out in their respective sciences" (Heger, ib; n. 26).

achieved except through concepts fixed by definition, rather than by 'pre-scientific' concepts . . . . (K. Heger, "Les bases méthodologiques de l'onomasiologie et du classement par concepts," in *TraLiLi* III[1], 1965, pp. 18, ff.).[13]

The classification of the vocabulary of a given language can present inherent structures and distribute the words according to principles which are appropriate to the case: the conceptual system cannot do that. The concept 'jaundice' for example is expressed in French by *jaunisse* and by *ictère* (see below, Part II, Chapter 4g); both words express the same concept. But when I classify the vocabulary of French, I can properly classify *jaunisse* within the general language and *ictère* under scientific medical vocabulary.

(f) ITS SUPRANATIONAL CHARACTER

Hallig and Wartburg aim to classify concepts, not words; that is, they naturally classify words that are thought of as being mental objects (concepts), since only with the help of words can concepts be expressed. But *Tisch* or *mesa* could take the place of *table*; that is, they are concerned with the mental object (schema of representation, concept) and not with its formal expression. We have already insisted that concepts are formed through language. If each language has created a different linguistic image of the world, this means, if we interpret it strictly, that there can be no supranational conceptual system. However, such an extreme view – Weisgerber and his school appear to be very near it, and might therefore be expected to reject in advance any supranational conceptual system – surely goes too far. Not only because the Romance Languages have approximately the same structure, which depends on their common Latin origin and on a considerable common tradition; one could even go further and speak of a common Western tradition, which also includes the Germanic Languages (cf. Whorf's Standard Aver-

---

[13]See also K. Heger, "Temporale Deixis und Vorgangsquantität", in *ZRP*, 83, 1967, §1.3.2.

age European); but especially because it is possible to deduce from natural languages conceptual schemata which do not depend on a given language. Heger tried to prove this[14], and we shall give an example of that later (Part II, Chapter 3). Without the possibility of conceiving mental objects which are independent of a given language, the onomasiological method would prove to be impossible. As for the Hallig/Wartburg system, we have more reservations. Their mental objects are neither analysed nor defined, with the result that their supranational character is not guaranteed. The farther we get from Western culture, the more difficult will it be to use the system without introducing profound modifications.

A conceptual system which depends on a given language would be no more than a tautology and could not serve as a starting-point for onomasiological studies. A conceptual system has to be 'supranational,' that is, independent of any given language. The fact that many languages may not have words to express this conceptual system does not make the system void. There are any number of possible conceptual systems, but it must be remembered that we cannot construct total conceptual systems, but only partial ones. The Hallig/Wartburg system claims to be a total conceptual system, but it is not.

(g) ITS "SUPRATEMPORAL" CHARACTER

The conceptual division of the world – as reflected by each language – changes. Hallig and Wartburg also take note of this. W. von Wartburg writes in *Problems and Methods in Linguistics:*

> As we have seen, the system of classification cannot be exactly the same for any two periods. But, for obvious reasons, it is also desirable that the different systems should not be more widely divergent than is absolutely necessary. The more nearly uniform the classification remains, the easier it becomes to establish the

---

[14]Klaus Heger, "Les bases méthodologiques de l'onomasiologie et du classement par concepts", in *TraLiLi* III[1], 1965, pp. 7–32.

organic connection between one period, or one locality, and another. The domains most subject to change are those which derive from human action, such as those of political and social institutions, professions and trades, military organisation, dress, etc. Granted that these domains change, that they may expand or contract according to the circumstances, it should nevertheless be possible to assign them a stable position in the lexicological system as a whole[15].

But it is precisely the *totality* of the conceptual system envisaged by Wartburg which does not exist. There are only partial conceptual systems, which are not only independent of a given language but also of the time factor. A conceptual system cannot change. What change are the meanings of a given language. If, for example, in Old Provenzal, the same word means "work" and "suffering," this does not mean that the concept for "work" was something different, but rather that a relation was established between two different concepts (see the *Appendix*, part 2.) If the form *mire* (<MEDICUS) was so popular (along with the regular form *miege*) in Old French, because of the influence of MIRACULUM (see FEW 6, 605 b), this is not a question of the conceptual system of 'doctor', but rather of the belief in miracles; that is, again, the combination of different concepts, combinations which can change with time, with social or geographical factors, etc.

We affirm once more that the semasiological structure of a language changes. Nor do we deny that the conceptual division of the world as reflected by language might change, but in this case other conceptual systems appear or disappear: they do not change. For example, the conceptual system that corresponds to the potato did not exist in Europe because the potato itself did not exist in Europe, but it already existed in America. A conceptual system can be without the words to

---

[15]W. von Wartburg, *Problems and Methods in Linguistics*, Revised edition with the collaboration of Stephen Ullmann, translated by Joyce M. H. Reid, Oxford (Basil Blackwell) 1969, p. 176 (= p. 177 of the third German edition of 1970; pp. 191, ff., of the second French edition of 1963; p. 298 of the Spanish edition of 1951).

express it, but once conceived of, the conceptual system exists as such, whether it is lexicalized or not in a particular language. Conceptions and meanings are born, change and disappear, but not conceptual systems, because they are not limited to any one language. Hallig/Wartburg correctly say in the Introduction to the *Begriffssystem* ([1]1952, p. x; [2]1963, p. 60): "Meaning changes; the concept, once grasped as an object by our consciousness, does not change; wherever it exists, it remains the same; it can only disappear and give way to another new concept"; which means that the designations of a conceptual system may disappear, but not the conceptual system itself (the passage just quoted contradicts what Wartburg says in the quotation at the beginning of this section).

10

Superimposing the Structures

Starting from Ullmann's triangle, we have postulated and examined four different types of structures with which the science of language is concerned: two microstructures (field of significations and field of designations) and two macrostructures (formal and conceptual macrostructures) as shown in Figure 19.

These four structures, with which lexicology is concerned, are open structures, in constant variation; furthermore, it can be said that macrostructures change more slowly than do microstructures. All these structures overlap, in such a way that the variations in one of them can have as a consequence variations in the others. On the level of mental objects we have postulated the possibility of constructing invariable conceptual systems (logical deductions): we shall deal with them later[1].

---

[1]The deduction of logical and coherent systems is possible at all levels, see Kurt Baldinger, "Structures et systèmes linguistiques," in *TraLiLi* V[1], 1967, pp. 123–39 (Second part of this study, chapter 1). Here, only the system on the level of content is of interest.

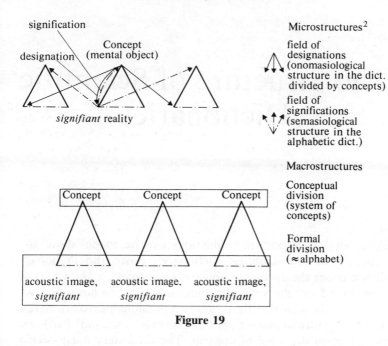

Figure 19

---

[2]In this model the linguistic sign is conceived of as the joining of a *signifiant* (= acoustic image) and *one* signification or *one* sememe (within the same triangle); this conception does not coincide with Saussure's definition (inseparable quantitative unity of *signifiant* and *signifié*), but rather corresponds to the normal use of a word in a context (unless there is a play on words). The other meanings are present as potentialities. See below, the conception in the trapezium of Heger (Part II, Chapter 7).

11

The Structure of Scientific Dictionaries

From all this important deductions can be made about the structure of the scientific dictionary[1]. Since the dictionary should order the entire vocabulary, or, at least, a great part of it, its task from the very beginning is *macrostructural*. But we have already seen that there are two possible macrostructures, one on the formal plane (level of expression, see part two) and the other on the level of content. The dictionary must decide on one of these two levels. If the formal level is chosen the alphabet provides a possible organizational principle (practical, not theoretical) for its structure. If the conceptual level is preferred, the conceptual system of Hallig/Wartburg serves as a possible basis for structuring. Both – formal as well as conceptual classification are equally valid and theoretically well-founded possibilities of organization. Therefore debate about

---

[1]See Kurt Baldinger, "Alphabetisches oder begrifflich gegliedertes Wörterbuch?", in *ZRP*, 76, 1960, pp. 521–36; F. de Tollenaere–A. Weijnen, *Woordenboek en dialect,* Bijdragen en Mededelingen der Dialectencommisie der Koninklijke Nederlandse Akademie van Wetenschappen te Amsterdam, 24, Amsterdam, 1963, 56 pp.; F. de Tollenaere, *Nieuwe Wegen in de Lexicologie*, with a summary in English (Verhandelingen der Koninklijke Nederlandse Akademie van Wetenschappen, Afd. Letterkunde, Nieuwe Reeks – Deel LXX – No. 1), Amsterdam, 1963, 150 pp.

whether a scientific dictionary should be ordered alphabetically or conceptually is pointless. Both kind of classification are necessary and mutually complementary. The often heard argument, that the alphabet is practical while the conceptual division is not, misses the point, because the evaluation of what is *practical* depends on the way the problem is posed. If I am looking for meanings, the alphabetical dictionary is practical and the conceptual dictionary is not, because here the meanings of a word are separated from each other. But if I am looking for designations, the conceptual dictionary is practical and the alphabetical dictionary is not, because designations for the same thing, "synonyms", are separated from each other. In fact, in the macrostructure of the alphabetical dictionary a multitude of semasiological microstructures (*fields of significations*) are found, and in the macrostructures of the dictionary arranged by concepts, there are a multitude of onomasiological microstructures (*fields of designations*). The alphabetical dictionary starts with the form (of expression) and is therefore *semasiological*; the dictionary which is arranged by concepts starts from the concept and is therefore *onomasiological*.

The dictionary ordered by concepts splits up the fields of meanings: *green* is found under the concepts "colour", "vegetable", "inexperience", etc, that is, its formal unity is destroyed. The alphabetically arranged dictionary breaks up the fields of designations: *green* is separated from the other designations of "colour", "vegetable", "inexperience", etc.

12

Hearer and Speaker

We have seen that the fundamental bipolarity of the linguistic sign as a unit of *signifiant* and *signifié* has far-reaching consequences for linguistic structures and also for the science of language. Bipolarity is, above everything else, the fundamental linguistic fact. This is confirmed if we consider language in its fundamental function, in its *communicative function*. Communication presupposes a duality, a sender and a receiver, that is, a speaker and a hearer. These two poles correspond exactly to the opposition, now familiar to us, between semasiology and onomasiology. The hearer receives from his interlocutor forms, the meaning of which he must determine in order to understand them. Thus, the hearer's task is semasiological. The speaker, on the other hand, has to communicate mental objects (concepts). He must select designations from the vocabulary placed at his disposal by his memory; he must link concepts to acoustic images, so converting them into *signifiants*; that is, his task is onomasiological.

In other words, the hearer must have in his head the fields of significations – a dictionary, so to speak, based on forms; the speaker must have in his head fields of designations – a dictionary based on concepts. Since in each conversation we are alternately speakers and hearers, we constantly change from one level to the other.[1] We are so accustomed to this

---

[1]Compare Luis J. Prieto, *Principes de noologie*, The Hague/London/

Paris (Mouton), 1964, p. 100:

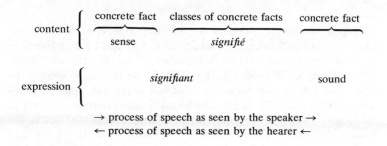

→ process of speech as seen by the speaker →
← process of speech as seen by the hearer ←

and the model by Franz Schmidt, *Zeichen und Wirklichkeit, Linguistisch-semantische Untersuchungen*, Stuttgart–Berlin–Köln–Mainz, 1966, p. 16:

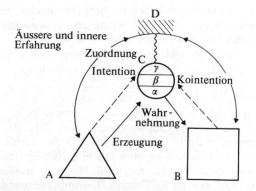

A = the person who writes, speaks or creates
B = the person who reads, listens, uses or understands
Cα = writing as bearer of sounds
Cβ = sounds as bearers of significations
Cγ = significations
D = piece of reality (real or imagined)

Aussere und innere Erfahrung = external and internal experience
Zuordnung = coordination
Erzeugung = creation
Wahrnehmung = perception

Compare with the model of K. Bühler, Part II, Chapter 5, section f.

switch of rôles that we do not even notice it. Conversation represents linguistic bipolarity[2].

---

[2]Eugen Wüster (†), known for his importance in international linguistic standardization, has established a model of four parts in his article dedicated to Leo Weisgerber, "Des Worten der Welt" (*Sprachform*, 3, 1959–60, pp. 183–204). There he tries to include the speaker and the hearer on the level of *parole* (speech, what the individual speaker actually does). Our triangle refers only to the level of the *langue* (language, language as a system of potentialities at the speaker's disposal). On this level of the *langue,* which Wüster conceives of as being the level of *concepts* (= Sprachsystem, linguistic system), he only distinguishes, however, between the sign (Zeichen) and the meaning (Bedeutung), see p. 188 (also p. 196: "The sign is as a general rule a concept, and the meaning of the sign is likewise a concept"). Thus Wüster does not distinguish between *concept* and *signification* (in our terminology), since for him the concept means something different. Nevertheless his article contains suggestive ideas, precisely concerning the interaction of both levels, *parole* and *langue*. Our model, in fact, is more differentiating than Wüster's, because of the distinction between acoustic image (*signifiant*), meaning, designation and concept.

An interesting Word-Reality model which includes the speaker and the hearer is given by G. P. Meredith, "Semantics in Relation to Psychology," in *Archivum Linguisticum,* 8, Fasc. 1 (p. 8).

In addition, it must be remembered that Saussure's opposition *langue-parole* greatly over-simplifies the linguistic situation. For this reason Coseriu establishes a trinomial: *Sistema, norma y habla,* Montevideo, 1952; reprint E. Coseriu, *Teoría del lenguage y lingüística general* Madrid (Gredos), 1962, pp. 11–113. In this introduction we have had in mind only the *sistema* (system) as "a group of functional oppositions" and not the *norma* (norm) as a "'collective' realization of the system, which contains the system itself and, in addition, the functionally 'extrinsic' but normal elements in the speech of a community" (p. 97); still less the *habla,* (speech) as an "individual concrete realization of the norm, which contains the norm itself and, in addition, the expressive originality of the individual speakers" (p. 98).

The *speaker-hearer* opposition also offers interest for other problems, cf., for ex., H. H. Christmann, "Wortbedeutung, Modus und das Prinzip der Unterscheidung von Sprecher und Hörer," in *Verba et Vocabula* (Festschrift to E. Gamillsheg), München (Wilhelm Fink Verlag), 1968, 121–126.

13

Résumé of the Fundamental Concepts Derived from Ullmann's Triangle

It would be rash to aim to define the essence of language. Language classifies the infinite variety of material and spiritual reality. This immense, incomprehensible reality is collected and reduced to concepts which are comprehensible and numerically limited, to notional schemata. Concepts become concrete in designations; therefore, they are conceivable only by means of acoustic images which, for their part, are not normally motivated directly by extralinguistic reality. The acoustic image is a word only when it is joined to a concept, to a notional schema (the *acoustic image*, as bearer of a signification, is called *signifiant*). The relation between the *acoustic image* and the *mental object* (concept) reflects the fundamental linguistic bipolarity of form (of expression) and content[1].

---

[1]Only in a 'play on words' can this bipolarity be made to disappear: for example, when, by means of new graphemes, or of a use of graphemes which goes against the normal standard, one tries to reflect directly the form of the content in the form of the expression: *Яeactionary*, *ddouble*, etc. (I owe these examples to Raul Ávila, México). Interferences of another type occur between both levels in

Signifiant + concept, mental image, (semasiological direction)
= word
Concept, mental object, + *Signifiant* (onomasiological direction) = word

Signification proceeds from the acoustic image (*signifiant*) towards the concept; designation proceeds from the concept towards the acoustic image (*signifiant*). Acoustic image and concept, signification and designation are found in four different structures or fields. Significations linked to a single *signifiant* form a field of significations (a *semasiological field*). Designations expressing a single concept form a field of designations (an *onomasiological field*). These two structures are microstructures, since they are bound to *one* form, and to *one* mental object (concept) respectively. A field of significations, polysemy, is made possible by the fact that between the acoustic image and the extralinguistic reality there is no direct relationship, nor any original motivation. Acoustic images form formal macrostructures among themselves (as a result of formal relations on the phonemic or morphemic level). The macrostructure on the conceptual level is more controversial: there are partial macrostructures, but there is no overall con-

---

contaminations of the type Germ. *jein* < *ja* + *nein*, Fr. *noui* < *non* + *oui* (for ex.. in the title of an article: "La concentration de plomb s'est-elle accrue dans l'air de Montréal? Noui" Le Devoir [Montréal] Aug. 3, 1972). José Luis Rivarola (Lima) has supplied me with the following examples gathered in Venezuela: *viasar* ("viajar por VIASA," traval by VIASA, in the advertisements for this airline), *chisparates* (*chistes* 'jokes' + *disparates* 'foolish remarks', on a TV programme), *telebridades* (*televisión* + *celebridades*, television celebrities). In these cases, a new *signifiant* is made up from elements of *signifiants* A and B, which is the bearer of a new meaning made up of elements of the *signifiés* of A and B. These phenomena should be differentiated from riddles such as this one in French: *G a* [which should be read as *G grand a petit* 'Big G little a', pronounced like *j'ai grand appétit*; I have heard it many times in Switzerland and Germany (there is the influence of *grosser Buchstabe* "capital letter")]; these cases should be included among plays on homonymic words.

ceptual pyramid. Accordingly, there are two kinds of dictionaries: the one that starts from a formal macrostructure and deals with semasiological relationships, and the other that starts from the mental object or partial conceptual macrostructures and deals with onomasiological relationships. The onomasiological type corresponds to the viewpoint of a speaker, the semasiological type to that of a listener, of the person who is interpreting the speaker.

A multitude of open structures interpenetrate each other and are subtly superimposed. For this reason, language is an extraordinarily flexible system of expression, in which each part, from the smallest structural unit to the largest, is conditioned by the other parts. These structural relationships, developed on the basis of Ullmann's triangle, are confirmed in lexicographical practice. Obviously only this practice permits us to give life to the skeleton of fundamental scientific-linguistic concepts developed here theoretically. Structures *are* skeletons.

"The reduction of languages to 'structures', that is, what is left of languages once those elements which the investigator considers irrelevant have been eliminated, is a most dangerous exercise, if it is not accompanied by frequent and intimate contacts with linguistic reality in the raw, with all its complexities, exceptions and irregularities".

This is the way André Martinet put it in 1953; it is not the opinion of a traditionalist (in which case it would not be remarkable), but of a prudent structuralist (*Word*, 9, 81). Nevertheless, a distinction must be drawn: on the conceptual level we are working with systems, schemata, mathematical constructions – it is the realm of onomasiology, the realm of the *esprit de géométrie* of which we shall speak in the Second Part. The situation is very different on the semasiological side where we find a large number of diverse factors, open structures, with lacunae and redundancies, which can change in every respect. In these structures, there is room enough for the *esprit de finesse* (of which we shall speak with reference to synonymy) and for what W. von Wartburg, in the prologue of the *French Etymological Dictionary* calls "free spiritual life", the area in which the individual continually puts into practice his freedom to be creative. Only the combination of the structural facts contained in language with the free human capacity to create forms language as a whole. Language, like man, lives in a dialectic tension between coercion and freedom.

When, in the motto we chose at the start of this book, Wilhelm von Humboldt alluded to the structural incorporation of the parts into the whole he did not fail to notice creative freedom as well, which cannot be grasped rationally. Therefore, we let Wilhelm von Humboldt's words end this first part:

Detailed consideration of present circumstances of political, artistic and scientific development leads to a long chain of reciprocally conditioned causes and effects, which extends over many centuries. As we follow this chain, we realize at once that there are two factors, of different kinds, with which investigation is not satisfied to the same extent. While, in reality, part of the successive causes and effects can be explained sufficiently by basing some of them on others of them, from time to time one stumbles, so to speak, against links that resist such a solution, as is demonstrated by every attempt at a cultural history of the human race. This is due precisely to that force of the spirit which can neither be entirely penetrated in its essence nor predicted beforehand. This force unites with what is formed by it and is around it, but manipulating it and shaping it, according to its own fashion. (*Über die Verschiedenheit des menschlichen Sprachbaues* . . . Berlin, 1936, p. 3).

Part II

HEGER'S TRAPEZIUM

1

Structures and Systems[1]

La langue est un système où tout se tient: language is a system
in which everything is related. This has been the creed of linguists (or of many linguists) since de Saussure. Mario Wandruszka, in a recent article[2] has just taken up a position against
this excessively general axiom. He affirms that the system or
systems (I would say structure or structures) of human language are neither consistent nor coherent ("weder konsequent
noch kohärent sind"). Wandruszka insists on the fact that
human language is a system of lacunae and of adjustments
("ein System von Aushilfen"); that each language possesses
several levels that help each other out when there are imper-
fections, ambiguities ("weil jede Sprache viele Register besitzt,
so dass, wo das eine schadhaft ist, ein anderes aushelfen
kann"); that the different levels help each other to such an
extent that redundancy (hypercharacterization) becomes a
completely natural phenomenon ("Die einzelnen Register
helfen einander so sehr aus, dass immer wieder Redundanz

---

[1]This chapter is the translation of pp. 123–30 of my article
"Structures et systèmes linguistiques," in TraLiLi V, no. 1, 1967, pp.
123–39; the English version derives from the Spanish translation by
L. López-Molina, with minor revisions.
[2]Mario Wandruszka, "Die maschinelle Übersetzung und die Dicht-
ung," in *Poetica* (ed. by K. Maurer), 1, 1967, pp. 3–7.

entsteht").[3] Wandruszka reaches the following conclusion: language is a system of programmes realized through a series of levels characterized by many lacunae and many redundancies, by deficiencies and surpluses ("Die Sprache ist ein System von Programmen in verschiedenen Registern, mit vielfältiger Defizienz und Redundanz, mit Mangel und Überfluss"). Language is a system of complementary information ("Die Sprache ist ein System komplementärer Information"). I now admit that I completely agree with all these remarks of Wandruska, which will perhaps surprise those who heard my lecture at the 1965 Madrid Conference. There I put forward a logical and coherent system, taking as my example the conceptual system of "se souvenir" (see below, Chapter 3). In reality, the two theses are in no way contradictory, but complementary, as we shall see. Wandruszka's thesis corresponds to a semasiological approach, the approach I put forward in Madrid is onomasiological.

First, let us place ourselves, with Wandruszka, on the level of semasiology, examining the different structures that are superimposed in French. The phonological structure of French is well-known. Let us take as an example the opposition *phoneme + õ*, limiting ourselves to this combination of only two phonemes:

/põ/ *pont* m., (il) *pond* (bridge, lays)
/bõ/ *bon* m. and adj., *bond* m. (good, bound)
/fõ/ *fond* m., *fonds* m., *fonts* pl., (ils) *font* (depth(s), fonts, they do)
/võ/ (ils) *vont* (they go)
/mõ/ *mont* m., *mon* pron., *m'ont* (mountain, my, they have me)
/tõ/ *ton* m., *ton* pron., *thon* m., *t'ont* (tone, your, tunnyfish, they have you)
/dõ/ *don* m., *dont, Don* (Sanche) (gift, whose, Don)

---

[3]For the concept and importance of "redundancy" see Peter Hartmann, *Theorie der Grammatik III*: *Allgemeine Strukturgesetze in Sprache und Grammatik*, 1961 (Mouton), pp. 316–18.

/sõ/ *son* m., *son* m., *son* pron., (ils) *sont* (bran, sound, his they are)
/zõ/ one of the few unrealized combinations (in initial position; cf. gazon, foison, blason, raison, etc.)
/šõ/ *chon* m., *chong* m. (A Korean coin, a Tibetan drink)
/nõ/ *nom* m., *non, n'ont* (name, no, haven't)
/žõ/ *jonc* m. (bullrush)
/kõ/ *qu'on*, etc. (which we . . ., etc)
/gõ/ *gond* m., *gong* m., (hook, gong)
/lõ/ *long, l'on, l'ont* (long, we, they have it)
/yõ/ *ion* m. (ion)
/rõ/ *rond*, (il) *rompt*, (round, he breaks)
/üõ/ *huons* (we boo)
/wõ/ *où on, ou on* (where we . . ., or we . . .)

This example shows us that, on one hand, the language does not use all the possibilities available in the phonological system (/zõ/, /uõ/, etc., are missing), while, on the other hand, in most of the realizations, the phonological oppositions result in ambiguous, polyvalent units. On the one hand, the phonological system does not take advantage of all its possibilities; on the other hand, it often gives us units that are not unambiguously determinate in content. This corresponds exactly to polysemy (or homonymy) on the lexical level. The phonological system is not exploited 100%; on the other hand, it is not able to provide us with unambiguous units. What it does do – and that is a great deal – is to preselect: the potential interpretations are reduced to one (the ideal case), to two, three, four, rarely more. The phonological system leaves it to other levels to go on with the determination.

Frequently it is even difficult to decide exactly whether or not we are dealing with one phoneme. It has often been said that the sounds [ç] and [χ] in German (as in *ich* and *ach*) are only combinatory variants of one and the same phoneme.[4] In

---

[4]See explicitly W. Rothe, *Strukturen des Konjunktivs im Französischen*, Beiheft of *ZRP*, 112, Tübingen, 1967, pp. 43, ff.: "Here (/niçt/'nicht', /naχt/ 'Nacht') we have automatic variants of the same one phoneme; [ç] and [χ] are never in opposition in German".

fact, after *i* and *e* the sound of *ich* is automatically used; after *a*, *o* and *u*, the sound of *ach* is automatic. This is so if the following syllable is not the diminutive suffix *-chen*. In this case, the two variants *ich* and *ach* are transformed into distinctive signs (I am not here claiming to solve the problem of their phonological status):

Kuchen ("cake")	: *Kuhchen* ("small cow")
tauchen ("plunge")	: *Tauchen* ("small rope")
fauchen ("spit", of cats)	: *v-chen* (dimunitive of the letter *v*)

We must admit, then, that *ich* and *ach* can be considered in the same language as either combinatory variants of the same phoneme or as two separate phonemes.

Let us proceed to the morphological level. French, as we know, is in a transitional phase from a 'postdetermined' structure (marked by suffixes) to a 'predetermined' structure (marked by prefixes)[5]. From the synchronic viewpoint the two structures complement each other and overlap.

The noun, in general, is predetermined: *le livre* – *la livre*:

sing.		pl.	
m.	f.	m	f.
ləlivr	lalivr	lẹlivr	lẹlivr
dülivr	dəlalivr	dẹlivr	dẹlivr
ọlivr	alalivr	ọlivr	ọlivr
ləlivr	lalivr	lẹlivr	lẹlivr

---

[5]See W. von Wartburg, *Evolution et structure de la langue française*, 1934, pp. 219, ff., and especially Harald Weinrich, "Ist das Französische eine analytische oder synthetische Sprache?", in *Mitt. des allgemeinen deutschen Neuphilologenverbandes*, 15, 1962, pp. 177–86; Kurt Baldinger, "Post- und Prädeterminierung im Französischen," in *Festschrift Wartburg*, I, Tübingen, 1968, pp. 87–106; ib. p. 94 also on the post-determined feminine of the adjective (on this subject, cf. now the more detailed study by Wolfgang Rothe, "Die Genusbildung des französischen Adjektivs auf der Ebene der Hörbarkeit", in *Neusprachliche Mitteilungen aus Wissenschaft und Praxis* 27, 1974, pp. 216–221).

The article serves to classify *livre* among the nominal elements. At the same time, the article determines the gender, number and case[6]. But none of these four structures, which overlap, is perfect:

(*a*) the *gender* remains ambiguous in the plural (and in the singular before a vowel).

(*b*) the *number* is not determined in the dative masculine (*au livre/aux livres*).

(*c*) the *case* is not determined for the nominative and accusative, neither in the singular nor in the plural (*le livre*, nom. sing. and acc. sing.; *les livres*, nom. pl and acc. pl.).

(*d*) there now remains the *classifying function*: the unit which follows *le, la*, etc., belongs to the nominal class. This seems to be evidence enough, but it is easy to show that this structure, too, has its ambiguities:

le battu (the tramp of a horse)
           – le bats-tu? (do you beat him?)
la tortue (the tortoise)
           – la tords-tu? (do you twist it?)
le tutu (the ballet-skirt)
           – le tues-tu? (do you kill him?)
le pointu (the pointed one)
           le poinds-tu? (do you hurt him?)
le tortil (the coronet)
           – le tord-il? (does he twist it?)
la curatelle (the trusteeship)
           – la cura-t-elle? (did she clean it?)
le castel (the small castle)
           – le casse-t-elle? (does she break it?)
la stèle (the monolith)
           lace-t-elle? (does she lace?)

---

[6] I am keeping the traditional classification without posing the problem of its justification, which could be attempted in different ways; see, for example, K. Togeby, *Structure immanente de la langue française*, Copenhagen, 1951, pp. 190, ff., [²Paris, 1965]; K. Heger, "Valenz, Diathese und Kasus," in *ZRP*, 82, 1966, pp. 138–70.

la tortelle (treacle mustard)
        – la tord-elle? (does she twist it?)
le pastel (the crayon)
        – le passe-t-elle? (does she pass it?)
la tutelle (the protection)
        – la tue-t-elle? (does she kill her?)
le v (the v)
        – lever; levée (to rise, embankment)
l'abattu/la battue (the depressed one, the beaten girl)
        – la bats-tu? (do you beat her?)
l'attelle, l'atèle (the splint, the spider-monkey)
        – l'a-t-elle?[7] (has she got it?)

The predetermined structure, therefore, is imperfect: the four categories (classification, gender, number, case) have weak points, ambiguities that are solved with the help of other categories.

'Postdetermination' of substantives has been almost entirely lost in French; admittedly there still remains a series of irregular plurals but these (*cheval/chevaux* etc) are being eliminated more and more in popular speech.

Table 14

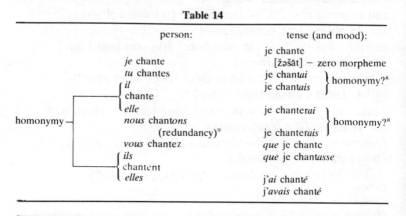

	person:		tense (and mood):
			je chante
	je chante		[žəšãt] – zero morpheme
	tu chantes		je chant*ai* ⎱ homonymy?[8]
	il ⎰		je chant*ais* ⎰
	chante		
	elle ⎱		je chanter*ai* ⎱ homonymy?[8]
homonymy ⎯	*nous* chant*ons*		je chanter*ais* ⎰
	(redundancy)[9]		*que* je chante
	vous chantez		*que* je chant*asse*
	ils ⎰		
	chantent		j'*ai* chanté
	elles ⎱		j'*avais* chanté

---

[7]In the title of a play, *Les caisses–qu'est-ce?* (as pointed out to me by A. Rey), the article serves, on the contrary, to distinguish between homonyms.

[8]Concerning the (controversial) phonological opposition/ę/:/ę/.

Let us consider the verb morphology shown in Table 14. Predetermination is most important for the differentiation of persons (including number) and gender (marked only in the third person); 'postdetermination' is most important for the differentiation of tenses (except for compound tenses). But both predetermination and postdetermination present ambiguities: homonymy of *il/ils*, *elle/elles*; homonymy in the first person of the future/conditional and in the imperfect/past (the homonymy present indicative/present subjunctive is avoided by *que*, that is, by a supplementary predetermination)[10].

Both types of determination work, but not perfectly. The redundancy *nous* chant*ons*, vous chant*ez* is unnecessary; from a logical point of view, it would have been better to keep the postdetermination for the third person, where there is ambiguity in the predetermination.

Word formation provides us, as a whole, with an example of a well-established system. Nevertheless, ambiguities and double functions are not unusual. We know that derivational prefixes in French never change the class of the base word. Suffixes are divided into two groups: some change the word-class and others do not[11]. Prefixes are always homogeneous, suffixes are homogeneous or heterogeneous. Prefixes never mark gender, suffixes may do so. But let us consider the French suffix -əte in Table 15.

One can avoid the problem by saying that in case I there is a suffix (-*eté*), and in II there is an infix (-*et*-), but the

---

see Hans-Wilhelm Klein, *Phonetik und Phonologie des heutigen Französich*, Munich, [2]1966, p. 65; Wolfgang Rothe, *Phonologie des Französischen*, Berlin, 1972, p. 62 f.

[9]The redundancy is greater in the past tense (1st, 4th, 5th, and 6th pers.).

[10]Cf. W. Rothe, *Strukturen des Konjunktivs im Französischen* (Beiheft *ZRP*, 112), Tübingen (Niemeyer), 1967, 427 pp.

[11]K. Togeby, *Structure immanente de la langue française,* 1951, pp. 224, ff.; B. Pottier, "Les infixes modificateurs en portugais," in *Boletim de Filologia,* 14, 1953, pp. 237, ff.; *Systématique des éléments de relation,* 1962, pp. 96, ff.

Table 15

	I. Noun + feminine gender	II. Verb
a) change of class (adj. > noun)	fermeté, âcreté, tendreté propreté, etc. (firmness, sourness, tenderness, tidiness)	
b) without change of class (verb > verb)		souffleter (to slap), vergeter (to whip), craqueter (to crackle), etc.

homonymy remains as an established fact. The determination of the class is effected by the article (predetermination) or by the context.

Let us take the words in *-eur*. Three factors come into play: Determination by the suffix *-eur* proceeds thus: the word in question is a noun or an adjective: if the root is a verb or a noun, the word in *-eur* is masculine; if the root is an adjective, the word in *-eur* is feminine; if the word in *-eur* can be preceded by the article *le/la*, it is a masc./fem. noun; if not, it is an adjective. See Table 16.

The table shows ambiguities (*-eur*: ambiguity of gender) as well as redundancies (the gender is determined at the same time by the root word in combination with the suffix and by the article).

Table 16

Class of the base word	*-eur*	
	noun	adj.
v.	m. le vainqueur (victor)	vainqueur (victorious)
v.	le crâneur (boaster)	crâneur (boastful)
v.	le critiqueur (criticiser)	
v.	le demandeur (plaintiff)	
v.	le relieur (binder), etc.	
adj.	f. la lenteur (slowness)	
adj.	la froideur (coldness)	
adj.	la fadeur (insipidity)	
adj.	la grandeur (size)	
adj.	la maigreur (thinness), etc.	

The lexicon, finally, is the level of ambiguities par excellence. Homonymy or polysemy – the terminology matters little – is the most convincing proof of that. There is hardly a word that does not have at least two meanings. Each word, it is true, reduces the infinite number of possible meanings to a small number of potential meanings. Thanks to polysemy, we can bring under our control the infinitude of the entire world, material or spiritual, with the help of a limited number of lexical elements (see Part I, Chap. 6). Each element, in general, has a whole series of semantic functions (Part I, Chapter 3a). The lexicon, then, is not an autonomous and unambiguous level either; rather, it effects a preselection in the realm of content. Definitive determination is made by the context, the distribution (the compilation of a *dictionary* is possible only because the syntagmatic environment and the context are replaced by definitions).

Is context, then, the *deus ex machina*, the saving grace, that resolves all ambiguities? It must be recognized that distributional rules are very effective; but it is not difficult to prove that distribution is not always able to overcome ambiguities either. I take two examples from the structural grammar of Jean Dubois:[12]

two interpretations (in speech);
Leur(s) collègue(s) étai(en)t malade(s) (Their colleague(s)
    were ill)
three interpretations (in speech):
Leur(s) secrétaire(s) étai(en)t venu(e) (s) (Their male/
    female secretary(ies) had come)

Liaison, less current in ordinary language, could serve as a secondary indicator of the plural[13]. A supplementary device comes into play: the situation (or the greater context, if we are

---

[12]Jean Dubois, *Grammaire structurale du français. I. Nom et pronom,* Paris (Larousse), 1965, pp. 82, ff.
[13]See Klaus Heger, "Die 'liaison' als phonologisches Problem," in *Festschrift Wartburg,* I, Tübingen, 1968, pp. 467–84.

dealing with language in writing). If the situation is also ambiguous, there is misunderstanding, unless the hearer asks for further information (*feed-back*). In this case, the speaker has recourse to different linguistic structures to find another, more precise solution.

A number of conclusions are evident:

1. Language is not *one* structure; language works thanks to a whole *series of hierarchical structures*.

2. None of these structures is without lacunae or deficiencies; in other words, each of these structures permits ambiguities.

3. The different structures overlap, confirm each other (redundancy) and complete each other. Since morphological predetermination is defective in determining case function (subject/direct object), syntax (distributional regularity) takes over the task of differentiation, etc.

4. This interplay between structures assures comprehension, that is, communication.

5. The different structures work like fuses: if the fuse of one structure has burned out, the next structure or structures repair the damage and guarantee that the communication continues to work. If all the fuses have burned out (including the system of reference to the situation) there is a misunderstanding and communication breaks down. The language is not working. We must resort to the *feed-back* system, i.e., start all over again.

We have shown Mario Wandruska to be right: linguistic structures are defective and redundant at the same time. But Wandruszka speaks, without distinguishing them, of *structure* and of *system*. I propose to distinguish between the two terms. Everything we have said concerns *structures*, such as we find them to be realized in French. From all these imperfect structures, we can abstract and construct coherent and perfect *systems*. [14]

---

[14]For a different use of the terms *structure* and *system*, see B. Pottier, *Systématique des éléments de relation*, 1962, p. 114; Bohumil Trnka, *Principios de análisis morfológico,* Montevideo (Cuadernos

Table 17

Phonological structure of French[15]	Coherent articulatory system (can be completed)
i i ẹ ȩ a ö o ü u	i ẹ î ȩ ä ë a ö̧ ǫ ȯ̈ ǫ ü u

These systems are logical abstractions on the conceptual plane.

The phonological level is shown in Table 17: the predetermination of the noun in Table 18.

I said at the beginning of this chapter that we were placing ourselves on the semasiological level, with Wandruszka. In fact, the structure realized in a given language is always the starting-point for semasiology. The coherent system, on the other hand, is the starting-point for onomasiology. The *structure* or structures are always the structure or structures of a given language. The *system* is always of a conceptual order, going beyond any given language. This new manner of

del Instituto lingüístico latinoamericano, 6), 1965, p. 6: "As with other levels, the morphological plane appears as a *system,* the features of which may be referred to in any order, and as a *structure,* that is, as an organization of those features arranged in words and groups of words along the horizontal axis." (Trnka uses *system* for *paradigmatic* questions, and *structure* for *syntagmatic* ones!); for G. Mounin (*CahLex,* 6, 1965, p. 20) structure is the *system of the systems*; see also Peter Hartmann, "Begriff und Vorkommen von Struktur in der Sprache", in *Festschrift für Jost Trier zum 70. Geburtstag,* Köln-Graz (Böhlau), 1964, 1–22; K. H. Rensch, "Organismus–System–Struktur in der Sprachwissenschaft", in *Phonetica,* no. 16, 1967, pp. 71-84 (of historical orientation), etc. In most linguistic works the use of *system* and *structure* is more or less unconscious; for this reason the terms are quite flexible, with many different uses.

[15]As for the controversial opposition / ẹ / : / ȩ /, see above, note 8.

Table 18

structure realized (masc. article)		coherent system (can be completed)	
a	A	a	A
b	B	b	B
c ←→ c		c	C
a	A	d	D

distinguishing between what is realized within a given language and deductive, coherent, logical systems, will serve as a basis in the following chapters for a more coherent conception of *semasiology* and *onomasiology*. Georges Mounin rightly speaks of re-establishing the bridge between logic and language, and especially between logic and semantics[16].

---

[16]Georges Mounin, *Les problèmes théoriques de la traduction*, Paris, 1963, p. 133.

2

Heger's Trapezium[*]

In the first part of this work we took as a methodological basis Ullmann's triangle, with its three points; the *signifiant* (the form of the word, Wortkörper = form of expression), the *concept* (mental object) and the *extralinguistic reality* (Ullmann's terms are *name, sense* and *thing*). Klaus Heger, in his article which we have already quoted on the methodological bases of onomasiology and the classification by concepts[1], an article of great theoretical importance (semasiological and onomasiological fields), says that I have distorted its original meaning, transferring it from the level of the first metalan-

---

[*]The nucleus of this chapter was presented as the first part of my lecture in the Congreso de Lingüística Románica in Madrid, 1965. The complete text (including the second part, which constitutes the next chapter) was published in French in 1966: "Sémantique et structure conceptuelle (Le concept 'se souvenir')", in *CahLex*, 8, 1966, pp. 3–46; an abbreviated version has been published in the Acts of the Conference ("Problèmes fondamentaux de l'onomasiologie", in *XI Congreso Int. de Lingüística y Filología románicas, Actas, I*, Madrid, 1968, pp. 175–213). This English version is from the Spanish translation of José Luis Rivarola (Lima).
[1]Klaus Heger, "Die methodologischen Voraussetzungen von Onomasiologie und begrifflicher Gliederung," in *ZRP*, 80, 1964, pp. 486–516 = "Les bases méthodologiques de l'onomasiologie et du classement par concepts," in *TraLiLi* III[1], 1965, pp. 7–32.

guage[2] to the level of the second:

> 3: level of the second metalanguage (level of linguistic methodology)
> 2: level of the first metalanguage (application of linguistic methodology; level of applied grammar)
> 1: level of the object language

At the same time, the modified triangle has lost the quantitative consubstantiality between meaning and *signifiant*; Heger, as a result, attempts to separate the meaning and the concept. Heger's criticism seems to me to be fully justified, at least in the sense that in my treatment of the triangle I changed, without realizing it, the conception of the linguistic sign. In my interpretation of the triangle, the uniting of the *signifiant* (Wortkörper) and the meaning (concept) does not constitute the whole of a linguistic sign, because the content of a form (Wortkörper) is an entire semasiological field (which contains more than one concept or mental object) and because, furthermore, a concept (mental object) can be realized by more than one form (*signifiant*). The definition of the linguistic sign, in the triangle conceived in this way, does not correspond to de Saussure's definition (sheet of paper: you cannot cut the front without cutting the back). The linguistic sign, in my application of the triangle, is the combination of a *signifiant* and (in the same triangle) a signification; the concept is a mental object which can be realized (within the same triangle) by a *signifiant*. This conception is legitimate (and in many cases it will be profitable to work with it), but it destroys the Saussurian unity of the linguistic sign. The triangle has another

---

[2]See A. J. Greimas, *Sémantique structurale*, Paris, 1966, pp. 14–15. Since Ullmann's triangle can be conceived of as a methodological model on the level of the second metalanguage (applicable on the level of the first) this criticism by Heger seems to me to be well-founded only in the sense that neither Ullmann nor I have distinguished clearly and consciously between the two levels (Heger, in subsequent discussions, agreed with this interpretation).

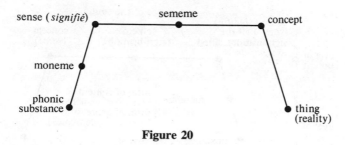

Figure 20

disadvantage: the concept contained in the triangle is a two-sided unit, a fact which has brought about many misunderstandings. On one hand, it is the mental unit, just as we have described it – a unit which serves as the starting-point for onomasiology. On the other hand, the concept is joined to the *signifiant* by way of the signification (sememe) (see above, Chapter 5c).

Heger, for these reasons, worked-out a more sophisticated model, the trapezium, which restores the unity of the linguistic sign and offers the possibility of analyzing the content (allowing room for sememes and semes). This model is Figure 20.

Figure 21 shows this in other terms (taking into account Hjelmslev's terminology)[3]. This diagram, I repeat, is "a methodological model which serves to represent the questions which linguistics poses; its application is transferred from the level of the first metalanguage to that of the second" (Heger, *TraLiLi* III[1], p. 13; *ZRP* 80, 493). This avoids the disadvantages of the triangle we have already mentioned. The term

---

[3]"The different Hjelmslevian levels are becoming more and more accepted, but at the same time they are being made more subtle; this is leading to a distinction between additional levels, to subdivisions of Hjelmslev's levels (the idea of substance of content, for example, is insufficient); at the same time, the complex relationships between the various levels are being explored much better" (Ruwet, "La linguistique générale aujourd'hui," in *Arch. europ. de Sociol.*, 5, 1964, p. 282; see also p. 287).

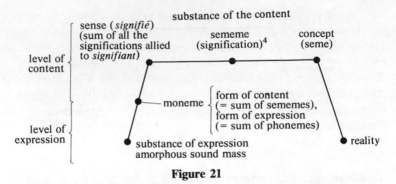

Figure 21

moneme[5] is understood as the minimal unit which bears a meaning (see Figure 22).

The moneme is at the same time a form of expression (as the sum of phonemes) and a form of content (as the sum of sememes); the moneme is at the same time *signifiant* and *signifié*. While the *signifié* depends on the structure of a given language, the concept, which figures on the right of the trapezium, is independent, according to Heger. It is defined by its position within a partial pyramid of concepts or of a logical system of relations[6]. Beginning with *structures* formalized in

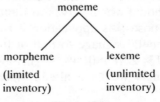

Figure 22

---

[4]Heger only makes use of the term *sememe* and rejects *signification*, in order to avoid misunderstandings. Later we shall distinguish between the two terms (Part II, Chap. 6).

[5]See Part I, Chapter 3c.

[6]"The ways in which the relationships that bind several concepts together can be presented are well known; you define the *species* with the *genus* and the *differentia specifica*; you divide a *genus* exhaustively

one language, it is possible to arrive at *systems* which are independent of a given language (see the preceding chapter). For Heger, semasiology and onomasiology are situated exclusively on the level of the substance of content. Semasiology starts from the *signifié* (sense, *Bedeutungsumfang*) and examines the different significations or sememes, by fixing the boundaries of the semes or *differentiae specificae* (cf. the analysis of Pottier, Part I, Chap. 5):

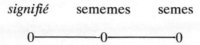

Onomasiology, on the other hand, starts from the concept, which is, I insist, independent of the structure of any given language, in order to find its designations, its linguistic realizations, in one or more languages. Onomasiology looks for the monemes which, through one of their significations or sememes, serve to express the concept in question (onomasiology, as a result, goes from the right to the left in the trapezium). Semasiology examines the combination of a *signifié* linked, through having the same content, *to only one moneme*; it offers, then, a number of significations or sememes. Onomasiology – starting from the opposite side – examines a number of significations or sememes linked to a multiplicity of senses (*signifiés*), and, through the senses, to *a number of monemes*. The semasiological field represents the internal structure of a single sense linked, through having the same content, to a single moneme. The onomasiological field represents the structure of all the sememes that belong to different *signifiés*, that is, to different monemes, but all of which realize one and only one concept. To symbolize these theoretical data geometrically, it will be necessary to resort to depth as a third dimension (see Figures 23 and 24).

---

into two *species* by introducing a *differentia specifica* and its negation, which thereby form a contradictory opposition; concepts are defined by their places in a logical system of relationships organized through axiomatic premises", Heger, p. 19.

SIDE VIEW

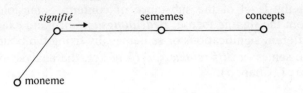

TOP VIEW
(of a hypothetical case)

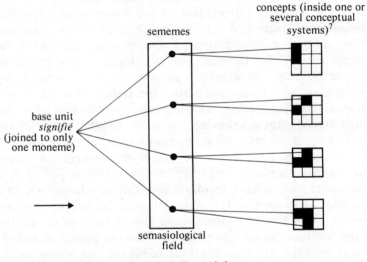

Figure 23 Semasiology

---

[7]The semes contained in the system of concepts can be of a very heterogeneous nature. See below, semes which form part of the conceptual system "remember."

SIDE VIEW

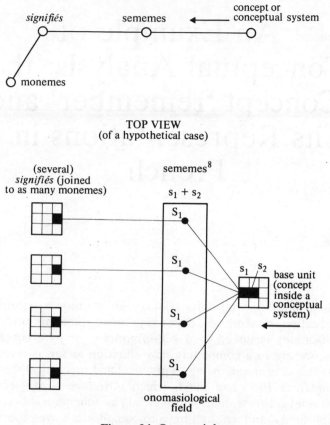

TOP VIEW
(of a hypothetical case)

Figure 24 Onomasiology

---

[8]Combination of semes ($s_1 + s_2$) which corresponds to a position in the conceptual system given (see the next chapter for the positions in the conceptual system "remember").

3

An Example of Conceptual Analysis: the Concept 'remember' and its Representations in French*

Both semasiology and onomasiology, then, study a system of significations or sememes, depending on whether this group of significations is linked to a sense/moneme or to a concept. Thus, we are in a completely new situation as far as level of content is concerned, owing to practical and theoretical studies dating from 1963 and 1964, which introduce a perspective more relevant to semantic problems. The schema has become complicated – and we shall have to complicate it even more in Part II Chapter 6 – but as it gets more complicated it comes closer to being a more accurate representation of the complexity that is characteristic of linguistic reality.

---

*This chapter was given as the second part of my lecture at the Madrid Congress of Romance Linguistics (in 1965); see the note in the previous chapter. (The editor is grateful to Dr. M. Carroll and Dr. S. Kay of the University of Liverpool for their help in translating the French examples in this chapter).

160

To illustrate this, we now turn to the study of a particular case. I have chosen as object of this demonstration the concept of "remember" and its linguistic realizations in French. First we shall examine these realizations on the synchronic level to continue later, in a very fragmentary manner, on the diachronic level. What I am about to present represent the results of a year of discussion with the students at Heidelberg, who have also prepared several synchronic cross-sections. I am also especially thankful to Professor Heger for his suggestions made during the course of numerous evening discussions, which were especially valuable to me.

First of all, one must realize the complex nature of the concept "remember." It can be defined as the "psychic presence" (P_ψ) of something belonging to the past $(A \xleftarrow{p})$ in the memory of a living being (M_B);[1] this gives us a base formula:

$$\boxed{P_\psi(A \xleftarrow{p}; M_B)}$$

This base formula presupposes in a schematic way the existence of the *categories* of *time* and *spirit*, and the existence of *persons* and of *things* (or realities). A is the object of memory under consideration; B is the person by whom the remembered object (= A) is evoked. The psychic presence is indicated by the verb or verbal expression:

Je /*me souviens*/ de mon enfance   (I remember my childhood)

B P_ψ A

---

[1] A passage in the *Bestiaire d'amour rimé* (about 1250) gives the same definition in poetic form:
"A homme [Dieu] une vertu donna,
Par coi il puet *ramentevoir*
les fais trespassés et savoir
Trestout en autretel samblance
Com se il fussent en presence." (V. 66–70).
(God gave a power to man by which he can recall things past, and know everything, presented in another way, just as if it were present)

Of these three fundamental elements, only P_ψ is always present, while B and A can be absent but considered as understood, as we shall see. But a fourth element, C, can be added, which indicates the cause that evokes or produces the remembrance:

> Ger. C *erinnert mich an* A
> Span. C *me recuerda* A
> Eng. C *reminds me of* A

When we try to translate the German or Spanish sentence into French or English, we notice that we cannot use the same word (remember, *souvenir*): in French

> C me *rappelle* A
> ce jouet me *rappelle* mon enfance (that toy *reminds* me of my childhood)

From this point on, we are dealing with the so-called synonymy between *rappeler* and *souvenir: je me souviens* (de mon enfance) is involuntary; *rappeler*, on the other hand, has a voluntary or causal character (at least in our example):

> (1) *je me souviens* de mon enfance (I remember . . .)
>   B P_ψ A
>
> (2) *je me rappelle* mon enfance (I am reminded of . . .)
>   C B P_ψ A

(1) is a sentence with two actants (A and B), following the terminology of Lucien Tesnière,[2] 2) is a sentence with three actants (in which B and C are the same). *Je* and *me* have different functions in the two sentences. Let us keep hold of this first distinction between involuntary and voluntary or causal which characterizes the difference between *se souvenir* and

---

[2] Lucien Tesnière, *Eléments de syntaxe structurale,* Paris, 1959, pp. 102, 105, ff.

rappeler in its etymological use (which, as we shall see, is now going out of date)[3]. It is this difference between *involuntary* memory and *voluntary* memory which stands out so clearly in the work of Proust[4]. Racine makes use of this opposition, for example, in *Mithridate* 201–204:

> Ne *vous souvient-il* plus, en quittant vos beaux yeux,
> Quelle vive douleur attendrit mes adieux?
> *Je m'en souviens* tout seul. Avouez-le, Madame,
> *Je vous rappelle* un songe effacé de votre âme.

> ("Do you no longer remember what deep distress beset my tender farewells on leaving you? I alone remember. Admit it, my Lady, I am reminding you of a dream which you had expelled from your soul")

Tout seul emphasizes the involuntary character of *se souvenir; effacé* emphasizes the voluntary character of *rappeler*[5].

---

[3]For *se souvenir* and *se rappeler* in the seventeenth century, see our article "Se rappeler – se souvenir" in *Mélanges de Grammaire française offerts à M. Maurice Grevisse* . . . , Gembloux (Belgique, Editions Duculot), 1966, pp. 21–37.

[4]See Elizabeth Gülich, "Die Metaphorik der Erinnerung in Prousts 'A la recherche du temps perdu' " in *ZfSL*, 75, 1965, pp. 51–74, especially pp. 55 and 59; Elizabeth R. Jackson, *L'évolution de la mémoire involontaire dans l'œuvre de Marcel Proust*, Paris, 1966, 280 pp.; S. Ullmann, "Images of Time and Memory in 'Jean Santeuil' ", *Currents of Thought in French Literature* (*Essays in Memory of G. T. Clapton*), ed. by J. C. Ireson, [1966], pp. 209–26.

[5]Henri Vernay (Heidelberg) has proved, in a special investigation, that in contemporary French literature *se rappeler* is still used primarily to express voluntary memory, *se souvenir* involuntary memory (see, however, below, concerning the tendency towards a new distribution of the two verbs). If Alain Fournier uses *se rappeler* almost exclusively in *Le Grand Meaulnes,* while Saint-Exupéry, in *Terre des Hommes,* prefers *se souvenir,* these preferences are explained by the character of the two novels. Alain Fournier calls to mind events from his childhood and youth (act of voluntary memory); in Saint-Exupéry, the remembrance, in most cases, is caused involuntarily by acts and thoughts in the present.

But there is a second fundamental opposition within the concept "remember": the remembrance can be presented either as an *act* or as a *state*. On the level of voluntary memory one can either *evoke* the memory or *retain* it. In the same way, in the realm of involuntary memory, the remembrance can either *return* or *remain*. The memory, then, can be *transformative* or *non-transformative*[6,7]. Let us take, by way of example, two sentences from Proust:

Brusquement *le souvenir* de sa femme morte lui *revient* (suddenly the memory of his dead wife comes back to him)
(Swann I, 28, *NRF*, 1919.)
(un rêve) dont *le souvenir durera* davantage (a dream whose memory will last longer)
(Swann I, 126, *NRF*, 1919.)

The first phrase is transformative, the second, non-transformative. In reality, it is often difficult to distinguish between transformative and non-transformative memory:

Il faut que *je me rappelle* bien que je n'ai pas dormi
(I have to tell myself that I have not slept)
(Proust, *Swann* I, 78, *NRF*, 1919.)

. . . mais *souvenez-vous*: au-dessous des mers de nuages . . . c'est l'éternité

---

[6]Following the terminology of M. Sánchez-Ruipérez, *Estructura del sistema de aspectos y tiempos del verbo griego antiguo,* Salamanca, 1954, p. 53, and K. Heger, "Valenz, Diathese and Kasus," in *ZRP*, 82, 1966, p. 142, note 7 and p. 151.

[7]The Czech language has available two forms which contain the root *men* (information from my Heidelberg colleagues Schröpfer and Schallich):

1. one form with no prefix: *pamatovati* "I have in my memory; I am keeping in my memory";

2. two forms with prefixes: *vzpomináti* and *připominati*. The two prefixes *vz* and *pri* have an inchoative function. An analogous situation is found in other Slavic languages.

(but remember: if you go below the cloud base . . . there lies eternity)

(St-Exupéry, *Terre des Hommes*, p. 14, *NRF*, 1939.)

These phrases are very similar to "il faut que je n'oublie pas . . .," (I must not forget . . .) ". . . n'oubliez pas" (do not forget). They have, therefore, a non-transformative character, just as do the non-transformative expressions *garder dans sa mémoire, retenir en sa mémoire*, etc. (keep in one's memory), all of which approach the neighbouring concept "ne pas oublier" (not to forget) and "penser à" (to be thinking of)[8].

These few observations and examples supply us with the necessary elements to build up the conceptual system of logical

---

[8]The distinction is even more complicated because of the existence of an intermediate *iterative* category which we have classified as transformative: "Souvent, plus tard, lorsqu'il s'endormait après avoir désespérément essayé de *se rappeler* le beau visage effacé, il voyait en rêve passer des rangées de jeunes femmes . . ." ("Often, later, when he was going to sleep after trying desperately to recall the beautiful face he had lost, he used to see pass in a dream lines of young women . . .": *Le Grand Meaulnes* I, XV, Coll. Livre de Poche). "Je ne *me rappelle* jamais cette partie de plaisir *sans* un obscur regret, comme une sorte d'étouffement" ("I never remember this bit of pleasure without an obscure feeling of regret, like a kind of choking . . .": ib. III, V). "Le directeur avait coutume de *rappeler* leurs devoirs à tous ses subordonnés" ("The director had the habit of reminding all his subordinates of their duties . . .": Duhamel, *Pasqu.* VIII, II, Robert). "Sans être belle, elle avait une figure difficile à oublier et que je *me rappelle* encore, souvent beaucoup trop pour un vieux fou." ("Without being attractive, she had a figure hard to forget and which I can still remember, often much too well for a foolish old man . . .": Rousseau, *Confess.* I. Robert, s. v. *difficile*). This iterative character becomes very clear in the combination *revenir + sans cesse*: "Cette idée *lui revenait, sans cesse*, d'une prison atroce dans laquelle on l'eût enfermé pour quelque crime inconnu" ("This idea kept on coming back to him of a fearsome prison where he had been shut in for some unknown crime": Bloy, *Le Désespéré*, p. 78, Robert, cit. 15). [Cp. "il pensait sans cesse à", "he kept on thinking of"].

relationships, which can serve as a basis for onomasiology, both for French, from which we have taken the examples, for other Romance Languages, and the Germanic Languages. If we take into account all the possibilities suggested for French, the conceptual system "remember" can be organized in the following way:

$$\boxed{P_\psi(A \underset{p}{\leftarrow}; M_B)} = \text{base formula (see above)}$$

This formula can be realized totally or in part. On the level of expression one can do without (= consider "understood") either $A \underset{p}{\leftarrow}$ or M_B, while the psychic presence is necessarily given form if one does not wish to leave the conceptual domain of "remember". This leads us to at least three sections: formalization of $P_\psi(A\underset{p}{\leftarrow}M_B) + (A) + (B)$; formalization of $P_\psi(A\underset{p}{\leftarrow}; M_Y) + (A)$; formalization of $P_\psi(X\underset{p}{\leftarrow}; M_B) + (B)$; formalization of the whole formula to which one can add a causal element. At the same time, we distinguish the number of formalized actants; the so-called *valencies* (Wertigkeit) (how many nouns or pronouns are allied with the verb). Heger has written a seminal article which develops Lucien Tesnière's theory of the valency of the verb[9]. I am giving in Figure 25

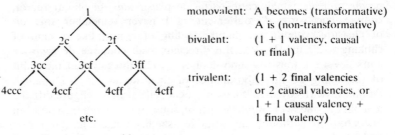

monovalent: A becomes (transformative)
A is (non-transformative)
bivalent: (1 + 1 valency, causal or final)
trivalent: (1 + 2 final valencies or 2 causal valencies, or 1 + 1 causal valency + 1 final valency)

etc.

valency 0 = avalent = without actant
valency 1 = monovalent = 1 actant
etc.

Figure 25

[9]Klaus Heger, "Valenz, Diathese und Kasus," in *ZRP,* 82, 1966, pp. 138–70 (the diagram is found on p. 146).

only those results which are essential to our subsequent considerations.

On applying this system of valencies to the concept "remember" we get:

$$P_\psi (X \xleftarrow{\text{P}}; M_Y) \quad \Big\} \quad = \text{valency 0 (avalent)}$$

$$\begin{aligned} P_\psi (X \xleftarrow{\text{P}}; M_B) \\ P_\psi (A \xleftarrow{\text{P}}; M_Y) \end{aligned} \quad \Big\} \quad = \text{valency 1 (monovalent)}$$

$$\begin{aligned} P_\psi (A \xleftarrow{\text{P}}; M_B) \\ {}_cP_\psi (A \xleftarrow{\text{P}}; M_Y; C) \\ {}_cP_\psi (X \xleftarrow{\text{P}}; M_B; C) \end{aligned} \quad \Big\} \quad = \text{valency 2 (bivalent)}$$

$$_cP_\psi (A \xleftarrow{\text{P}}; M_B; C) \quad \Big\} \quad = \text{valency 3 (trivalent)}$$

Taking into account the base formula, the different valencies and the total or partial formalization, and adding the transformative (t) and non-transformative (t̄) variants, we get Figure 26, which will allow us to classify all the possible formalizations. The transformative side corresponds exactly to the non-transformative side. That is, each formalized example offers at least two interpretations to be examined[10]. This diagram, which contains the logical possibilities, will allow us to determine to what extent a given language realizes it, which realizations are preferred, which are very rare (such attestations could correspond either to a mistake or to a very elevated stylistic value), and which realizations are left empty. In

---

[10]Cp. the following example pointed out to me by K. Heger:

—monovalent and transformative: "la voiture se met en marche", "the car is starting to move";

—monovalent and non-transformative: "la voiture est (se trouve) en marche", "the car is moving";

—bivalent and transformative: "le moteur met la voiture en marche", "the motor starts the car moving";

—bivalent and non-transformative: "le moteur maintient la voiture en marche", "the motor keeps the car moving."

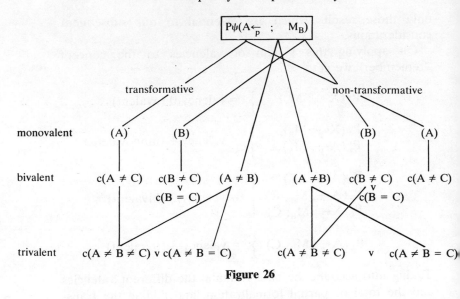

Figure 26

addition, the diagram will often help us to grasp the *differentiae specificae* between supposed *synonyms* (see, also, Part II, Ch. 5).

Let us go back to the conceptual diagram, numbering the positions, and explaining them verbally (see Table 19, p. 174).

This diagram systematically brings together all the possible realizations that I have found in Modern French. It is a detailed diagram, which, however, does not claim to be complete, although I am sure it covers the essential realizations. When we fill out the conceptual outline with expressions from the object language, we apply to this object language, on the level of the first metalanguage, the methodological system acquired on the level of the second. The diagram is filled with monemes and expressions formed with several monemes, but the position of these monemes within the conceptual system fixes the signification (to a certain extent, as we shall see when we discuss synonymy). In reality, we have made an abstraction from the semasiological field of each moneme, retaining only those significations which come into the conceptual field of "remember." Thus, we have classified significations or sememes joined to monemes that can have still other significations. We are dealing with *onomasiological fields*, structured according to the conceptual system from which we have set out. Each position within the conceptual system constitutes a (minimal) *onomasiological field* (see the list of onomasiological fields, Table 20, p. 176). I shall first include a series of examples in Modern French to document the different positions. (See also Table 19, p. 174.)

Examples in Modern French

1-1 "Puis *renaissait le souvenir* d'une nouvelle attitude" ("Then the memory sprang to mind again of a new attitude": Proust, *Swann* I, 16, ed. N.R.F., 1919).

1-2 "Enfin Bury releva la tête, parut m'entendre, *se souvenir*, et partit brusquement dans un rire clair" ("At last Bury lifted his head, seemed to hear me, remember, and suddenly burst out laughing": St-Exupéry, *Terre*, 12f., N.R.F., 1939).

2-1 ". . . car les excuses *rappellent* la faute plus certainement qu'elles ne l'atténuent" (". . . for excuses recall the fault more surely than they attenuate it": Louys, *Avent. roi Pausole*, III, XI, Robert, s. v. *excuse*). "Il est un peu petit, et c'est pour excuser sa taille qu'*il rappelle* à tous propos son grade de lieutenant dans la cavalerie de réserve" ("He is rather small, and to make allowances for his height he reminds (people) at every opportunity of his rank of lieutenant in the reserve cavalry": V. Garbaud, *Barnabooth Journal* II, p. 200, Robert, s. v. *petit*). "*Rappellerai-je* encore *le souvenir* affreux/Du jour qui dans les fers nous jeta toutes deux?" ("Shall I evoke again the frightful memory of that day that saw us both imprisoned?": Racine, *Iphig.* II, 1, Robert). "Une existence quasi fraternelle qu'il m'est impossible d'*évoquer* sans que mes yeux s'emplissent de larmes" ("An almost fraternal existence which I am unable to recall without my eyes filling with tears": Courteline, *Boubour.*, cf. Robert). "Il en est ainsi de notre passé. C'est peine perdue que *nous cherchions à l'évoquer*" ("And so with our past. It is no use trying to recall it": Proust, *Swann* I, 69, ed. N.R.F., 1919). "Tout *parlait* du Grand Meaulnes" ("Everything had the mark of the Grand Meaulnes": A. Fournier, *Le Gd Meaulnes* III, XI, Coll. Livre de Poche).

2-2a ?

2-2b "J'ai fini par ne plus m'ennuyer du tout à partir de l'instant où *j'ai appris à me souvenir.* Je me mettais quelquefois à penser à ma chambre . . ." ("I ended up by not being bored any more from the moment when I discovered how to remember. I would sometimes begin to think about my room . . .": Camus, *L'Étranger*, p. 112, Robert). "Horloge! dieu sinistre, effrayant, impassible./Dont le doigt nous menace et nous dit: *"Souviens-toi!"* ("Clock! Sinister, frightening, impassive God; whose finger threatens us and says: "remember!" . . ."; Baudelaire). "*Rappelle-toi,* Barbara!" ("Remember, Barbara": refrain of a song by Jaques Prévert, cf. 3-1b).

2-3 "Brusquement *le souvenir* de sa femme morte *lui revint*" ("Suddenly the memory of his dead wife came back to him": Proust, *Swann* I, 28, ed. N.R.F., 1919). "Il retrouvait son ami, comme vous *revient* une musique oubliée" ("He rediscovered his friend, as a forgotten tune comes back to one's mind": Montherlant, *Le Songe* I, III, Robert [or = 20-3?]). "Mais quel était l'objet de mes amours? Peut-être cela *me reviendra-t-il* comme beaucoup de choses me *reviennent* en écrivant" ("but what was the object of my love? Perhaps that will come back to me, as many things come back to me as I write": Stendhal, *Vie de H. Brulard*, 13, Robert). "*Je me souviens/Des* jours anciens/Et je pleure" ("I remember days gone by, and I weep": Verlaine, *Poèmes saturniens*, Robert).

3-1a "La vue de la petite Madeleine ne *m'avait* rien *rappelé* avant que je n'y eusse goûté" ("The sight of the small madeleine had not reminded me of anything before I tasted it": Proust, *Swann* I, 72, ed. N.R.F., 1919). "*rappelez-moi* à son souvenir" ("Remember me to him": traditional polite formula). "Tu veux, en les niant, qu'on *te les remémore*" ("Rejecting them, you want people to remind you of them": Littré). "Tu *me fais souvenir* que j'ai tout oublié" ("You've reminded me that I have forgotten everything": Hugo, *Hernani*, Robert). "Je vous *ferai souvenir* d'une petite histoire" ("I will remind you of a little story": Racine, ed. Mesnard, IV, 284, Imag., see also VI, 307).

"Il lui *remet devant les yeux* ce qu'Ajax a fait pour les Grecs" ("He reminds him vividly of what Ajax has done for the Greeks": Racine VI, 435, *Cin*., 1137).

3-1b   Je *rappelai* à moi le peu que je savais" ("I summoned up the little I knew": Valéry, *Regards sur le monde actuel*, 13, Robert).

"je passais la plus grande partie de la nuit à *me rappeler* ma vie d'autrefois . . . à *me rappeler* les lieux" ("I used to spend most of the night turning over my past life . . . recalling the places": Proust, *Swann* I, 19, ed. N.R.F., 1919).

"*Rappelle-toi cela*, Barbara!" ("Remember that, Barbara!": variant of the refrain of a song by Jacques Prévert, cf. 2–2b).

"Tiens, disait ma tante en se frappant le front, cela *me fait penser* que j'ai point su si elle était arrivée à l'église après l'élévation" ("Heavens, said my aunt tapping her forehead, that reminds me – I don't know if she arrived at the church after the elevation of the host": Proust, *Swann* I, 148).

"*Remets dans ton esprit*, après tant de carnages, De tes proscriptions les sanglantes images" ("Call to mind, after so much bloodshed, the blood-stained image of your purges": Corn., III, 435, *Cin*., 1137, Littré). "Plus je vous envisage, moins *je me remets*, Monsieur, votre visage" ("The more I look at you, the less, Sir, I remember your face": Racine, *Plaid*., 380).

"Ne vous *remettez-vous* point son visage?" ("Can't you place his face at all?"; Ac 1694).

"La nuit, sur l'oreiller, il *se remémore* ces délicieuses soirées" ("At night, in bed, he remembers those delightful evenings": Rolland, Robert).

"Tel qu'un homme qui s'éveille le matin et qui *rappelle* peu à peu de loin le songe fugitif qui a disparu à son réveil" ("Like a man who wakes in the morning and who gradually remembers the fleeting dream which disappeared as he awoke": Fén. *Tél*. VIII, Littré).

"un nom qu'on *cherche à se rappeler* et à la place duquel on ne trouve que du néant" ("A name which one seeks to remember and instead of which one only finds nothing": Proust, *Rech. temps perdu* I, p. 530, Pléiade).

10-1   "(un rêve) dont *le souvenir durera* davantage" ("A dream whose memory will last longer": Proust, *Swann* I, 26, ed. N.R.F., 1919).

10-2   "C'est tout, si *j'ai mémoire*" ("That's all, as far as I remember": La Fontaine, ed., Regnier, IV, 386). "Il n'est pas vieux, mais il *se souvient* de loin" ("He is not old, but he has a long memory": Ac 1694).

"J'ai connu, sur les bancs du collège, un garçon qui avait de l'ambition et des moyens; il s'appliquait, il comprenait, *il retenait*" ("I knew, at school, a boy with ambition and means: he worked hard, he understood, and he could remember things": Alain, *Propos*, 18 févr. 1911, Grandet).

20-1   "Ces gradins, qui *rappellent* ceux des amphithéâtres de Rome" ("These tiers, that bring to mind those of the amphitheatres in Rome": Gautier, *Voyage en Espagne*, Robert, s. v. *gradin*).

20-2a   ?

20-2b   ?

20-3   "Ah! je *me souviendrais* du serpent de Motril!" ("Ah! I would remember the stream near Motril!": (St-Exupéry, *Terre*, p. 17, ed. N.R.F., 1939).

"Il *s'en souviendra!*" (menace: "He'll remember all right", different interpretations possible).

"Il *se souvient* d'un goût de pleine mer qui, s'il est une fois savouré par l'homme, n'est jamais oublié" ("It recalls the taste of the open sea which, once tasted by man, is never forgotten": St-Exupéry, *Terre*, p. 184).

"Ce vieil omnibus a disparu, mais son austérité, son inconfort *sont restés vivants dans mon souvenir*" ("That old bus has gone, but its bareness and discomfort live on in my memory": ib., p. 20).

"Je *me rappelle* encore cet être singulier" ("I still remember this extraordinary being": A. Fournier, *Le Gd Meaulnes* II, III, Coll. Livre de Poche).

"Je *revoyais* les grandes armoires solennelles de la maison" ("I saw in my mind's eye the great sombre cupboards of the house": St-Exupéry, *Terre*, p. 75, N.R.F., 1939 [or = 2-3?]).

"Je *n'ai point mémoire* d'en avoir vu qui m'ait semblé si doux" ("I don't remember having seen one that seemed so sweet": La Fontaine, *Orais*).

"si j'en *ai mémoire*" ("As far as I remember it": La Fontaine, VIII, 291).

30-1a   "Par sa seule présence il me *fait* sans cesse *souvenir* de mon enfance." ("By his very presence he continually makes me think of my childhood")

"*Grâce* à ce bruit permanent *je me souvenais* toute la matinée *de . . .*" ("Thanks to that continual noise I kept remembering all morning (something) . . .").

"Par la diversité de son humeur . . . elle *allait rappellant en* lui mille désirs, évoquant des instincts ou des réminiscences" ("According to the variety of her moods . . . she kept on raising in him countless desires, evoking instincts or memories": Flaubert, *Mme Bovary* III, 5, Robert, s. v. *humeur*).

"L'horizon . . . donne une place d'honneur à notre soif d'infini, en même temps qu'il nous *rappelle* nos limites" ("The horizon . . . exalts our thirst for the infinite, at the same time as reminding us of our limitations": Barrès, *La Colline inspirée* II, 18, Robert).

30-1b   "il faut que *je me rappelle* bien que je n'ai pas dormi" ("I have to tell myself that I have not slept": Proust, *Swann* I, 78, ed. N.R.F., 1919).

"Parce qu'on *se rappelle* toujours ce qu'on a médité long-temps" ("Because one always remembers what one has considered deeply": Hugo, *littér. et philos. sur Walter Scott*, Robert).

"*Rappelle-toi* bien d'employer tout ce que tu as d'esprit à être aimable" ("Don't forget to put all your effort into being pleasant": Stendhal, *Corresp.* II, 174, Robert).

"Seurel, je te demandais l'autre jour de *penser à* moi. Maintenant, au contraire, il vaut mieux oublier" ("Seurel, I asked you the other day to think about me. Now, on the other hand,

Table 19

THE CONCEPT "REMEMBER" $[P_\psi(X_{\bar{p}}; M_Y)]$

transformative

monovalent	1-1 "A comes to the memory" $[P_\psi(A_{\bar{p}}; M_Y) + 1 + t + (A)]$	1-2 "B begins to remember" $[P_\psi(X_{\bar{p}}; MB) + 1 + t + (B)]$	
bivalent	2-1 "C evokes the memory of A" $[cP_\psi(A_{\bar{p}}; M_Y; C) + 2c[C \rightarrow (A_{\bar{p}}; M_Y)] + t + (A \neq C)]$	2-2a "C evokes the memory in B" $[cP_\psi(X_{\bar{p}}; M_B; C) + 2c[C \rightarrow (X_{\bar{p}}; M_B)] + t + (B \neq C)]$	2-3 "A is realized in the memory of B" $[P_\psi(A_{\bar{p}}; M_B) + 2 + t + (A \neq B)]$
		2-2b "C evokes its memory"; "B: evoke your memory!" $[cP_\psi(X_{\bar{p}}; M_B; C) + 2c[C \rightarrow (X_{\bar{p}}; M_B)] + t + (B = C)]$	
trivalent	3-1a "C evokes in B the memory of A" $[cP_\psi(A_{\bar{p}}; M_B; C) + 3c[C \rightarrow (A_{\bar{p}}; M_B)] + t + (A \neq B \neq C)]$	3-1b "B evokes in himself the memory of A"; "B: evoke the memory of A!" $[cP_\psi(A_{\bar{p}}; M_B; C) + 3c[C \rightarrow (A_{\bar{p}}; M_B)] + t + (A \neq B = C)]$	

it would be better not to": Fournier, *Le Gd Meaulnes* II, XII, Coll. Livre de Poche).

"Et maintenant encore, au seul mot de fontaine, prononcé n'importe où, c'est *à* celle-là, pendant longtemps que je *pense*" ("And even now, at the very word *fontaine*, whenever I hear it, that's the one I continue to think of": ib. III, I) [or = 3-2?]

Seigneur, ne vous souvenez point de mes offenses" ("Lord, hold not my sins against me": Ac 1694).

"De vos nobles projets, Seigneur, qu'il *vous souvienne*" ("Don't forget, my Lord, your noble plans": Rac., *Bér.* 555).

"*Ayez mémoire de* qch" ("Remember (something)": Ac 1694).

non-transformative

monovalent		10-2 "B is in a state of remembering" $[P_\psi(X^-_{\bar{p}}; M_B) + 1 + \bar{t} + (B)]$	10-1 "A remains in the memory" $[P_\psi(A^-_{\bar{p}}; M_Y) + 1 + \bar{t} + (A)]$
bivalent	20-3 "B keeps the memory of A" $[P_\psi(A^-_{\bar{p}}; M_B) + 2 + \bar{t} + (A \neq B)]$	20-2a "C keeps alive the memory in B" $[cP_\psi(X^-_{\bar{p}}; M_B; C) + 2c[C{\to}(X^-_{\bar{p}}; M_B)] + \bar{t} + (B \neq C)]$ 20-2b "B makes its memory remain"; "B, keep the memory!" $[cP_\psi(X^-_{\bar{p}}; M_B; C) + 2c[C{\to}(X^-_{\bar{p}}; M_B)] + \bar{t} + (B = C)]$	20-1 "C makes the memory of A remain" $[cP_\psi(A^-_{\bar{p}}; M_Y; C) + 2c[C{\to}(A^-_{\bar{p}}; M_Y)] + \bar{t} + (A \neq C)]$
trivalent	30-1a "C makes the memory of A stay in B" $[cP_\psi(A^-_{\bar{p}}; M_B; C) + 3c[C{\to}(A^-_{\bar{p}}; M_B)] + \bar{t} + (A \neq B \neq C)]$	30-1b "B makes the memory of A stay in B"; "B keep the memory of A!" $[cP_\psi(A^-_{\bar{p}}; M_B; C) + 3c[C{\to}(A^-_{\bar{p}}; M_B)] + \bar{t} + (A \neq B = C)]$	

Glossary:

A = object which is remembered (= X if it is indeterminate).
B = bearer of the memory; "the person who remembers" (= Y if he is indeterminate).
C = cause of the memory; "that which evokes the memory."
P_ψ = psychic presence.
c = causal valency.

The description of the sememes offers no difficulties once the conceptual field is established. The first part is composed of the group of semes which serves as a base:

$$s_1^{\ 1} \qquad P_\psi(A \xleftarrow{\bar{p}}; M_B)$$

or the two elliptical variants

$$s_1^{\ 2} \qquad P_\psi(A \xleftarrow{\bar{p}}; M_Y)$$
$$s_1^{\ 3} \qquad P_\psi(X \xleftarrow{\bar{p}}; M_B)$$

which is clear from the title of the diagram in Table 19.

Table 20

ONOMASIOLOGICAL FIELD(S) OF "REMEMBER" IN MODERN FRENCH[11]

1-1	1-2	
le souvenir renaît	se souvenir	

2-1	2-2a?	2-3
rappeler **(le souvenir de) (something)	2-2b	*se rappeler* (something) que
*(something) rappelle (something)	*se rappeler (in infinitive)	**se souvenir* de
(≈ ressemble à, fait penser à) évoquer (something)	*se souvenir (in infinitive)	il me souvient (archaic, literary)
chercher à évoquer (something)	souviens-toi! (absolute use)	*revenir* (à la mémoire, à l'esprit, au coeur, en sa
*(tout) parle de		pensée) (Racine)
		le souvenir de revient à
		se ressouvenir (archaic, literary)
		*revoir

3-1a	3-1b	
rappeler (something) à (someone) (including ≈ *ressembler à)	*se rappeler* (something), que se rappeler le souvenir de	
*faire souvenir de (including ≈ *ressembler à)	se rappeler de (something) se remémorer (something)	} (≈ répéter)
*faire penser à, remettre (something) devant les yeux de (someone) (Racine)	remémorer (something) se mettre à penser à (something from the past)	
remémorer (something) à (someone) faire		

---

[11]The system could be expanded. We have not considered, for example, this possibility: 2-1b, or perhaps better 20-1b (C evokes and causes the memory of A to remain); realized, for example, in this passage:

"*l'odeur* et *la saveur* restent encore longtemps, comme des âmes, à *se rappeler,* à espérer" ("Its smell and its taste still linger on like ghosts, to be recalled and hoped for": Proust, *Swann* I, 73).

L'odeur and *la saveur* are at the same time the cause and the object of the memory. This possibility is also found on the trivalent level; I have here an example from the sixteenth century:

3-1c [C evokes in B the memory of A (A = C ≠ B]:

"*Dieu se ramentoit à nous* par elles, afin de nous amender" ("God used them (diseases) to remind us of Him, for our salvation": Pasquier, *Lettres am.*, no. 14).

God, with the help of the illnesses, is at the same time the cause and the object of the memory evoked in "us," that is, in men.

revenir (something) (en
mémoire) à (someone)

*penser à (something from
the past)
se souvenir (in the imperative)
remettre (something) dans
son esprit (in the imperative) (Corneille)
se remettre (le visage) de
(someone) (Racine, Ac 1694)
[cf. *noter: il faut noter
qu'il était alors bien jeune;
*prêter attention à (some-
thing) → neighbouring concepts ("take into account")]

	10-2	10-1
	avoir mémoire (La Font.)	le souvenir
	retenir	de (something) durera
	se souvenir	

20-3	20-2a?	20-1
se souvenir	20-2b?	rappeler (something)
		(≈ ressembler à, faire penser à)

*se rappeler (something)
se ressouvenir (archaic,
literary)
rester vivant dans son
souvenir
*revoir
retenir
garder le souvenir, la
mémoire de
avoir mémoire de (La
Fontaine)
subsister dans son souvenir

30-1a	30-1b
*rappeler (something) à (someone)	*se rappeler toujours
*faire souvenir (something) à (someone)	ayez mémoire de (something) (Ac 1694)
*se souvenir de . . . grâce à	ayez souvenance de
*faire souvenir de (including ≈ ressembler à)	(also in Ac 1694)
	retenir (in the imperative)
*aller rappelant (something) en (someone)	*se rappeler (in the impera-tive)
	*se souvenir (in the impera-tive)

---

*It is difficult to distinguish here between transformative and non-transformative.
**Forms printed in italics are very frequently found.

We indicate:

by s_2 the valencies ($s_2{}^1$ = monovalency, $s_2{}^2$ = bivalency $s_2{}^3$ = trivalency),

by s_3 the opposition causal/non-causal ($s_3{}^{c\cdot}$, $s_3{}^{\bar{c}}$),

by s_4 the opposition transformative/non-transformative ($s_4{}^t$ = transformative; $s_4{}^{\bar{t}}$ = non-transformative),

by s_5 the opposition between B ≠ C and B = C ($s_5{}^{\bar{i}}$ = non-identity between B and C; $s_5{}^i$ = identity between B and C).

Let us take, by way of example, the sememe of *se rappeler* in position 3-1b:

$$S = s_1{}^1 + s_2{}^3 + s_3{}^c + s_4{}^t + s_5{}^i$$

It is easy, then, to transcribe the formulae of the diagram in terms of sememes.

The diagram and the examples pose a series of problems. I have found no examples for certain positions. This, on the other hand, shows that the diagram is not tautological and that it is not limited to reflecting significations suggested by the language in question (French). Some of these *empty positions* will be filled when we turn to Old French. Especially in these cases, the empty space can be the result of chance, and perhaps a more detailed investigation would supply some examples, which must in any event be rare. It is more significant that we have found almost no examples, neither in Modern French nor in Old French, for positions 2-2a and 20-2a, that is, for the combinations of B and C (non-identical), transformative and non-transformative. One could almost say that this is not the result of chance. It is at the least unusual to speak of B and C without speaking of A[12]. As regards the

---

[12]Examples of 2-2b and of 20-2b (it is anyway difficult to determine whether it is a case of one position or the other) are also very rare. Three examples in Baudelaire, Proust, and Camus are for that reason particularly striking.

other positions, the density of the examples is very uneven. Certain positions – for example, the monovalent positions – are rarely formalized, which is understandable, since the concept "remember" normally presupposes two actants (A and B). As a result, all the monovalent positions have an elliptical character; either A or B is left understood (which corresponds to X in place of A and Y in place of B in the base formula). On the other hand, non-elliptical positions, bivalent and trivalent, are well documented. Examples abound. These last positions can be classified into two types:

1. *B se souvient de A* with variants which are causal /non-causal and transformative/non-transformative; they are 2-3 and 20-3, 3-1b and 30-1b, which gives us the following formula:

$$P_\psi(A \xleftarrow{}_{\overline{p}}; M_B) + (t \vee \overline{t}) + ([2 + (A \neq B)]v$$
$$[3c(C \rightarrow (A \xleftarrow{}_{\overline{p}}; M_B)) + (A \neq B = C)])$$

2. *C rappelle A à B*, transformative and non-transformative (but in which C is not identical to B): they are positions 3-1a and 30-1a, which gives us the following simple formula:

$$P_\psi(A \xleftarrow{}_{\overline{p}}; M_B) + (t \vee \overline{t}) + 3c(C \rightarrow (A \xleftarrow{}_{\overline{p}}; M_B)) +$$
$$(A \neq B \neq C)$$

The second formula corresponds (or corresponded, see below) to the central domain of the verb *rappeler* (something) *à* (someone); the first corresponds (or corresponded) to the central domain of *se souvenir de* (something: B remembers A). In these cases, *rappeler* is distinguished from *se souvenir* by its causal character[13].

---

[13]This nature of the base is well reflected in the following passage: "telle femme incapable de *se rappeler* les événements les plus grands, *se souviendra* pendant toute sa vie des choses qu'importent à ses sentiments" (Balzac, *Femme de trente ans*, Robert) (such a woman, unable to recall the most important events, will remember all her life things that matter to her emotionally). The interpretation of the fol-

But this diagram also shows us the possible interferences; from the moment we put *se souvenir* in the imperative, we introduce a causal element, and the verbal expression changes from bivalency to trivalency: in *souvenez-vous des choses du passé*,[14] (remember the things of the past), B becomes identical to a new causal element, C, and we enter the causal realm of *rappeler*. In fact, *souviens-toi de ta jeunesse* can be replaced by *rappelle-toi (de) ta jeunesse* (remember your youth). If there is a stylistic difference between the two expressions it is because the two verbs have different semantic nuclei. The semasiological field intervenes in stylistic nuances (see my article "Sémasiologie et onomasiologie," *RLiR* 28, 1964, especially p. 257, and in the appendix to this book; Benveniste in *Word*, 10, 264)[15].

---

lowing example is more difficult: "Marius, nous l'avons dit, *ne se rappelait rien. Il se souvenait seulement* d'avoir été saisi in arrière par une main énergique . . ." (Hugo *Misér.* V, V, VIII, Robert). An English translation would be something like: "Marius told us that he couldn't (really) remember anything. He only had a vague memory that he had been snatched from behind by a strong hand. . . ." Is this a conscious nuance, or a stylistic variation to avoid repeating the same word (since, basically, it is a matter of a causal memory, voluntary in both cases)? However, in the following cases, one would expect the verb *se rappeler*: "Oubliée par qui, je vous prie? Par ceux-là qui, ne sentant rien, ne *peuvent se souvenir* de rien" (Baudelaire, *Art romant.*, XXII, III, Robert) (Forgotten by whom, I ask you? By those who feel nothing and can remember nothing). "Je les *prie* de *se souvenir que* ce n'est pas à moi de changer les règles" (Racine) (I beg them to remember that it's not for me to change the rules). Here, as in *faire souvenir, pouvoir* and *prier* take on a causal meaning.

[14]This is the first model example given by Larousse for *se souvenir*. Another example:

"Mais *souvenez-vous*: au-dessous des mers de nuages. . . . c'est l'éternité" (Saint-Exupéry, *Terre*, p. 14, *NRF*, 1939).

Already in Boileau: "*Souvenez-vous* bien qu'un dîner réchauffé ne valut jamais rien" (*Lutr.* I) (Don't forget that a re-heated dinner has never been any good).

[15]See, for example, Middle French *lui ramentevoir sa faim*

On the other hand, along the same lines, *rappeler* approaches the realm of *se souvenir* when it is constructed in the same way as a pronominal verb. In *il se rappelle* (something) the object pronoun has, above all, the full value of an indirect object, but C is identical to B. *Se souvenir* in the imperative and *se rappeler*, a reflexive verb with three valencies, are properly found in position 3-1b:

"B évoque son souvenir de A" (je me rappelle (something), I remember something) or
"B: évoque le souvenir de A!" (souviens-toi de (something) = rappelle-toi (something): Remember (something)!)

This point of contact[16] could serve as a starting point for the analogy; *se rappeler* (something)→*se rappeler de* (something) (attested from the time of Marivaux, *Jeu* I$_7$, and Rousseau, *NHél* I, 22)[17] based on the model *se souvenir de* (something)

(Chastellain) > "faire sentir à (someone)," or Old French, *tous les barons ne puis mie ramentevoir* (1288, *RenN*) > "énumérer" (enumerate). Both examples prove the importance of the context. See also Uriel Weinreich, "On the semantic structure of language," in *Universals of Language*, 1963, p. 142.

[16]There is another, for example: *faire souvenir* = *rappeler* (*faire* assuming the causal element). See the following note.

[17]But already in 1694, in the Dictionary of the French Academy: "*Je me rappelle d*'avoir dit telle chose" (I can remember having said such a thing). This construction is still found today; it is classified as wrong by grammarians: "*Je me rappelle d*'un certain civet de sanglier" (I remember a certain stewed boar) (P. Brasillach, *Le Voleur d'étincelles*, p. 82); "Quand il m'arrive de *me rappeler de* mon âme" (When I happen to remember my soul) (Claudel), etc. (See Grevisse, *Le Bon Usage*, § 599, p. 19, n. 4; § 757, p. 6).
In Proust: "Mais comme ce que *je m'en serais rappelé* m'eût été fourni seulement par la mémoire volontaire, la mémoire de l'intelligence" ("But as what I would have remembered of it had been only provided for me by voluntary memory, intellectual memory, . . .": Proust, *Swann* I, p. 68, *NRF,* 1919), but with causal value.

and on the movement of *rappeler* from the realm of voluntary memory to involuntary memory[18].

The movement of *se rappeler* from the area of voluntary memory to that of involuntary memory removes at the same time the awareness of the etymological link with *appeler*. The

---

[18]The following example is particularly curious (paradoxically causal): "Car *chaque fois qu'il venait de quitter M. Vinteuil,* il *se rappelait* qu'il avait depuis quelque temps un renseignement à lui demander . . ." ("For every time he had just left M. Vinteuil, he used to remember that for some time he had had something to ask him . . .": Proust, *Swann* I, p. 216, *NRF,* 1919).

Other examples of *se rappeler* in position 2–3: "*Je me rappelle* combien je le trouvais beau" ("I remember how beautiful I found it. . .": A. Fournier, *Le Grand Meaulnes* I, VI, Coll. Livre de Poche); "De ce déjeuner, *je ne me rappelle* qu'un grand silence et une grande gêne" ("All I remember of that meal is a long silence and great discomfort": ib.); "Elle nous demande, *je me rappelle,* pourquoi nous ne canotions pas sur le lac des Aubiers, comme les autres" ("She asks us, I remember, why we are not rowing on the lake at Aubiers, as the others are": ib. III, VI). "Mais à l'instant où je quitte le bureau, j'entends comme un "Plouff!" de plongeon. Un de ces bruits sourds, sans écho. *Je me rappelle* à l'instant même avoir entendu un bruit semblable: une explosion dans un garage" ("But at the moment I leave the office, I hear a noise like the *Plouff!* of a dive. One of those dull sounds with no echo. At that very moment I can recall having heard a noise like it; an explosion in a garage": Saint-Exupéry, *Terre,* p. 133, *NRF,* 1939). This last example shows that the causal use and the final use may be interchangeable: the French expression *je me rappelle à l'instant même* might be expressed in German by *in demselben Augenblick fällt mir ein* (non-causal), but the memory of the sound is caused by the sound mentioned in the preceding sentence. Involuntary memory itself also has its causality which provokes it. If we join the two phrases: "Le 'Plouff!' de plongeon *me rappelle* à l'instant un bruit semblable . . ." non-causal *se rappeler* is turned into causal *rappeler.* We find an analogous case in Verlaine: "Pourquoi voulez-vous donc qu'*il m'en souvienne?*" ("So why do you want it to come back to me?"). In spite of the causal expression which precedes it, *se souvenir* keeps its non-causal value (which is confirmed by the impersonal form).

introduction of *se souvenir* seems to be preparing the way for a new structural distribution (I am suggesting this with all appropriate reservations; it is still unrecorded by either lexicographers or grammarians). *Rappeler*, because of its causal value and its etymological value of *re* + *appeler*, is much more tied to the transformative realm than is *se souvenir*, in which it is sometimes difficult to perceive its transformative or non-transformative value. After studying hundreds of examples, both Henri Vernay and I have the impression that *se souvenir* is tending to lean toward the non-transformative side, progressively yielding the transformative position (its only etymologically justified position[19]) to *se rappeler*[20]. In any case, *se*

---

[19]We would have to find out whether there was at one time a tendency to distribute *il me souvient* (transformative) and *je me souviens* (non-transformative) in the same way. Littré still gave the following definitions:

    il me souvient "venir à l'esprit" (to come to mind);
    je me souviens "avoir mémoire de qch." (to have a memory
      of something

But it is not difficult to find examples which contradict this distribution ("*Il m'en souviendra* longtemps" Ac 1694; it will come back to me for a long time).

[20]Compare *il faut qu'il se rappelle* (he must remember, transformative) and *il faut qu'il souvienne* (≈ he must keep it in his memory, non-transformative). The opposition between transformative and non-transformative can also be expressed by the opposition imperfect/past definite.

The infinitive can present the extreme case of the reduction of valencies to zero (avalency). In this case the infinitive gives only a conceptual orientation with no indication of actants [formula $P_\psi(X \xleftarrow{}_{\overline{p}}; M_Y)$: ". . . percevoir finit par n'être plus qu'une occasion de *se souvenir* . . ." ("the act of perception ends by being no more than an opportunity for remembering": Bergson, *Matière et mémoire*, p. 68, Robert). Another example, from the fifteenth century: "Aincores vous dy que Dieu et raison deffendent le parler ou le *ramentevoir,* devànt aucune femme mariée en eage de porter enfans, ou qui est enchainte, *de quelconque chose* pour mengier" ("Again I tell you that God and reason prohibit talking or bringing to mind, before any married woman of child-bearing age, or who is pregnant, of anything to *souvenir* is losing ground (as to its lesser vitality on the non-transformative side, see below). Some scholars who worked out statistics demonstrated that *se souvenir* is attested 58 times in 37 texts, while *(se) rappeler* is attested 116 times in 56 texts, which corresponds to a frequency classification number of 269 for *(se) rappeler* and 482 for *se souvenir*[21]. As a result, *se souvenir* has not been considered by the authors as part of the fundamental vocabulary of French!

There is another problem suggested by the application of the diagram: the formalization can be realized by means of a *moneme*, by a more or less lexicalized combination, or by means of a *periphrasis*. This is, in any case, a recognized fact in onomasiology. There is a scale which begins with periphrasis and allows numerous variations – especially interesting from the viewpoint of stylistics – before reaching lexicalization through one moneme, the domain of pure lexicology. There is no precise limit between the two realms of study; it is of interest to the lexicologer to find out that certain positions in the conceptual diagram are formalized only through periphrasis, and similarly to find out, on the diachronic level, that there has been progressive or decreasing lexicalization. On the other hand, it is evident (and the onomasiological field in Old French will confirm this for us) that formalization through one moneme is far more frequent on the transformative side. This, in my opinion, is explained by the fact that a memory presupposes a transformative movement which makes it possible to bridge the distance between the present moment and the object which belongs to the past (the temporal distance in $A \xleftarrow{}_{\overline{p}}$ and P_ψ of the base formula). Furthermore, the causal element, so often linked to the concept "remember", is inclined to the transformative side,

---

eat": *Les Evangiles des Quenouilles,* ed. P. Jannet). Here, the infinitive neutralizes the causal actant (while A is expressed by *de quelconque chose*); notice that *le ramentevoir* could be translated by *the mention.* The base formula in this second example is $cP_\psi(A \xleftarrow{}_{\overline{p}}; \dot{M}_Y; C)$.

[21]Gougenheim – Michéa – Rivenc – Sauvageot, *L'Élaboration du français fondamental* (1.er degré), Paris, 1964, pp. 74, 78, 108, 110.

SIDE VIEW   TOP VIEW

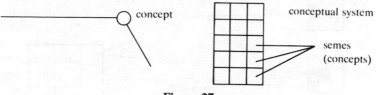

Figure 27

and less amenable to non-transformative formalization, which
is mostly done with auxiliary verbs which emphasize the
duration of the memory (*avoir* en mémoire (to have), *garder* le
souvenir de (to keep), *rester* vivant dans son souvenir (to
remain), etc.).

Finally, I should like to emphasize that the conceptual diagram can help in the interpretation of texts, both modern ones
and, especially, texts from earlier periods, since, if it is valid, it
offers all the possible interpretations, including unusual ones
which would not have occurred to one without a previous conceptual analysis.

We have spent quite a bit of time on the conceptual diagram, but we must remember that it is the basis of onomasiology. The essential result, in my view, is the complexity of the
concept "remember", since it is composed of various conceptual elements or semes. The situation on the conceptual side of
the trapezium, then, is presented in Figure 27. The
conceptual system allows us to find the distinctive features
which differentiate between 'synonyms' and to set up the
methodological procedure of onomasiology shown in Figure
28 (hypothetical case on the level of the first metalanguage).

I can only refer briefly here to the problem of the
relationships between the concept "remember" and
neighbouring concepts – we have already seen that the
non-transformative side approaches the concept "forget", or
rather "not forget" –. "Forget" would bring us to an opposite
and complementary conceptual structure.

The non-transformative side of the conceptual diagram
"remember" shows still more relationships; for example, with

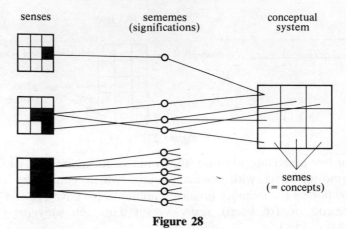

Figure 28

the concept "narrate." These relationships have had semantic consequences, especially in Old French (the noun *mémoire* (memory: dissertation), furthermore, has evolved semantically in a similar way). With the phrase "Ce portrait *me rappelle* une amie de jeunesse" (this portrait reminds me of a girlfriend of my youth) we enter the conceptual realm of "resemble". "Tu t'en *souviendras!*" (you'll remember this!), spoken in a threatening tone, brings us close to the conceptual domains of threat and regret (the expression has been attested since *Ac* 1798, *FEW* 12, 376, with the definition "tu t'en repentiras", you'll be sorry for this). Semantics has to concern itself with the realm of metaphor on the conceptual level. Contacts like these, of which I have given only a few examples, ought to be examined closely and in detail. I must make it clear that neither Heger nor I claim a complete conceptual pyramid, which has for a long time been criticized by logicians as utopian. Nevertheless, partial pyramids, which can have multiple and complex relationships, do seem possible to us. This in no way diminishes the practical utility of the Hallig/Wartburg *Begriffssystem*.

Having studied closely the conceptual system and the onomasiological field, we return to the *semasiological* side. I am not going to study it in a very detailed manner. Semasiology examines the different sememes brought together in one sense

Table 21

$$2\text{-}3 = S_1 \left[P_\psi(A \xleftarrow{p}; M_B) + 2 + t + (A \ne B) \right]$$

$$20\text{-}3 = S_2 \left[P_\psi(A \xleftarrow{p}; M_B) + 2 + \bar{t} + (A \ne B) \right]$$

$$3\text{-}1b = S_3 \left[cP_\psi(A \xleftarrow{p}; M_B; C) + 3c[C \to (A \xleftarrow{p}; M_B)] + \right.$$
$$\left. (\text{in imperative}) \ t + (A \ne B = C) \right]$$

$$30\text{-}1a = S_4 \left[cP_\psi(A \xleftarrow{p}; M_B; C) + 3c[C \to (A \xleftarrow{p}; M_B)] + \right.$$
$$\left. \bar{t} + (A \ne B \ne C) \right]$$

$$1\text{-}2 = S_5 \left[P_\psi(X \xleftarrow{p}; M_B) + 1 + t + (B) \right]$$

$$10\text{-}2 = S_6 \left[P_\psi(X \xleftarrow{p}; M_B) + 1 + \bar{t} + (B) \right]$$

$$2\text{-}2b/20\text{-}2b = S_7 \left[cP_\psi(X \xleftarrow{p}; M_B; C) + 2c[C \to (X \xleftarrow{p}; M_B)] + \right.$$
$$\left. (t \vee \bar{t}) + (B = C) \right]$$

and given a single collective form by one moneme. If we consider the different monemes which formalize the concept "remember", we find out that there are words such as, for example, *se souvenir*, in which every sememe (every meaning) comes from within the diagram of our concept, and that there are others, such as *revenir*, which have other additional meanings that have no seme in common with the concept "remember". Given that the pronominal verb *se souvenir* has no meanings outside the concept "remember", its semasiological field is completely included inside our conceptual system. We have only to situate it in our model; it occupies there the positions shown in Table 21.

This is the catalogue of the significations or, in other words, the catalogue of the sememes ($S_1 - S_7$), or the polysemy, that constitutes the *semasiological field* of the verb *se souvenir*. This semasiological field, taken altogether, constitutes the sense of the moneme *se souvenir*. If we want to, we can reduce the sememes into one very complicated formula bringing together all their elements. This is the formula of the meaning of *se souvenir* (see Table 22). The semasiological field, brought together by this formula, can be symbolized geometrically as in Figure 29.

Sememe S_3 is found only in the imperative (*souviens-toi!*); this is explained by the fact that (in all verbs) the imperative

188 *An Example of Conceptual Analysis*

Table 22

$$U = ((P_\psi(A \leftarrow_{\overline{p}}; M_B) + t \vee \overline{t}) + 2(A \neq B))$$

$$v(cP_\psi(A \leftarrow_{\overline{p}}; M_B; C) + 3c(C \rightarrow (A \leftarrow_{\overline{p}}; M_B) + ([t + (A \neq B = C)] \vee [\overline{t} + (A \neq B \neq C)]))$$

$$v(P_\psi(X \leftarrow_{\overline{p}}; M) + (t \vee \overline{t}) + 1 + (B))$$

$$v(cP_\psi(X \leftarrow; M_B; C) + 2c(C \rightarrow (X \leftarrow_{\overline{p}}; M_B)) + (t \vee t) + (B = C))$$

---

implies an increase of one in valency. So we are entitled to disregard it, since it is more a fact of grammar than of the lexicon. S_4 is also debatable; I have only found one example:

"*Grâce à* ce bruit permanent *je me souvenais* toute la matinée *de*" (because of this continual noise, all morning I was remembering . . .)

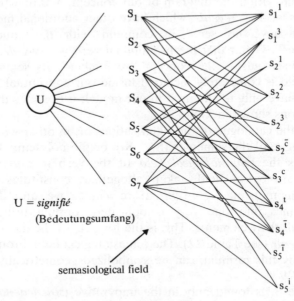

U = *signifié*
(Bedeutungsumfang)

semasiological field

Figure 29

in which the causal value is due to the expression *grâce à*, so that it would be better to classify it under the final position 20-3 (=S_2). As a result, the centre of the semasiological field is made up of S_1 and S_2, which are bivalent with no causal value, transformative or non-transformative. All the other sememes correspond to elliptical uses, which are somewhat rare and accidental. The formula could be reduced considerably, then, by leaving aside these rare and accidental examples:

$$U = [P_\psi(A \leftarrow_{\overline{p}}; M_B) + (t \vee \bar{t}) + 2 + (A \neq B)]$$

The structure of *se rappeler* and of *rappeler* is much more complicated, since this verb has grown beyond the area of trivalent uses and is in the process of taking over the transformative bivalent realm (to say nothing of the meanings which go beyond the conceptual domain "remember"). Other monemes faithfully maintain their trivalent positions, such as *se remémorer*, which is only found in position 3-1b, and *remémorer* in positions 3-1a and 3-1b (all trivalent and transformative), while *revenir, revenir à l'esprit, revenir en mémoire* always occupy the transformative bivalent position 2-3. *Remémorer* and *revenir*, then, are in clear opposition within the conceptual field "remember"; they occupy the positions which were long and firmly held by *rappeler* and *se souvenir*. But this is by now a diachronic question. I intend to return to the problems posed by the semasiological fields of these verbs, such as *rappeler* or *revenir*, which have significations beyond the concept of "remember". At the same time, this will necessarily raise the problem of metaphorical use[22].

---

[22]The interesting and complicated problem of metaphor goes beyond the scope of this book. The reader is referred to the illuminating articles of Harald Weinrich, "Typen der Gedächtnismetaphorik" in *Archiv für Begriffsgeschichte* 9, 1964, 23–26; "Semantik der kühnen Metapher" in *Deutsche Vierteljahresschrift für Literaturwissenschaft und Geistesgeschichte* 37, 1963, 325–344; "Semantik der Metapher", *Folia Linguistica* 1, 1967, 3–17; "Linguistik des Widerspruchs" in *To honor Roman Jakobson*, The Hague-

Up to this point, we have not gone beyond the synchronic level, and we are still far from having exhausted it[23]. I am going to add, however, a few observations concerning diachrony. We can only do this by examining several synchronic cross-sections and attempting a historical explanation of the modifications found to have occurred (the borderline case is the diachronic explanation of a synchronic state on its own, for example, of a dialect the past of which is unknown to us). If we compare the onomasiological field of the concept "remember" in Old French with that of Modern French, we discover profound differences. We could say that there has been a total modification of the means of expression (see below, Table 23, "onomasiological field of the concept 'remember' in Old French" and the list of examples)[24].

Paris (Mouton), 1967, 2212–2218; *Linguistik der Lüge*, 1966. See also, for ex., Segundo Serrano Poncela, *La metáfora*, Caracas (Univ. central de Venezuela, Fac. de Humanidades y Educación, Cuadernos del Instituto de Filología "Andres Bello"), 1968, 67 pp.; Albert Henry, *Métonymie et métaphore*, Paris (Klincksieck), 1971, 161 pp.; Werner Abraham, *Zur Linguistik der Metapher*, Trier (Linguistic Agency University of Trier), 1973, 42 pp.; Michel Le Guern, *Sémantique de la métaphore et de la métonymie*, Paris (Larousse), 1973, 126 pp.; Georges Lüdi, *Die Metapher als Funktion der Aktualisierung*, (Romanica Helvetica, 85), Bern (Francke), 1973, 359 pp. [a work of the school of G. Hilty; ib. more bibliography will be found]; Hartmut Kubczak, *Die Metapher, Beiträge zur Interpretation und semantischen Struktur der Metapher auf der Basis einer referentialen Bedeutungsdefinition*, Habilitationsschrift (accepted by the University of Heidelberg, 1976; not yet published).

[23]In Italian we would have to study especially *ricordare, ricordarsi, rammentare; venire in mente; richiamare qualche cosa alla memoria di qualcuno; far notare, osservare*, etc. In Spanish: *recordar una cosa a alguien, recordarse, acordarse, venir a la memoria, evocar alguna cosa, traer a la memoria una cosa a uno, hacer presente una cosa a uno, hacer pensar en*, etc.; see also J. Casares, *Diccionario ideológico de la lengua española*, Barcelona, 1959, s. v. memoria.

[24]It is worth while making a similar synchronic cross-section in

Latin. Some manuals give us a preliminary idea of the distribution: Ch. Huré *Dictionnaire Universel de l'Ecriture Sainte*, 2 vols., Paris, 1715 (*recordari*, 2, pp. 461, ff.; *meminisse, memorare*, etc., 2, pp. 99, ff.; *reminisci*, 2, p. 481; *commemorare*, etc., 1, p. 347; *rememorari*, 2, p. 481; *mens*, 2, p. 103 b; *retinere*, 2, p. 501 a; *immemor*, 1, p. 796 a; *recognoscere*, 2, p. 460 a; *recogitare*, 2, p. 460 a; *recolere* ib.; *colligare*, 1, p. 338 b; *commonefacere*, 1, 350 a; L. Ramshorn, *Synonymisches Handwörterbuch der lat. Sprache*, 1835; Ludwig Doederlein, *Lateinische Synonyme und Etymologien*, I. Teil, Leipzig, 1826, pp. 166–73 (*meminisse, reminisci, recordari, memorare*); Barrault et Grégoire, *Traité des synonymes de la langue latine*, pp. 136, 567–68 (the same verbs). "*Meminisse* means "se souvenir" when one has kept something in one's memory, when one still knows it, when one has not forgotten it at all, equivalent to *memoria tenere*. *Memorare*, and more normally *commemorare*, "rappeler" something, to show by one's words that one has not forgotten it at all. The first "(*meminisse*)" describes a state of mind also expressible as *memorem esse*; the second "(*memorare*)" expresses an act, the manifestation of a "souvenir". So these two words are more or less in the same relationship as *fugere* and *fugare*, or *misereri* and *miserari* . . ." (p. 136). *Reminisci* " "se souvenir de" something, after forgetting it; re-encounter something among one's "souvenirs" (*in memoriam revocare*)". *Recordari* " "ramener" " (bring back) "something before one's mind and place one's attention on it for some time" (ib. p. 567).

We should add *in mentem venire, in mente habere* (*ThesLL*, see below), *subvenire* (see below), *rememinisse* and *rememorari* (see below for the importance of *re-*). This evidence (collected in a study done by Karl Brademann, one of my students), gives us the following provisional pattern of distribution;

non-causal	transformative	non-transformative
	in mentem venire	in mente(m) habere
	in memoriam regredi, etc.	*meminisse*
		commemini
		retinere
		memor (esse)
		non immemor (esse)
		inoblitus (esse)
		memoriter . . .

Rappeler, se rappeler are entirely missing[25] – the earliest attested examples are found in D'Ablancourt, Patru, Cor-

---

causal	*reminisci*	
	recognoscere	
	repetere	
	revocare	
	rememorari	
	recomminisci	
	comminisci	
	(minisci)	
	memorare	
	commemorare	
	commonefacere	
	recordare ⟷	*recordari*
	memorari (Eccles. Lat.) ⟷	memorari
	recogitare ⟷	recogitare
	recolo ⟷	recolo
	memoria + verb ⟷	memoria + verb

Cicero, in part of a speech given in 46 or 45 B.C., makes use of some of these verbs, indirectly confirming our arrangement: "Equidem, cum tuis omnibus negotiis interessem, *memoria teneo* qualis T. Ligarius quaestor urbanus fuerit erga te et dignitatem tuam. Sed parum est *me hoc meminisse,* spero etiam te, qui oblivisci nihil soles nisi iniurias, – quam hoc est animi, quam etiam ingeni tui! – te aliquid de huius illo quaestorio officio, etiam de aliis quibusdam quaestoribus *reminiscentem,* recordari" Cicero, *Discours,* t. XVIII (Collection des Universités de France, publiée sous le patronage de l'Assoc. Guill.-Budé), a text established and translated by Marcel Lob (Paris, 1952), who gives the following French translation: "Quant à moi, pour avoir été mêlé à toute ton activité, *je garde le souvenir de* ce que T. Ligarius, alors questeur urbain, fut pour toi et pour ta dignité. Mais il ne suffit pas que moi *je m'en souvienne,* j'espère que toi aussi, qui n'oublies jamais que les injures – comme c'est bien ton caractère et ton esprit! – *tu te rappelles* les bons offices de ce questeur, quand tu repenses à certains de ses collègues" (Cic., *Lig.* XII, 35).

[25]One early example stands in isolation;

"*Rapele a ta memore* ton anemi et ne toi semblerat pas dure chose ce ke tu soffres" (Job; see Littré).

neille, Racine and Molière[26]. *Se souvenir*, used only im-
personally (*il me souvient*), is well documented, but the verb
also means "aid, help"[27]; the same is true of *ressouvenir*[28],

[26]See my article "Se rappeler – se souvenir," in *Mélanges de Grammaire française offerts à M. Maurice Grevisse* . . . , Gembloux (Belgique, ed. Duculot), 1966, pp. 21–36.

[27]In Latin, SUBVENIRE had the following significations (according to Georges):

I. (a) *dazukommen*: "arrive unexpectedly, happen, supervene"; (b) *vorkommen*: "come forth, happen, occur, take place," etc.; (c) *in die Gedanken kommen, einfallen*: "occur to someone (i.e., to one's mind)", documented only once, in Apuleius in the second century (around 170 A.D.): "Sed mihi sero quidem, serio tamen *subvenit* ad auxilium civile decurrere et interposito venerabili principis nomine tot aerumnis me liberare." "It was indeed late, but in earnest, that *it occurred to me* to resort to the protection offered by the law, that is, to interpose the sacred name of the emperor and thus to escape so many misfortunes . . ." (Apuleius, *Metamorphosis,* Latin text according to the edition of Rudolf Helm, Darmstadt, 1957, 3, 29). See also the passage from Gellius 19, 7, 1–2 quoted by Forcellini: "Ut quaeque vox digna animadversione *subvenerat, memoriae mandabamus*"; according to the edition of Hertz (A. Gelii, *Noctium Atticarum,* libri XX ex recensione et cum apparatu critico Martini Hertz, Berolini, 1883–1885): "Eo saepe nos ad sese vocabat et olusculis polisque satis comiter copioseque invitabat. Atque ita molli quodam tempestatis autumnae die ego et Iulius Celsinus, cum ad eum cenassemus et apud mensam eius audissemus legi Laevi Alcestin rediremusque in urbem sole iam fere occiduo figuras habitusque verborum nove aut insigniter dictorum in Loeviano illo carmine ruminabamur et, ut quaeque vox indidem digna animadverti *subvenerat,* qua nos quoque possemus uti, *memoriae mandabamus.*" (He often invited us there to visit him and entertained us very pleasantly and generously with vegetables and fruits. And so one mild day in autumn, when Julius Celsinus and I had dined with him, and after hearing the *Alcestis* of Laevius read at his table were returning to the city just before sunset, we were ruminating on the rhetorical figures and the new or striking use of words in that poem of Laevius', and as each word occurred that was worthy of notice with reference to its future use by ourselves, we committed it to memory.) (Trans. by J. C. Rolfe; Loeb, London, 1927–8).

which was very common in the seventeenth century. Table 23 gives us a whole series of verbs documented in the sense of "rappeler" and of "se souvenir" which, in Old and Middle French were extremely frequent, already disappearing in the sixteenth century and, especially, the first half of the seventeenth: thus the verbs *membrer* (*MEMORARE*)[29], (*remembrer* converged[30] with this and was increasingly taking its place until

---

The two texts prove that the sense "se souvenir" can be linked to meaning I. a. (Gellius) or perhaps in Apuleius to the following meaning:

II. (a) come to the aid of; > Old Fr. *sovenir* v. a. "secourir" (Huon SQuentin), *sovenir a qn* "venir au secours de qn" (Aimé), still alive in the fifteenth and sixteenth centuries (see *FEW*, 12, p. 376), but progressively replaced by the learned form *subvenir* from 1370 on (oresme). (b) correct a wrong, stand up against an evil (c) help with legal aid.

In French the impersonal form, *me souvient de*, I am concerned with, (from about 1150 to about 1350), *me souvient que, de*, I can remember (*Roland*, fourteenth century), *il me souvient*, (from the fifteenth century), converged with *se souvenir que, de* only from Estienne 1538; *souvenir* someone *de* something with a causal value is documented only in Monet 1636. Compare It., *sovvenirsi*, Old. Cat., *sovenir* 1215, R 15, 67. "Originally, the preposition probably described the emerging of the memory image from the subconscious to the conscious" Wartburg, *FEW*, 12, p. 378 a. Indeed, *souvenir* has always kept its "involuntary" value.

For *sovenir* and (*re*)*membrer* in Old Fr., see also A. Stefenelli, in *Moderne Sprachen*, 9, 1965 (*Festschrift Gossen*), p. 168, and his book *Der Synonymenreichtum der altfranzösischen Dichtersprache*, Vienna, 1967, 327 pp. (especially pp. 216–22).

[28](a) Old French *resouvenir* v. a. "subvenir à" (Flandr. 1248). (b) Old French *me resovient de* "je me souviens de" (twelfth and thirteenth centuries); *il me ressouvient de* (from the fourteenth century); *se ressouvenir* "avoir mémoire de" only from Montaigne. In the seventeenth century, La Bruyère states: "L'usage a préféré *faire ressouvenir* à *ramentevoir*" (Usage has chosen . . .).

[29]See MEMORARE, *FEW* 6[1], 695–698 (1968).

[30]It goes back to Ecclesiastical Latin *rememorari* (a formation based on *commemorari*); compare Old Italian *rimemorare*, Cat.,

both verbs finally gave way to the learned forms *mémorer* and *remémorer*)[31]; *mentevoir* (MENTE HABERE)[32] with which converged *amentevoir*[33] and later *ramentevoir*[34], subsequently to

Span., Port., *remembrar* (now literary). In French: *remembrer* something *à* someone (*Roland* – 1542, Rabelais), *remembrer* something (Wace *Nic*-Gace), *il me remembre de* something (*Alexis* – 1406), *remembrer de* (thirteenth century; Chastell), *se remembrer de* (*Roland* – 1569, "vieux au XVIIᵉ s." archaic by the seventeenth century, Br 3), *estre remembrant* (thirteenth century to 1487). English *remember* comes from French. See REMEMORARI, *FEW*, 10, pp. 237–39 (entry by M. Müller). Unfortunately, the graphic variants with *ra-* are not distinguished from the forms in *re-*!

[31]Middle French *rememorer* v.n., "commemorate" (1374), *rememorier,* "remember again" (OlMarche; "vulg." BL 1808 – Platt 1835), *remémorer* (from 1499; "vieilli" (archaic) Ac 1694–1935; "comique, marotique" (quaint) Fér 1788), *remémorer* someone *de* something (a hapax of the sixteenth century), *se remémorer* something (from 1579, Lac; Br 4; "vieillit" Fur 1690 – Ac 1878).

[32]I drew up the entry MENTE HABERE for the *FEW* myself: Old French *mentaveir* v. a. "rappeler, rapporter, retracer, mentionner" Wace, *mentevoir* (Saisn-MPol), *mentovoir* BrunLat, etc. (*FEW* 6¹, 732).

"The expression *aliquem in mente habere* 'think of someone, remember' is documented for the first time only around the year 200 in Tertullian, then frequently with an inanimate object in the Itala, in the Vulgate, and other ecclesiastical texts, and in inscriptions; beginning with the Itala the form *in mente habere* is also found, *ThesLL*. There are glosses explaining *in mente habeo* by *reminiscor* (*ALL*, no. 3, p. 529). Because of the frequent use of the imperative (*in mente habe*, Itala), we can infer that the remembering has an active meaning ..." Now we can state it precisely: the imperative adds the causal value and its frequency explains the change from non-transformative *mente habere* to transformative and causal *mente habere* (*FEW* 6¹, 734).

[33]Old French *amentevoir* someone, mention (Chrestien – around 1300), "se rappeler qn à l'esprit" Gace, Middle Fr. *amentevoir* someone *à* someone, MirND; Old Fr., Mid. Fr. *amentevoir* something *à* someone (around 1170 – JAvesnes), *amentiveir* GuernesSThomas, *amentevier* BensSMH, *amantevoir* "remémorer, rappeler" MirND ... There follow other related meanings (*FEW* 6¹, 732b).

replace it; finally, *recorder* (*RECORDARI*)[35] and *recoler* (ca. 1370 – Oud. 1660).

---

[34]Old French *ramantevoir* someone, to mention Chrestien, *ramentevoir* to cite (Coucy; Perc; Aiol; Lac), to name RenBeaujIgn, to enumerate RenN, *ramantevoir* someone (around 1210), Middle Fr. *ramentevoir* Baïf; Old Fr. *ramantevoir* someone, to have a happy memory of (around 1220), to have in mind (1327, Lac), Middle Fr. *ramentevoir* someone MirND; Old Fr. *rementevoir* someone *de* something, to remind PMor, Middle Fr. *ramentevoir* someone *de* something (1573; 1601; Fr. de Sales), *ramentevoir* someone *de faire* something, to remind to do Marot; *ramentevoir* someone *à* someone, remind (MirND; SainéanRab; Malherbe, v. CabSat); *tenir ramenteu* someone *en sus bonnes graces* to have a happy memory of (1585); Mod. Fr. *ramentevoir le chat qui dort,* to awake the sleeping cat (1622, Gdf). – Old Fr. *ramantevoir* something, to tell of Chrestien, Fr. *ramentevoir* something (around 1210 – La Font, still in Malherbe, Racan, Molière) . . . Old Fr. *ramentevoir* something Ruteb., Middle Fr. id. (Baïf; 1563; Montaigne; Scève; Pasquier), *ramentevoir* something *en sa teste*, CentNouv, Mod. Fr. id. La Fontaine; Fr. *ramentevoir* something *à* someone (twelfth century – Pom 1671, still in Fr. de Sales, Malherbe, Richelieu, Racan, Scarron; Voltaire, *Rhlitt*, 28, p. 108) . . . Middle Fr. *se ramentevoir* v. r. (hapax, fifteenth century; Rons; CabSat), to have unhappy memories of Chastell, to come to mind Pasquier, Middle French and Mod. Fr. *se ramentevoir* something (Marot-Malherbe, Hu; *ZFSL* 9[1] 288; Fr. de Sales; Astrée, Liv), *se ramentevoir de* (1559–1605), Mod. Fr. *se ramentevoir que* (1652, Liv); Middle Fr. and Mod. Fr. *se ramentevoir à* someone, to be remembered by (BPériers; Pasquier; Malherbe; Ménage, in 1660 does not accept it in poetry, see Livet); Mod. Fr. *se ramentevoir,* to be remembered, Malherbe; it still lives in pic., ang., poit., etc. "In Northern France *mentevoir* had competitors in its compounds with AD and with AD+RE (compare here Latin expressions such as *ad memoriam, ThesLL* I, 538 b) from as early as the twelfth century; at the end of the thirteenth century *mentevoir* disappears completely. But *amentevoir* is kept only in Northeastern France after 1300 until it, in turn, was replaced by *ramentevoir,* which better expressed the idea of making something recur to the memory, and took its place in the series in *re-* which included *remembrer, recorder, ressouvenir* and *remémorer.* But even *ramentevoir,* which was still very widely used in the sixteenth century, became old-fashioned, along with *recorder,* at

Examples in Old French

1-1 ?"en la fureur des seize, cest arrest *se ramentoit*" = "on se souvient de," ("The fury of the sixteen makes people remember this arrest": Pasquier, Gdf).

1-2 ?

2-1 "Dunc se prist mult a contrister E en sun quer a *recorder* Les biens dunt tanz aveit eüz" ("And so he began to feel very sad, and recall in his heart the good things of which he had had so many": Wace; Keller defines as "Se souvenir de" instead of "(se) remettre à l'esprit", causal and transformative, confirmed by all the examples).

---

the beginning of the seventeenth century. Even so, Malherbe uses it frequently, which provoked censure from Chevreau in 1660; Chevreau says that even in prose it is used only by "quelques antiquaires, et dans le style épistolaire". Furetière, in 1690, agrees; Miege, in 1677, calls it old-fashioned. La Bruyère states: "L'usage a préféré *faire ressouvenir* à *ramentevoir*". The grammar of Regnier-Desmarais, in 1706, counts it among those verbs already fallen from use long before. In the eighteenth century, only Voltaire uses it, but sporadically. In the nineteenth century, the written language sometimes borrows it again from the dialects" (*FEW* 6^1, 734).

[35]Fr. *se recorder* v. r. (Alexis – Fur 1690), *recorder* de v. n. (PsCambr-Chastell), *recorder* v. a. (Wace-Hardy). *Recorder* has the additional meanings of 'to relate' (Chrestien-Cotgr 1611), 'to recite' (PsCambr – *Ac* 1878), 'to teach' (sixteenth century) – which confirms its eminently transformative and causal character (as a result, it would be necessary to replace the first definition "se souvenir de," given by the *FEW*, with "se rappeler, se remettre à l'esprit.") – Among the Romans, the heart was considered the seat of the spirit, which explains the designation (*recordari* "make something present by means of the memory, think of something which occurred in the past"; it includes in contrast with *meminisse* the idea of the participation of the heart, *cor*; for *meminisse* simply refers to the activity of the memory which has retained something in itself, or which would be able to evoke it again by means of reflection, *FEW*, 10, p. 161 a). Cp. It., *ricordarsi*, Cat., Span., Port. *recordar*. English *to record* (with a somewhat different meaning) was taken from French (*FEW* RECORDARI).

Table 23

ONOMASIOLOGICAL FIELD(S) OF THE CONCEPT "REMEMBER"
IN OLD FRENCH[36]

1-1	1-2	
?	?	
2-1	2.2a	2-3

remember **someone, something[37]   ?   *me membre* de something, someone
ramembrer something, someone   se membrer de something, someone
recorder something, someone   me sui amembré que (+ sentence)
mentevoir something   me remembre de something, someone
[≈ mention]   2-2b   *me sovient* de something, someone
amentevoir someone, something   ?   me resovient de something
ramentevoir someone   recorder de something, someone
*metre (something) en memoire   [se recorder de something = 3-1b?]
faire ramembroison de something   s'amentevoir de something (once, ca.
                                                1330)
                                                se ramentevoir (de) something (?)
                                                venir à memoire à someone (GaceB,
                                                TL)
                                                venir à membrizon
                                                il me vient souvenement de
                                                (15th cent.)
                                                se porpenser que (Wace)

3-1a	3-1b

recorder (something) *à* someone   recorder (something) en sun quer
recorder (someone) de something   (Wace)
mentevoir (someone, something) à   *se recorder* something
someone   *amentevoir* something
amentevoir (something) à someone,
(someone) à someone, (someone) de   s'amentevoir something
something   *ramentevoir* something
[≈ mention]
rementevoir (someone) de something   se ramentevoir something
(PMor)   se vouloir ressouvenir envers
ramentevoir (someone) de something   someone (1592)

---

[36]The doctoral thesis of my assistant Karl Brademann (which was finished in 1976, and will be published as a supplement to the ZrP) on the onomasiological field of "remember" in Old and Middle French, is the result of a wider and more detailed study, which includes neighbouring concepts and starts from a slightly different understanding of "actants".

[37]*Difficult to distinguish between transformative and non-transformative

**Italicized forms are very common.

(someone) à someone (something) à
someone
ressouvenir (something) à someone
(1572)
apeler (someone) de something
vos di, si en soiez membrez
faire remembrance de (something)
à (someone)

se remembrer
se membrer de (imperative)

se sovenir (imperative, impers. form)

	10-2		10-1
	?		est remembrance de
			est memoire de (Wace)
			memorer something (epitaph)
			(someone) est tenuz en memoire
			(something) soit remembrez

20-3	-20-2a	20-1
aveir (someone, something) *en*	?	mettre (something) en memoire,
memorie		(to preserve the memory of . . .)
tenir memoire de someone		tenir memoire de someone
ramentevoir someone,		faire memoire de someone
(to have a happy memory of . . .)	20-2b	remembrer something
(ca. 1220)	?	mettre (something) en remembrance
remembrer something, someone		*memorer (something)
*me sovient de [= 20-2b?]		
me ressovient de		
me va resovenant		
*recorder something		
aler recordant (something) en sun quer		
estre recordans de		
estre remembrans de		
avoir en sa remembrance		
(Chrestien)		

30-1a
affermer la memoracion de
(something) en someone
faire avoir remembrance de
(something) à someone

30-1b
[often difficult to distinguish from
20-3]

aveir (someone) en memoire, en
remembrance (imperative)
tenir (someone) *en memoire*
faire memoire de someone
remembrer something
noter/something (to keep in the
memory: cp. écrire en son coeur)
noter (something) en sun quer (Wace)
retenir something (en son memoire)
recorder something (imperative)

"Et les droitures *ramembrerent* ("And they remember there their rights": *Dolop.*, 86, Gdf).

"As blanches Pasques en *font ramembroison*/Et un et autre, li prestre et li clerçon" ("At Easter-time, both the priests and the scholars remember it"; *Cour. Louis*, 991, Gdf).

"Memoire *remembre* les choses/*recorde* sentenses et gloses" ("Memory calls things to mind, registers sentences and interpretations": 1518, Gdf).

2-2a   ?

2-2b   ?

2-3   "De son compaignon *li membra* ("He remembered his companion": *Eneas*, 5139, TL).

"Bien *li* devroit de moi *membrer* et *sovenir*" ("Indeed it is his duty to remember me": *Rom. u. Past.*, ed. Bartsch, TL)

"Or me sui d'un eirre *amembré*/Que a une cité faision . . ." ("Now I am reminded of a journey which we made to a city": Chast., XVI, 2, TL).

"Si *li sovint* par avanture Que feite avoit cele costure Soredamors" ("And so he happened to remember that Soredamors had made that seam": Chrestien, *Cliges* 1551, Schwake).

"Lors *lor sovint de* Salemon" ("And then they remembered Solomon": ib. 5802).

"Ignaures si tres biel s'acointe/a chascune . . . que de l'autre ne *li souvient*" ("Ignaures gets on so well with each of the women . . . that he forgets his other love": *Lai d'Ignaure*, Bartsch-Horning, 1887, p. 555).

"Des sunges qu'out sungié suvent *li suveneit*" ("He often used to remember the dreams he had dreamed": Wace, *Rou* II 496, Keller.)

"ung jour m'avint a Dovre sur la mer/qu'*il me souvint* de la doulce plaisance que souloie ou dit pais trouver" ("One day, by the sea at Dover, the thought came to me of the sweet pleasure that I used to find in that country": Charles d'Orléans).

"De sa mere *li resovient*/Que il vit pasmee cheoir" ("He remembers his mother again, who he had seen fall in a faint": *Perc.*, 2918).

"Or *m'est il venu a memoire*/Que je n'é pas solu encore . . ."
("Now I remembered that I still had not paid . . .": *GaceB*
11031, TL).

"De la franche pucele *li vint a membrizon* . . ." ("He
remembered the noble girl . . ." *Charles le Chauve*, Gdf).

"Il *m'est venu souvenement*/D'une fleur plaisante et jolye"
("I have remembered a pretty and pleasant flower": *Chans.
du XV*^e *s.*, Gdf).

"Puis que la messe fu finee/Si s'est la mere *purpensee*/Que
ele out lessé son enfant/Einz al bain sur le feu ardant"
("When the mass was over, then the mother remembered
that she had left her baby in the bath over the burning fire":
Wace, *Nic.* 180, Keller).

3-1a   ". . . an mon non a de la color, A cui li miaudres ors
s'acorde, Et la fine amors *me recorde*" ("My name
(Soredamors) has in it the colour of finest gold, and reminds
me of true love": Chrestien, *Cliges* 966, Schwake).

"Et molt lor *amentoit* sovent/L'ermite le Dé jugement"
("And the hermit often reminded them of the judgement of
God": Béroul, *Tristan* 1397, ed. Muret).

"Le luy *ramentevant*, non pas une fois seulement, mais fort
souvent" ("Reminding him of it very often, not just once":
A. Le Masson, Gdf).

"Une chose vos di, si *an soiez membrez*: Se . . ." ("I tell you
one thing, which you must not forget": J. Bod., *Sax.*,
CCLXXXIV) [= je vous rappelle; or "n'oubliez
pas!" = 30-2?].

"Dites al duc que jo li mant/Qu'il ne *m'apelt de* covenant"
("Tell the duke that I command him not to remind me of
my promise": Wace, *Rou* III 6838).

3-1b   "*Amentevoir* son nom ne puis" ("I can't remember his
name": *Ste Leocade*, Gdf).

"Quant *se recorde en sen corage*/Dou bel vergier, mout se
demente" ("When he recalls to his mind the beautiful gar-
den, he is deeply distressed": Rencl. de Moil., Gdf)
[or = 2-3?].

"Ki fait ad pechet bien *s'en* pot *recorder*" ("He who has
sinned could remember it well": *Alexis*, Gdf).

"Remembre toy ou te souviengne" [= qu'il te vienne le
souvenir = non-causal] "du bon propos que Dieu t'avoit
donné" ("May the memory come back to you of the wise
council that God had given you": *Intern. Consol.*, III, XXV).
"Mesdisans, pleins de felounie/qui de feme dis vilounie/Car
te recorde et *te ramembre*/comment furent fourmé ti
membre" ("Slanderer, full of treachery, you who speak ill of
women, remember and recall how your body was formed":
Jeh. de Cond., Gdf).

10-1   "Si *ert remembrance de* mei" ("So shall I be remembered": Wace, *Nic.* 391, Keller).
"Pour *memorer* la louenge et la vie/Dudit deffunct" ("To
call to mind the fame and the life of this man now dead":
Epitaphe de Phelippes d'Austrice, Gdf).
"Pour ceo que tant vus ai amez/Voil que mis doels *soit
remembrez*" ("Because I have loved you so well, I want my
grief to be remembered": Marie, *Lais Chaitivel* 201, Gdf)
[or = 1-1?].

10-2   ?

20-1   "Une cité, ço dist l'estorie/Fist pur *tenir* de lui
memorie" ("The story goes that he built a city as a monu-
ment to his memory": Wace, *Brut* 1598, Keller) (A = C!).
"Ainsi que Asculepius le *memoire* et *remembre* en son livre"
("And thus Aesculapius records it in his book": *Jard. de
santé* I, 486, Gdf) [or = 2-1? Very near *raconter*].

20-2a   ?

20-2b   ?

20-3   "Onques mes, dom *il me remanbre*/N'ot mal don je
l'oïsse plaindre" ("Never thereafter, as far as I remember,
did he endure any suffering of which I heard him complain":
Chrestien *Cliges* 5418, Schwake).
"Mes celi don plus *li remanbre*" [≈ penser à]/"N'ose
aparler" ("But he dares not speak to the one who is most on
his mind": Chrestien, *Cliges* 574, Schwake).
"Tant le delite a *remanbrer*/La biauté et la contenance/Celi
. . ." ("He delights so much in recalling her beauty and her
face": Chrestien, *Cliges* 614, Schwake).
"Les lermes et la contenance/a toz jorz *an sa remanbrance*"

("Every day he remembers her tears and expression": Chrestien, *Cliges* 4322; see also 3844, Schwake).

"La volanté de son corage/Toz jorz en un panser le tient:/De Fenice *li ressovient*/Qui loing de lui se retravaille" ("The determination of his heart keeps him thinking of one thing all the time: he remembers Fénice, who also suffers far away from him": Chrestien, *Cliges* 5018, Schwake).

"En sun quer *alot recordant*/les paroles e le semblant" ("He kept on remembering her words and her expression": Marie, *Guigemar* 411, Gdf).

"Et por çe *c'as* Deu *en memorie*,/Est preste ta corone en glorie" ("And because you have remembered God, your place in heaven is assured": Wace, *VieSMarg* 395, mscr. A; TL).

"Quant de ma ciere amie *me va resovenant*" ("Whenever I remember again my sweet love": *Naiss. de Chev. au Cygne*, Gdf).

30-1a "Mout m'abelist la crueus *ramembrance*/Que bone amors *me fait* de li avoir" ("I enjoy the painful memories that sweet love makes me have of her": *Jaq. de Cisoing*, Gdf).

"Pour en euls *affermer la memoracion* (du vœu)" ("To strengthen their memory of their promise": *Restor du Paon*, Gdf).

30-1b "Sor tos cex qui me nomeront/Et *en memoire* me tenront/Li Sains Espir del ciel descende!" ("May the Holy Spirit descend from the heavens upon all those who call my name and remember me": Wace, *VieSMarg* 658, mscr. A; TL).

"La feste *deit om remenbrer*/Que Jüeu suelent celebrer" ("That festival should be remembered which the Jews celebrate": Wace, *Conception NDame* 219, Keller).

"Des œuvres Deu *fui recordans*/Et *serai* tous jours *remembrans*" ("I remembered the works of God, and I always shall": *Lib. Psalm.*, Gdf).

"Mais *retien* bien *en ton memoire*: Por nulle (dame) ne t'en desespoire!" ("But remember well: never lose your head over a woman": *Jak. d'Am.* I, 340, TL).

"Mes le comandemant saint Pol/Fet boen garder et *retenir*" ("It is a good idea to observe and remember the commandment of St Paul": Chrestien, *Cliges* 5265; see also 4409, Schwake).

"*Recorde ke* tu fus enoins/De chel tres saint prechious ole" ("Remember that you were anointed with that most holy precious oil": Renclus de Moiliens, *de Carité* XXXV, 3, Gdf) [or = 3-1b?].

"Johanz, dist ele, ore te pri/Que tu *aies en remembrance* . . ." ("John, she said, I beg of you that you remember . . . ." Wace, *Conception NDame* 1401, Keller).

"*Aions*, seinors, cel saint homme *en memorie!* ("My Lords, let us always preserve the memory of this holy man!": *Alexis* 125*a*, TL).

The explanation of this evolution will have to take into account the system of monemes on the morphological level, since the prefix *re-* plays a fundamental rôle (*recorder, remembrer, recoler, ressouvenir*). This no doubt explains the step from *amentevoir* to *ramentevoir* and the vacillation between *rementevoir* and *ramentevoir*. *Rappeler* is the latest important inheritor of this system in *re-*, accompanied in Modern French by *revenir*[38], *remémorer, retenir, revoir*[39] and others. The important rôle of the moneme *re-* is explained by our base formula for the concept "remember": *re-* expresses the establishment of a relationship between the present and the object of the memory situated in the past (between P_ψ and $X \leftarrow_{\overline{p}}$). I shall not here undertake a closer investigation of the evolution of the onomasiological field and the various semasiological fields (though it would be well worth while, especially

---

[38]Middle Fr. and Mod. Fr. *revenir* "se représenter à l'esprit, par le souvenir" (from 1553), in *FEW*, 10, 351a. It would be necessary to modify the definition, since *revenir* does not have a causal value. The meaning "remember" has been led to by *revenir au fait*, à *un sujet*, etc. (to talk, bother about again) (from the *Alexis*).

[39]The *FEW* (14, 423a) does not give it except for Sancoins *se*(?) *revoir* "repasser ses souvenirs"; see, however, *revoir* in Robert.

in the case of *se souvenir* and *rappeler*). Such a study would have to take into account not only internal linguistic causes, but external historical causes as well. Nor shall I now examine the "synonymy" of expressions which occupy the same position in the conceptual system (a most interesting problem, to which we shall return in Chapter 5; at that time it will be necessary to take into consideration stylistic and emotional values). What I am concerned with now – the real objective of this chapter – is that it should have become obvious that there are several structures that come into play, and that they are not independent of each other; we shall return now to the four structures mentioned in Part I, Chapter 10.

4

The Four Structures: Semasiology and Onomasiology in the Trapezium

We can now integrate the four structures (Part One, Chapter 10) into Heger's trapezium (see also the diagrams in Part Two, Chapter Two):

1. Structure on the morphological level (the importance of *re-* in the onomasiological field of the concept "remember"; the parallelism of the structure *il me souvient* and *il me membre*; the two verbs occupy above all the non-causal transformative positions in Old French, etc.). The study of prefixes and suffixes is of special importance for the lexicologer. These elements behave like lexemes, but they are distinguished from the latter in that they constitute a closed set. On the diachronic plane, a structure on the level of expression (form of expression) frequently can have repercussions on the level of content, which we have not mentioned (see my article "La pesadilla de los etimólogos", *RFE* 48, 1965, 95–104; in a more systematic way, Otto Ducháček, "L'attraction lexicale", *Philologica Pragensia* 7, 1964, 65–76)[1].

---

[1]When editing the entry Mansuetinus for the *FEW*, for example, I hesitated whether to attribute the proverb *qui a bon voisin a bon*

matin (*mâtin*, in some dictionaries) "he who has a good neighbour can sleep peacefully" to MANSUETINUS (the neighbour would be the mastiff keeping guard) or to MATUTINUS, for lack of ancient testimony (*FEW*, 6, p. 257a). At that time, I did not know of the testimony of the Proverbes au vilain *Qui a mal voisin, si a mal matin* (*Hundert altfranzösische Bauernsprüche*, edited by E. Lommatzsch, XLIV (104), p. 11), which decides the question in favor of MATUTINUS. But due to the subsequent coincidence on the level of expression, there has been a modification on the level of content (as interpreted by popular etymology) (s. my article "Qui a bon voisin, a bon matin (mâtin)," in *Philologica Romanica, Erhard Lommatzsch gewidmet*, Munich (Fink) 1975, pp. 23–29). Examples documenting these interferences abound. The *sansonnet* (starling) became *chansonnet* (Cotgr 1611; Besch 1845 – Lar 1867) although it is not a songbird (popular etymology often "modifies" reality to its taste; see also our article "Être soûl comme une grive – Être larron comme une chouette, deux cas de psychologie linguistique des animaux", in *Omagiu lui Alexandru Rosetti*, Bucharest, 1965, pp. 43–45).

Other examples: the deformations of *porc-espin* (Old. Prov. *porc-espi*) "porcupine" into *porc-épi*, (based on *épi*, ear of corn), into *porc-espic* (based on *piquer*, to prick) and into *portépi, porte-pic* (based on *porter*, to have on), in *FEW*, 9, p. 191b, etc. *HURSLO: "hornet": saint. *grelon* (+ CRABRO), pic. *hurlon* (+ *hurler*), Montbél. *frondon* (+ *fronde*), bress. *fyacon* (+ *flocon*), in *FEW*, 16, p. 271. *Hanneton*: > *kenneton* (+ *cane* "duck"), *jeanneton* (+ *Jeanne*), *arnicho* (+ *Arnoud*), in *FEW*, 16, p. 144a. Ollon, etc. *mayuntse* "titmouse", because titmice appear in the month of May, in *FEW*, 16, p. 548a. Compare *près de* (< PRESSE, in *FEW*, 9, p. 366a) and *prêt de, à*, prepared to (< PRAESTO, in *FEW*, 9, p. 317a), interferences especially in the eighteenth century (*Nouv. Héloïse*, éd Pléiade, p. 1483). Play on words: liégois *èsse måvi* "être mauvis" (thrush) = "être mort" (dead: interpreted as *mal vif*), in *FEW*, 16, p. 469 + n.4. See the article HIRUNDO in the *FEW* with numerous interferences on the level of expression and on the level of content; the article *BAWA (interferences between *BALCOS, BROD, BULLARE and BULLIRE), in *FEW*, 1, 302b. Centr. *amoissoner* (rent a section of land) (< MODIATIO), cut by *moisons* (sections of a particular length) (< MENSIO), Middle Fr. *moissonnier* adj. (milky) (1542 in Rabelais, < MULSIO; Gdf defines "qui constitue une redevance", which was a form of rent), etc. See other examples in Ducháček's article, referred to in the text.

2. Structure on the conceptual level (level of the substance of content). We have discussed this in more detail because, in our view, semasiology as well as onomasiology hinges on it. Besides, Coseriu has demonstrated the importance of changes that occur in the domain of the substance of content on the diachronic plane. A whole series of problems concerning the conceptual plane needs a deeper study: the complex nature of concepts and the relationship between those conceptual structures and the sememes; the problem of micro- and macro-structures on the conceptual level; the problem of the determination of concepts by denotation or connotation (see the next chapter) and the ontological problem of their relationship with extralinguistic reality.

3. Semasiological structure (or semasiological field). We have defined this as a group of sememes linked to a single *signifié*, which in its turn is linked, having the same content, to a single moneme (but often linked to *different conceptual systems*).

4. Onomasiological structure (or onomasiological field). We have defined this as the sum of sememes linked to *a single concept* – determined by its position in the conceptual system – which forms part of different *signifiés*, linked, having the same content, to *different monemes*[2]. We now return, then, to the four fundamental structures, but integrated now into the better differentiated and more satisfactory system set up by Heger.

The interferences between semasiology and onomasiology are now seen in a new light, more clearly than before, as shown in Figure 30.

Semasiology and onomasiology examine the two fundamen-

---

[2]The conceptual system we have established for the concept "remember" has shown us that there is no verb in French which occupies or formalizes all the positions of the conceptual system. If we have continued to talk about the concept "remember" it is for practical reasons. From the viewpoint of scientific accuracy, we should refer only to the conceptual system "$P_\psi(X\overleftarrow{p}; M_Y)$", – making in this way a strict distinction between the conceptual system and its linguistic realizations.

signifiés (senses, each linked to a single moneme)

sememes (significations)

concepts

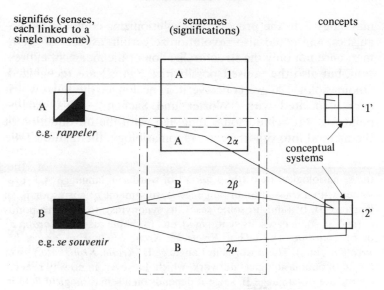

e.g. *rappeler*

e.g. *se souvenir*

conceptual systems

———— Semasiological field of A.

— — — — Minimum onomasiological field, of 'absolute' synonyms with identical symbolic sememe – in this diagrammatic example A 2α = B 2β –, see Part II, Chapter 5a.

— · — · — Micro-onomasiological field, including all the positions of the conceptual system "remember", in this example.

Figure 30

tal microstructures of the lexicon. Onomasiology especially (combined with the structural evolution on the level of concepts, suggested principally by Coseriu) promises many new results: it lets us see the lexical structure of each individual language, and makes it possible to compare different languages from one structural basis[3]. We can even claim that ono-

---

[3]See also the interesting study by Herbert Ernst Wiegand, "Synchronische Onomasiologie und Semasiologie, Kombinierte Methoden zur Strukturierung der Lexik", in *Germanistische Linguistik* (Verlag Georg Olms, Hildesheim) 3, 1970, 243–384. – The relationship between the semasiological perspective and the onomasiological perspective is especially complicated in the case of a *bilingual dictionary*:

masiology is in the process of revolutionizing comparative linguistics, and could also revolutionize certain aspects of grammar, once not only the structuralization of the means of expression, but also the unused possibilities ('gaps') are recognized. Onomasiology, as we conceive it, is no longer the narrow science associated with "Wörter und Sachen"[4]. This starting point was left behind some time ago, with the introduction of the method into other areas[5]. Onomasiology, then, studies the

---

the semasiological field (the *signifié*) of word *a* in language A is presented with a translation in language B; to sememe a^1 corresponds, in language B, b^1 (and, in some cases, its synonyms), to a^2 corresponds c^2 (and, in some cases, its synonyms), etc. (a simple case: Sp. *corona* a^1 or Fr. *couronne* a^1 → Ger. *Krone* b^1, *Kranz* b^2, or Eng. *crown* b^1, *wreath* b^2, etc.). These words in Language B (*Krone*, *Kranz*, etc.) form a kind of onomasiological network, which, however, in no way reflects a structure of language B, since it depends on a semasiological field in language A. Cf. in this regard Kurt Baldinger, "Semasiologie und Onomasiologie im zweisprachigen Wörterbuch", in *Interlinguistica* (Festschrift Wandruszka), Tübingen (Niemeyer), 1971, 384–396.

[4]See, for example, the works by Ulrich Ricken, *"Gelehrter" und "Wissenschaft" im Französischen* (Deutsche Akademie der Wissenschaften zu Berlin, Veröffentlichungen des Instituts für Romanische Sprachwissenschaft, 15), Berlin (Akademie-Verlag), 1961, 323 pp., and his articles "Bemerkungen zur Onomasiologie", in *Wissenschaftliche Zeitschrift der Karl-Marx-Universität Leipzig*, 10, 1961, pp. 409–19; "Onomasiologie oder Feldmethode? Bemerkungen zur Methode und Terminologie einiger neuerer wortkundlicher Arbeiten", ib. 833–40, and in *Beiträge zur Romanischen Philologie*, 1, 1961, pp. 190–208; in addition, his ideas set forth in the *Résumés des Communications* (Congress of Romance Linguistics, Strasbourg, 1962), p. 28.

[5]See, for example, K. Heger, *Die Bezeichnung temporal – deiktischer Begriffskategorien im französischen und spanischen Konjugationssystem* (Beihefte zur ZRP, 104), Tübingen, 1963, and the discussion provoked by this book; Heger answers in his article "Temporale Deixis und Vorgangsquantität ('Aspekt' und 'Aktionsart')", in *ZRP*, 83, 1967, pp. 512–82. Heger also started from a conceptual system in his article "Personale Deixis und grammatische Person", in *ZRP*, 81, 1965, pp. 76–97.

linguistic realization of concepts in any area of the vocabulary (and even in all the realms of language, as long as it is concerned with the level of the first articulation, following Martinet's terminology).

Semasiology, however, is far from having lost its importance. Linguistic realization (the object of onomasiology) is carried out by means of "words", words subject to polysemy, and whose semasiological structure has to be taken into account. In other words, the onomasiological elements needed to study the realization of the concept in question are each embedded in a semasiological structure. The study of these semasiological structures, then, should precede the study of the onomasiological field. On the other hand, it is precisely the distribution of lexical elements within an onomasiological field which determines, to a great extent, the semasiological value of each element. First, then, we have to study the different onomasiological fields in which, by virtue of its polysemy, each word participates, in order to be able to determine subsequently its different semasiological values within a semasiological field. In other words, we have to start at both ends – which is impossible. It is easy to see why: it is necessitated by the fundamental bipolarity of the linguistic sign, recognized by de Saussure, which we have taken as our starting-point. This basic bipolarity means that the two methods are at the same time opposite and complementary. *Onomasiology* corresponds to the situation of the speaker who, having at his disposal the structured repertoire of the language, has to *express* his thought; *semasiology*, on the other hand, corresponds to the situation of the listener, who perceives forms already selected – that is, words subject to polysemy – and who must determine the significations in question (see Part One, Chapter 12). During a conversation we continually move between onomasiology (while speaking) and semasiology (while listening). We switch back and forth between onomasiological and semasiological analysis. It is the object of linguistics to study, on the level of the first metalanguage, what happens – usually unconsciously, but sometimes consciously – on the level of the object language.

5

The Problem of
Synonymy: Symbolic
Values and Symptomatic
Values

The problem of synonymy is one of the main preoccupations
of semantics[1]. Ludwig Söll, in a very fine article[2], has brought

---

[1]This chapter was presented as a paper at the Round Table on
Semantics in Mainz (November 1966), published in French in the
Probleme der Semantik (*ZFSL*, Beihefte 1), Wiesbaden, 1968, pp.
41–61 ("La synonymie – problèmes sémantiques et stylistiques"). An
abbreviated version was published as the second part of my article
"Structures et systèmes linguistiques", in *TraLiLi* V[1], 1967, pp.
123–39 (second part pp. 132–39). This English version, with some
additions and modifications, is from the Spanish translation by José
Luis Rivarola (Lima), which also modified the original.

[2]Ludwig Söll, "Synonymie und Bedeutungsgleichheit", in *GRM*,
16, 1966, pp. 90–99; see also S. Ullmann, *Semantics, An Introduction
to the Science of Meaning*, 1962, p. 141. Inger Rosengren, *Seman-
tische Strukturen*, *Eine quantitative Distributionsanalyse einiger mittel-
hochdeutscher Adjektive*, Lund-Kopenhagen, 1966, works carefully
with distributions and statistics (see the chapter *Synonymie,
Bedeutungsnähe und Polysemie*, pp. 14–16). G. S. Sčur, "Some

together a number of answers to the question of whether there are absolute synonyms (*bedeutungsgleiche Wörter*), whether '*yes*' or '*no*' or the uncertainty of an evasive answer. I shall try to show that the question is badly put. We have to distinguish between different planes or levels; when this is done, we get clear and precise results.

(a) SYNONYMY ON THE CONCEPTUAL LEVEL

The analysis of the concept "remember" (II, Ch. 3) gave us a base formula:

"remember" is the psychic presence (P_ψ) of something belonging to the past ($X \leftarrow_P$) in the memory of living being (M_Y):

$$\boxed{P_\psi(X \leftarrow_P; M_Y)}$$

The linguistic realization of this formula showed us that there is a complete system of variants on the conceptual plane. I shall merely recall the three or four most important positions within this system:

	transformative	*non-transformative*
bivalent	2-3: "A is realized in the memory of B" $[P_\psi(A \leftarrow_P; M_B) + 2 + t + (A \neq B)]$	20-3: "B keeps the memory of A" $[P_\psi(A \leftarrow_P; M_B) + 2 + /t + (A \neq B)]$

Thoughts on Synonymy in Language", *Orbis* 22, 1973, pp. 177–183 [it has nothing substantially new]; Hans-Martin Gauger, "Zum Problem der Synonyme", with a résumé in French: "Apport au problème des synonymes" (*TBL*, 9, Tübingen, 1972, 149 pp. ["En comparant les contenus des mots dits 'synonymes', on découvre toujours entre eux des différences plus ou moins marquées, quoique souvent difficilement exprimables" 122 (When we compare the content of words said to be "synonyms", we always find differences between them, more or less fixed although often hard to express)]; Hartmut Kleineidam, "Lexikalische Synonymie unter kontrastivem Aspekt", in *Lebendige Romania* (Festschrift H.-W. Klein), Göppingen 1976, pp. 177–195.

transformative

trivalent	3-1a: "C evokes in B the memory of A" $[cP_{\psi}(A \leftarrow_{p}; M_B; C) + 3c + t + (A \neq B \neq C)]$	3-1b "B evokes in itself the memory of A", $[cP_{\psi}(A \leftarrow_{p}; M_B; C) + 3c + t + (A \neq B = C)]$

Position 2-3 corresponds to *involuntary memory* (transformative):

"*Je me souviens*
Des jours anciens
Et je pleure" (Verlaine)

(I remember days gone by and I weep)

Positions 3-1a and 3-1b correspond to *voluntary memory* (transformative): a memory is evoked in oneself or in another:

"*Je rappelai à moi* le peu que je savais" (Valéry) (I summoned up the little I knew)
"*ils lui rappeloient* ses victoires passées" (They reminded him of his past victories) (to *Nestor*: Fénelon, *Télémaque*, ed. Grands Ecrivains II, 257).

Position 20-3 is among the most important of the non-transformative ones:

"Ce viel omnibus a disparu, mais son austérité, son inconfort *sont restés vivants dans mon souvenir*". (That old bus has gone, but its bareness and discomfort live on in my memory) (St.-Exupéry, *Terre*, p. 20).

The analysis of a great number of examples has given us a whole series of synonyms for each position, each realizing the same formula:

2-3 se rappeler (something), que . . .
se souvenir
il me souvient
revenir à la mémoire, à l'esprit, au coeur, en pensée

le souvenir de . . . revient à
revoir [often = 20-3]

3-1a rappeler (something) à someone
faire souvenir de
faire penser
remettre (something) devant les yeux de someone
remémorer (something) à someone
faire revenire (something) à someone

3-1b se rappeler (something), que . . .
se rappeler le souvenir de
se rappeler de something
se remémorer something
se mettre à penser à (something from the past)
penser à (something from the past)
se souvenir (in the imperative)[3]
remettre (something) dans son esprit (in the imperative)[3]
remettre (for example, the face) de someone
noter (il faut noter qu'il était alors bien jeune, you must remember that he was quite young then)
[neighbouring concepts]

20-3 se souvenir
se rappeler (something: rare and doubtful in this position)
se ressouvenir
rester vivant dans son souvenir
revoir
retenir
garder le souvenir, la mémoire de
subsister dans son souvenir.

---

[3]The imperative adds the value of one actant; so it can move a verb which expresses an involuntary memory (position 3) by adding a causal actant. Cf. our article in *CahLex*, 8, 1966, pp. 5–46, especially p. 28; K. Heger, "Valenz, Diathese und Kasus", in *ZRP*, 82, 1966, pp. 138–70, especially p. 158.

Two conclusions become clear from this analysis:

1. We have obtained a whole series of onomasiological fields: each position in this conceptual system is realized by means of a small onomasiological field, a *minimal ono-masiological field*[4]. These onomasiological fields join together to form the onomasiological field "remember," the *micro-onomasiological field*. (It would be necessary to add the *macro-onomasiological field*, which would go beyond the conceptual system of "remember"; we have not examined this).

2. From the conceptual viewpoint, the monemes or groups of monemes which realize the same formula (which are found in the same position) are synonyms, and in more precise terms they are *absolute synonyms* from the conceptual point of view. Synonyms which are brought together into the same position are absolute synonyms in the sense that they *all realize the same conceptual formula*. This can be verified by substitution[5]: in each position I can replace any synonym within the group with any other without modifying the conceptual substance. This is not valid for the micro- and macro-onomasiological fields: for example, it is impossible to replace *se souvenir de*, in position 2-3, with *remémorer* (something) (which is found in position 3-1b) without modifying the conceptual substance. *Je me souviens de mon enfance* and *je remémore mon enfance* are not synonyms on the conceptual level: the first implies involuntary memory and the second implies voluntary memory. In the same way, I cannot replace *revenir à la mémoire*, which is found in position 2-3, with *garder le souvenir de*, which is found in position 20-3: the first is transformative, while the second is non-transformative, etc. Therefore, a precise conceptual analysis is indispensable before speaking of absolute syn-

---

[4]In the article "Sémantique et structure conceptuelle", in *CahLex*, 8, p. 24, I speak, in this sense, of *micro-onomasiological field*. Now I prefer the tripartition as it is defined below, and as in the diagram in the last chapter.

[5]As for substitution, see S. Ullmann, *Semantics*, 1962, p. 143.

onyms on the conceptual level[6]. Let us remember this initial conclusion: *there are absolute synonyms on the conceptual level* (minimal onomasiological field).

This corresponds exactly to what Heger has demonstrated concerning *soixante-dix* and *septante*: they are absolute synonyms on the level of an onomasiological analysis which starts with the same conceptual formula ("dass ein und derselbe Begriff zwei verschiedene Bezeichnungen hat. In dieser Sicht ist es völlig legitim, von Synonymien (oder Allomorphien) zu sprechen, denn der Begriff "70" hat im Französischen die zwei Bezeichnungen *septante* und *soixante-dix*.")[7] The situation is altogether different in the semasiological field.

(b) SYNONYMY OF TWO SEMEMES AND SYNONYMY OF TWO *SIGNIFIÉS*[8]

Heger's trapezium distinguishes, on the plane of the substance of content

signifié	*sememe*	*seme*
(brings together all the sememes linked to a moneme).	(= 'meaning' in traditional terminology).	(= concept; system of semes = conceptual system).

If the *signifié* has but one sememe, *signifié* and sememe are identical; if, on the other hand, the *signifié* contains several

---

[6]*Frêle* 'weak', and *fragile*, 'fragile, brittle', for example, which have the same etymon, are not synonyms at all any more (they realize different conceptual systems). This is valid for the whole list given by Ullmann, *Semantics*, 1962, p. 148; see also Ullmann, *Précis de sémantique française*, [2]1959, p. 191 = *Introducción a la semántica francesa* (Spanish translation and notes by Eugenio de Bustos Tovar), Madrid (C. S. I. C.), 1965, p. 261.

[7]Klaus Heger, "Homographie, Homonymie und Polysemie", in *ZRP*, 79, 1963, p. 478: now updated in *Monem, Wort, Satz und Text* 1976, pp. 61–65, 94 ff.

[8]This paragraph came about from a discussion with Heger, on the occasion of the Mainz Round Table.

signifié 1 (= only one sememe) of moneme A

they are identical

signifié 2 (= only one sememe) of moneme B

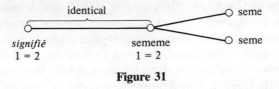

Figure 31

sememes, it constitutes a semasiological field. As far as synonymy is concerned, this basic formulation allows us to distinguish between two kinds of synonymy on the plane of the substance of content:

A synonymy of two signifiés (if the two *signifiés* linked to two different monemes, contain but one sememe each; see Figure 31).

A synonymy of two sememes which are linked by means of two complex *signifiés* (which contain more than one sememe), to two different monemes; see Figure 32.

In this second case, the synonymy is produced, not on the level of the *signifié*, but on the level of the sememe (more exactly, on the level of sememe 2, which is common to *signifiés* 1 and 2, which are linked to monemes A and B). All of this concerns the symbolic function of the linguistic sign (see below, relative to K. Bühler). In German, these two kinds of synonyms can be called *symbolbegriffliche Signifiésynonymie* and *symbolbegrieffliche Sememsynonymie*; these might be translated into uncouth English as "symbol-conceptual *signifié*-synonymy" and "symbol-conceptual sememe-synonymy"; in any case, we

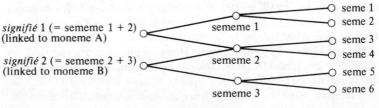

Figure 32

have to distinguish between the synonymy of two *signifiés* on the symbolic-conceptual level and the synonymy of two sememes on the symbolic-conceptual level.

If there is identity between *signifié* and sememe, the two monemes in question are *absolute synonyms* with regard to their symbolic function on the level of the substance of content (= identity of one of their sememes or meanings). In this second case – this is the most important conclusion – the two monemes in question, which have one sememe (one meaning) in common, are distinguished by the potential presence of the sememes (meanings) which they do not have in common. In other words, the potentialities present in two semasiological fields create a difference between two monemes (lexemes or morphemes) which have one meaning in common[9]. Since our definition of a moneme (Part II, Chapter 2) includes both morphemes and lexemes, the distinction we have just established concerns lexicology (the semasiological field of a lex-

---

[9]Cp. Josette Rey, concerning *Les haricots sont lourds* [two meanings] *Les haricots sont indigestes* [one meaning]: "The use of a word is rarely unconnected with its phonetic substance, if we consider as homonyms the several "senses" – collection of uses corresponding to a definition – of a lexical unit" [i.e. semasiological field]. "For *lourd*, there are a number of homonyms (the senses of the polysemic *lourd*), and the sense elements "heavy", "carry", "laborious" " [cp. Coseriu's *solidarities*] "are present in one's mind. For *indigeste*, the homonymy of the *digest* – monemes, in *indigeste*, *digestion*, recalls the sense elements "to digest", "passage", "assimilation" " [The word family and its solidarities come in here, see **3** below] "In speech, the phonetic substance could easily evoke *all the potential signifiés* to begin with, and it would only be by decoding and reference to a context that one *signifié* alone would be grasped. If the hearer feels a difference between *lourd* and *indigeste*, this would then be the reminiscence of the *signifiés* of the same phonetic substance [lur], forming a *kind of fringe around the signifié* "indigestible", without becoming part of the sememe of *lourd* "indigestible" " [the presence of the semasiological field of *lourd*]. "This sememe of one *signifiant lourd* is in practice isolated by the semanticists, but the user of the language is not bothered with such distinctions" (*Cahlex*, 8, 1966, pp. 88, ff.)

eme), morphology and word-formation (the semasiological field of a morpheme).

The very structure of the moneme, that is, the polysemy inherent in the linguistic sign, provides us with our first principle for distinguishing between synonyms (absolute synonymy of sememes on the conceptual level):

1. Potential presence of the semasiological field[10].

Therefore, two monemes (lexemes or morphemes) which have two or more meanings are never absolutely synonymous, although one may use them with the meaning (or one of the meanings) that they have in common, because the other meanings are still potentially present.

The polysemy of two "synonyms" is the basis for numerous jokes and puns. Thus, in Mexico, it is said that the Duke of Windsor "exchanged a *corona* (crown) for a *bohemia destapada* (open Bohemian)", since *corona* and *bohemia* are also two well-known brands of beer. The pun is completed in that *destapada* also means 'eloped' in part of Latin America.

In the following Mexican example, which in no way reflects a humorous intention, polysemy is indicated by means of inverted commas (except that these merely indicate a different register): "The local representative . . . today criticized here the strike called 48 hours ago by 153 *camiones "materialistas"* (i.e., drivers of lorries carrying building material) and said that if the government applies the law, it can cancel the concessions granted to these, and to the taxi drivers should they come out in sympathy" ("Possible cancellation of permits for *'materialistas'* and taxi drivers, in Acapulco"). *Materialista* 'lorry driver' naturally calls to mind "materialist" in the philosophical sense (*Excelsior*, a Mexican newspaper, May 20, 1972). [Similarly, this traffic sign is said to exist in Mexico City, 'PROHIBIDO

---

[10]See my article "Sémasiologie et onomasiologie", in *RLiR*, 28, 1964, pp. 249–72 (especially p. 256), published here as appendix 2 and S. Ullmann, *Mél. Delbouille*, 1964, pp. 646, ff.; E. Coseriu, "Pour une sémantique diachronique structurale", in *TraLiLi* II[1], p. 151 (The problem of 'neutralization').

A LOS MATERIALISTAS ESTACIONARSE EN LO ABSOLUTO' (Absolutely no parking for lorries); some future archeologist may wonder why materialists should be prohibited from stopping in the absolute.]

There remains the case of those moneme-synonyms which are synonymous in respect of their *signifiés*, whose semasiological fields contain only one member and which, as a result, could be absolute synonyms. This is valid with regard to their substance in symbolic content (*symbol* as used by Bühler, see below). As for the monemes themselves, this would be true if there were no other distinguishing factors. We shall mention this later on.

(c) STRUCTURES WHICH GO BEYOND THE MONEME

It is necessary to add to the potential presence of the semasiological field (1) a whole series of factors which are relevant to synonymy because the moneme does not lead an isolated existence within the language; it is related to other elements, both on the level of expression and on the level of content (one must not forget that the two levels are always united in the linguistic sign in such a way that the presence of the form of expression necessarily implies the presence of the form of content). Thus, the formal similarity to another moneme which could provoke disagreeable associations can determine the choice between two synonyms. In Argentina, for example, colloquial speech prefers *elegir* over *escoger* (choose), probably to avoid the association of *coger* (take: usually used in a sexual sense in Argentina).

In the same way, a Spanish speaker would avoid the erudite adjective *putativo* (putative) in some circumstances: *puta* means "whore". On the other hand, the speaker may consciously prefer the synonym which evokes another word (on the level of expression); this is what we call a play on words. Thus a Latin-American might use the European Spanish *votar* instead of the American *sufragar* (to vote) precisely in order to make a play on words with the identically pronounced *botar* (to throw away). In these examples, we discover a second differentiating factor[11].

2. The similarity of one of the synonyms to another moneme or lexeme on the level of the form of expression. This differentiating factor, too, is used in plays on words and jokes. In Mexico, for example, I heard the expression *flan quinquenal* (five-year crême caramel), which the hearer automatically takes to refer, on the basis of the similarity of form of expression, to the *plan quinquenal* (five-year plan), which is thus linked metaphorically with *flan*; and, vice versa, the dessert can be designated (also in Mexico) as *flan quinquenal* (on the analogy of the *plan quinquenal*), if service at the hotel is too slow[12].

---

[11]For morpho-stylistics, see Ullmann, *Mél. Delbouille*, 1964, p. 639; *Language and Style*, 1964, p. 111.

[12]The following anecdote clarifies this (*art scénique* 'scenic art' is replaced by the synonym *art théâtral* 'theatrical art', to avoid homonymy with *arsénique* 'arsenic'):

"At the time when Victor Hugo was admitted to the Académie Française, the trial of Marie Lafarge, suspected of having poisoned her husband with arsenic, was exciting public opinion. In the speech he gave in reply to the new member, M. de Salvandy unintentionally made a pun.

'At this time when *l'art scénique* has undergone such considerable development . . .' he began.

These unfortunately chosen words provoked in the audience an immediate and uncontrollable desire to laugh, which stopped the speaker.

While the audience were laughing, one of his companions whispered to him the reason for the amusement. Smiling and amused himself, M. de Salvandy then changed his phrasing:

'At this time when *l'art théâtral* . . .' " (Marius 1241, 29-3-1973)

Puns such as "Modern man lives in *taverns* instead of *caverns*" would not be possible with synonyms.

William C. Brown, translator, calls my attention to the consequences the use of one synonym for another can have, when they have nothing in common in phonetics, as can be seen in the following anecdote:

Related to this formal similarity is the fact that the majority of monemes belong to a *family of words*. Their diachronic de-limitation (which is done in certain etymological dictionaries such as the *FEW*) does not necessarily correspond to their syn-chronic delimitation, which is all that matters here. But even synchronically, the formal relation of one word to other words in the same family becomes a factor in synonymy.

3. The fact that two synonyms belong to two different word families. This difference implies a series of different associa-tions [solidarities, see Part I, Chapter 5, n. 15]. In French, *lourd* "heavy" can be a synonym of *indigeste* "indigestible"; the potential presence of *lourdeur* "heaviness" and of *digérer* "digest", etc., implies different associations for each synonym (see above, note 9).

Another factor is:
4. The motivation of compound or derived words. For example, two German words for "pavement", *Trottoir* and *Geh-weg*, are synonyms (absolute synonyms on the level of the sub-stance of content). But they are not synonyms as far as their motivation is concerned. For any German speaker, *Gehweg* is easy to analyze (*gehen* "go", and *Weg* "way"); *Trottoir*, on the other hand, is not (being a French loan-word). The speaker may prefer a motivated compound or derivative over its non-motivated synonym (whether this is a simple word or a com-pound or derived word from a diachronic viewpoint), which has lost its motivation because of phonetic evolution or other dia-chronic factors (such as loan-words, for example)[13]. The scien-

---

"A group of young women from a Mexican ranch went into town to have their picture taken. They had been told to say *rojo* ("red") as the photographer snapped the shutter, thus pursing their lips, which is supposed to be more attractive (analogous to the way English speakers are told to say "cheese", forcing a smile), but one girl forgot, using instead the synonym *colorado*, thus opening her mouth too wide and ruining the picture".

[13]Also see Ullmann, *Mél. Delbouille*, pp. 638, ff.

tific analysis of these compounds is performed (1) on the level of the form of expression and (2) on the level of the form of content. This 4th factor is also often used for plays on words. In Mexico, for example, I was once asked: "Do you know a synonym for *sequía* (drought)?". The answer was *aguacero* (downpour), interpreted as *agua-cero* (water-zero). The example is especially interesting because by means of a new analysis of the form of expression as a new form of content (motivated), an antonym becomes a synonym.

We should continue the analysis within the framework of more complex structures which go beyond the lexeme (but here we shall simply enumerate them, without making a thorough examination).

5. Phono-stylistics; see Ullmann, *Mél Delbouille*, 1964, 637, ff., especially 641, ff.; *Language and Style*, 1964, p. 111; L. Söll, "Murmurare in der Romania – Bedeutungswandel durch Lautwandel?" *Festschrift Wartburg*, 1968: "Phonetic motivation cannot take place within *one* word. An 'heureux arrangement des sonorités' (P. Delbouille, *Poésie et sonorités*, 1961, p. 35) is brought about only in a larger phonic context".

6. The syntagmatic environment and the context (principles of distribution; see, for example, Ullmann, *Semantics*, 1962, 143, concerning *broad/wide*); *Language and Style*, 1964, pp. 103, ff.; for *second* and *deuxième* in French, see Söll, *GRM* 16, 1966, 95)[14]. For Fr. *plus* and *davantage* (more), Maibrit

---

[14]Cf. the fine German anecdote told by Dornseiff (quoted by Söll, in *GRM*, 16, p. 96); to help the English-speaking reader interpret properly the ambiguities and puns of the German text, we give the following "translation" with commentaries:

"An ambassador, speaking to his superior (it is usually added that the Foreign Minister of the story is Bismarck, according to the translator of the Spanish edition): 'The German language is very difficult, since there are always two words for the same thing: *speisen* ('eat' and 'feed'), and *essen* ('eat'), *springen* ('crack' and 'jump') and *hüpfen*

Westrin draws the following conclusion:

It is possible to say with the same sense: 'Pierre travaille *davantage*' or 'Pierre travaille *plus*' (Pierre works more). Yet the two adverbs are not always interchangeable. The use of *davantage* is restricted by many rules. The restrictions apply to the words involved as well as to the complement. *Plus* should be chosen: 1. Before a comparative complement with *que*, 2. Before a partitive nominal complement with *de*, 3. with a quantitative complement with *de*, 5. to modify an adjective, 8. As an auxiliary of the negative to express the cessation of an action or of a state. *Davantage* would be preferable if no complement follows: 4. with *en* representing a noun: 6. with *le* representing an adjective. To use *plus* in cases 4 and 6 one would have to reinforce it with an adjective[15].

('jump'), *hauen* ('hit') and *schlagen* ('hit', 'strike the hour'), *senden* ('send'; substantivized participle *Gesandter* = ambassador) and *schicken* ('send', 'remit'; the adj. participle *geschickt* also means – for historical, etymological reasons – 'fit', 'capable', 'clever')'. The superior answered him: 'That is not true. You are wrong. One can feed ('speisen') a crowd, but not eat ('essen') a crowd; a cup cracks ('springen') but does not jump ('hüpfen'); the clock strikes ('schlagen') but does not hit ('hauen'); you are an ambassador ('Gesandter'), but not very clever ('geschickt')'. And addressing one of the ladies present: 'I may accompany you to a safe place (*'sicher'* = safe, certain), but not to a 'certain place' (*'gewiss'* = 'certain' and 'safe'; in colloquial speech 'der gewiss Ort' means the same as 'das Örtchen,' that is, 'toilet')' ".

Jean Dubois (*CahLex*, 4, 1964, p. 12) distinguishes, studying the distribution of *voie* and *chemin* (road) in French, a *common zone* and a *zone of exclusion* ("on appelle termes synonymes deux unités dont les distributions se superposent presque complètement," p. 8: "we call synonymous terms two units whose distributions are almost identical").

[15]Maibrit Westrin, *Etude sur la concurrence de* davantage *avec* plus *dans la période allant de 1200 à la Révolution, Comparaison avec l'usage actuel* (Etudes romanes de Lund, 21), Lund (C. W. K. Gleerup), 1973, p. 7.

7. Intonation[16] and rhythm (see Ullmann, *Language and Style*, 1964, p. 103).

8. Stylistic level (poetry, prose, etc.): *passing/death* (the first is poetic and archaic, Ullmann, 1962, 143); Fr. *mort/trépas/décès*; *dale/valley* (Ullmann, 1962, 147); *col* for *cou* (neck) in Gide (Ullmann, "Choix et expressivité" 1959, 220); Sp. *trabajar/laborar* (elevated style) (work), *blanco/albo* (poetic) (white); Ger. *sterben/hinscheiden* (die), *Träne/Zähre* (tear), *Gesicht/Antlitz/Visage* (face).

9. Conventional principles of style (principle of not repeating the same word; see Ullmann, *Semantics*, 1962, 152)[17].

---

[16]Intonation can be a symptomatic factor (with stylistic value), which justifies its inclusion in our list; but it can also be a symbolic factor (it would be necessary to investigate the problem of interrogation in French; in any case, in German, Swedish, Norwegian, and Serbo-Croat there are oppositions involving intonation – note by K. Heger). We have to distinguish intonation from tone, which in the Indo-European languages, is not relevant in the symbolic-conceptual field ("C'est le ton qui fait la musique; this is highly (but not absolutely) valid in Indo-European languages, in the sense that the *tone* is available for expression and appeal and is irrelevant for representation" (Karl Bühler, *Teoría del lenguaje*, 2nd. ed.; Spanish Transl. by Julián Marías, Madrid (Revista de Occidente), 1961, p. 71).

[17]A good example to illustrate the stylistic principle of non-repetition is found in Jean Vauquelin de la Fresnaye, *La Vie du Campagnard* (Satyres françaises, livre II) in the sixteenth century:

"(I) Il oit dans les forests des vents le doux *murmure*.
  (II) Il oit le *gazouillis* de ces mille ruisseaux.
  (III) Il oit mille oisillons qui sans cesse *jargonnent*."
("(I) He hears the soft murmur of the winds in the forests.
  (II) He hears the babbling of these countless streams.
  (III) He hears countless little birds chirruping ceaselessly")

Murmurer occupies paradigmatically positions I, II, and III: *gazouiller*, positions II and III; for III there is, in addition, a whole inventory (which comes in part from previous times). Syntagmatically, then, there is no other possible distribution, if the poet does not want to repeat one of the words" L. Söll, "*Murmurare* in der Romania –

(d) PRACTICAL EXPERIENCE OF ABSOLUTE SYNONYMY ON THE CONCEPTUAL LEVEL

Before I continue with the analysis, let me cite a pertinent experience of my own in Montevideo in early 1966. With my assistant, M. Höfler, I had gone to our favourite little restaurant; I asked the waiter for some coffee with milk and some peanuts (*un capuchino chico y unos cacahuetes*); the waiter turned round and shouted to the boy at the counter "¡*Un cortado grande y unos maníes!*" He brought me exactly what I wanted. This significant experience proves, by means of the extralinguistic realization (the waiter's actions), the absolute identity of the synonyms in question, on the conceptual level, extra confirmation of our theoretical results[18]. There is no need, however, to go so far to find examples of this kind: in Germany, if I ask for *ein Helles*, the waiter might change the expression to *ein Bier* (beer), etc.; in English, *spuds* for "potatoes", etc. All these synonyms have a

---

Bedeutungswandel durch Lautsymbolik?", in *Festschrift Wartburg*, 1968, 2, pp. 302, ff.

Another example of non-repetition: "Le peuple, mécontent des patriciens, se retira sur le Mont-Sacré: on lui envoya des députés qui l'apaisèrent; et comme chacun se promit secours l'un à l'autre en cas que les patriciens ne tinssent pas les paroles données, ce qui *eût* causé à tous les instants des séditions, et *auroit* troublé toutes les fonctions des magistrats, on jugea qu'il valoit mieux créer une magistrature qui *pût* empêcher les injustices faites à un plébéien ("The people were discontented with the patricians and withdrew onto the Sacred Mount: deputies were sent to them who calmed them down; and as each of them promised they would help each other should the patricians not keep their word, which *might* have led to revolts again and again, and *would* have upset all the workings of the magistracy, the decision was taken to establish a magistracy which *might be able to* prevent injustices being done to a plebeian": Montesquieu, *Considérations sur les causes de la grandeur des romains et de leur décadence*, Paris, 1852, p. 77 (= chap. VIII, § 5).

[18]For intensional and extensional synonymy, see below, paragraph 5 k.

sememe in common, a materially verifiable identity. Communication is guaranteed. The synonyms contain the same relevant distinctive features; from the conceptual viewpoint, they are *free variants*.

(e) ABSENCE OF SYNONYMY ON THE SEMASIOLOGICAL LEVEL

On the other hand, no one will deny that *cacahuete* and *maní*, *capuchino chico* and *cortado grande* are distinguished by easily recognizable elements. *Cacahuete* and *capuchino chico* are the Spanish terms current in Madrid, as well as in Montevideo; *maní* and *cortado* are regional terms. *Maní* comes from the Taino language of Haiti; it is a typically American word; *cacahuete* also comes from America (from Nahuatl), but it has taken over Spain. Thus *maní* has preserved an American character, both regional and popular. The speaker often needs to choose between two or more synonyms which are absolute on the conceptual level; he will make his choice according to his social position, regional origin, profession, age, etc.; also – this must not be forgotten – according to his intentions (artistic or otherwise), his environment, and the effect he might wish to have on that environment or on those he is talking to. He must choose. In doing so, he makes a *stylistic* decision. In other words, we now find ourselves in the realm of style[19]. The very definition of the word "style" implies selection; Ullmann has told us this on different occasions[20]. On the conceptual

---

[19]"Stylistics is usually regarded as a special division of linguistics; since however, it has a point of view which is peculiar to it and distinguishes it from all other branches of linguistic study, it would perhaps be more logical to regard it as a sister science concerned not with the elements of language as such, but with their expressive potential. On this reading, stylistics will have the same subdivision as linguistics" (S. Ullmann, *Language and Style*, 1964, p. 111).

[20]See, for example, S. Ullmann, "Choix et expressivité", in *Actes du IXᵉ Congrès International de Linguistique Romane* (Lisbon, 1959), 2, 1961, pp. 217–26; *Semantics*, 1962, p. 151 ("The possibility of choos-

symbolic level we can, or rather, we must make an abstraction from everything that comes from the speaker; the elements that are grasped are the relevant distinctive features, just as phonology makes an abstraction from phonetic variants. But when we come to the level of linguistic realization, when we relate the conceptual system to the monemes of a given language, we also simultaneously introduce, along with the conceptual content, all the wealth of style, a whole gamut of supplementary elements. Ullmann quotes the two lines from Shakespeare:

"What's in a name? That which we call a rose
By any other name would smell as sweet"
(Romeo and Juliet II, 2.).

The rose is still a rose, and coffee is still coffee, whether one calls it *capuchino* or *cortado grande*. The sememe they have in common is still identical[21].

---

ing between two or more alternatives is fundamental to our modern conception of style, and synonymy affords one of the most clearcut examples of such choice"); *Précis de sémantique française*, [2]1959, p. 192 ("Le mécanisme du *choix* qui est à la base de la notion du style" the method of *choice* which underlies the idea of style); *Language and Style*, 1964, p. 102 ("another key-concept of stylistics, the idea of *choice*"; see also p. 154). "Le style est un écart par rapport à une norme", style is a variation from a norm, (Valéry, see P. Guiraud, *La stylistique*, Paris (Que sais-je?), 1954, p. 105).

[21]William C. Brown told me the following anecdote, which shows that dogs do not follow the above rules:

"We used to have a dog named *Snubby*, but three-year-old Dick couldn't pronounce that, and called him *Flubby*. When we tried to correct him, he defended his pronunciation with the irrefutable logic: 'But he comes when I call him!' "

The dog, then, identifies the sememes of *Snubby* and *Flubby*. Joking aside, it is true that certain human beings, too, in the case of mistakes or slips of the tongue, can perform such identifications when the context allows one to recognize the *signifiant* which the speaker has meant to produce (a recognition which is a correction), and when

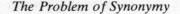

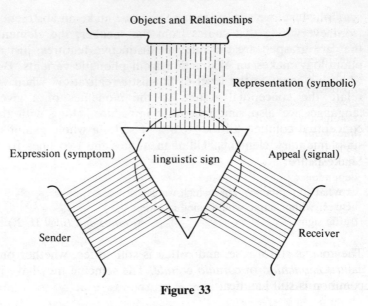

Figure 33

(f) KARL BÜHLER'S MODEL

We can relate this basic situation to the model given by Karl
Bühler[22], reproduced as Figure 33.

---

the *signifiant* actually produced has no meaning of its own which
might provoke a misunderstanding. In these cases, it is not a matter of
synonyms, in the normal sense, but rather of a neologism which, in
reality, constitutes a phonetic variant of the correct *signifiant*.ı

[22]Karl Bühler, *Sprachtheorie*, Jena, 1934, p. 28 (das Organon-
Modell der Sprache) = *Teoría del lenguaje*, Spanish translation by
Julián Marías, 2nd. ed., Madrid (Revista de Occidente), 1961, 497
pp. (the *órganon* model on p. 51).

See also the presentation and interpretation of this model by K.
Heger, "La linguistique et sa place parmi les sciences", *TraLiLi* X, 1,
1972, 7–34, particularly p. 10 (this article appeared first in German,
with the title "Zur Standortbestimmung der Sprachwissenschaft"
ZRP 87, 1971, 1–31, particularly p. 5). The model is presented again
in Heger's *Monem, Wort, Satz und Text* 1976, §1.2.

The circle in the middle symbolizes the concrete acoustic phenomenon. Three variable elements are able to raise it on three different occasions to the category of a sign. The sides of the inserted triangle symbolize these three elements. In one aspect the triangle covers less than the circle (principle of abstractive relevance). At the same time, in another sense, it covers more than the circle, to indicate that the perceptible datum always hints at something unperceived. The bundles of lines symbolize the semantic functions of the (complex) linguistic sign. It is a *symbol* (Darstellung) by virtue of its link with objects and relationships; a *symptom* (Ausdruck), by virtue of its dependence on the sender whose being (Innerlichkeit) it expresses; and a *signal* (Appell) by virtue of its appeal to the hearer, whose external or interior conduct it directs like other traffic signs (Bühler, pp. 28, ff.).

Language is at the same time *Darstellung* (a representation), *Ausdruck* (an expression of the speaker) and *Appell* (an appeal to the hearer): this corresponds exactly to what Ullmann has called *objective meaning, feeling-tone* and *evocative value*[23].

The *absolute synonymy* we have found on the conceptual level concerns only the symbolic function (*Darstellungsfunktion, Symbolfunktion*), that is, one of the three functions of the linguistic sign. The differentiation between absolute synonyms is made through the link with a sender, with a speaker, or, to put it another way, through the *symptomatic function* of the linguistic sign. Absolute synonymy, undeniable on the symbolic level, is destroyed on the symptomatic level, or, to put it more accurately, onto the absolute synonymy which comes from symbolic values are added differentiating elements which come from the speaker.

---

[23]Ullmann, *Semantics*, 1962, p. 142; "Very few words" [I would say none!] "are completely synonymous in the sense of being interchangeable in any context without the slightest alteration in objective meaning, feeling-tone or evocative value". As for *evocation*, see also Ullmann, *Mél. Delbouille*, 1964, pp. 643, ff.

(g) THE FUNCTIONS OF SYMPTOM AND OF SIGNAL

What kind of elements originating with the speaker can come into play? They could be called *connotative elements*, or *pragmatic elements*[24]. Here is an attempt – provisonal only – at classification:

FUNCTION OF SYMPTOM[25]

10. Geographical differentiation: French *soixante-dix/septante* (70); German *Samstag/Sonnabend* (Saturday), *Reinmachefrau* (charwoman) (more in the north)/*Putzfrau* (more in the south); English (Scots) *flesher/butcher* (Ullmann, 1962, 143); Spanish *tiza* "chalk"/*gis* (México), *fresa* "strawberry"/*frutilla* (Chile), *plátano* "banana"/*banana* (certain Latin American countries).

11. Social differentiation (including level of education): French *voiture* (bourgeois, "carriage")/*bagnole* (normal popular word, see *CahLex* 8, 1966, 89); *travail/boulot* "job"; English *turn down/refuse* (Ullmann, 1962, 143); Spanish *mi señor* (lower class)/*mi esposo* (upper class) "my husband"; *aliviarse* (lower class)/*dar a luz* (upper class) "to give birth to".

---

[24]On *denotation* and *connotation* see the clear approach of Georges Mounin, *Les problèmes théoriques de la traduction*, Paris (Gallimard), 1963, pp. 114, ff. ("Les connotations font partie de la *pragmatique*, qui désigne les relations entre les signes et leurs utilisateurs," p. 154, Connotations are part of *pragmatics*, concerning the relationship between signs and their users); *connotation*, however, needs a more detailed study. It seems that, alongside *pragmatic connotation*, there also exists a *symbolic connotation*. In German, if I say *ersticken* "choke, suffocate" instead of *sterben* "die," in a neutralized use (that is, when I prefer *ersticken* for stylistic reasons, not because of its symbolic difference), then the symbolic difference between the two sememes becomes reduced to a symbolic connotation.

[25]It goes without saying that, in a strict sense, the synonymous terms should coexist in the vocabulary (active or passive) of the same speaker.

12. Profession: English *death/decease* (Ullmann, 1962, 143); German *Fernrohr/Teleskop* (telescope); French *jaunisse/ictère* (med.) (jaundice: see Part I, Chapter 9e) *époux* (common language, "married couple")/*conjoints* (administrative language), *CahLex* 8, 1966, 87[26].

13. Religion (Cath., Prot., etc.): In Spanish *musulmanes* is used by Moslems, *mahometanos* by Christians. In German, Protestants refer to the *Papst* "Pope," and Catholics use the term *Heiliger Vater* "Holy Father"; on the phonetic level, for example, in French, *Jésus Christ* (Catholics pronounce [*Kri*] and Protestants [*Krist*]).

14. Political affiliation: in Germany, *vor Christus* "before Christ" becomes *vor der Zeitrechnung* ("before the Era") among Communists, to avoid referring to Christ; *Verteidigungsminister* (term for the National Defence Minister of West Germany)/*Kriegsminister* ("War Minister," Communist East German term for the same West German minister); *Chemnitz* (West Germany)/*Karl-Marx-Stadt* (East German name for the same city); French *planification* (leftist term)/*dirigisme* (rightist term); *free enterprise/capitalist oppression*[27].

15. Age (language of children, adults, etc.): English *daddy/father*; German *Wauwau/Hund* "dog"; French *faire*

---

[26]In a broad sense, one might include here cases such as *ping-pong* and *table tennis*: "*tenis de mesa* (Table tennis), a sport; *ping-pong* a pastime . . . a recreation" (*Ultimas Noticias* [Mexico], April 24, 1972); one must wonder, however, if the symbolic-conceptual sememe continues to be identical, even if the rules of the game are the same.

[27]In principle, each social group, including the *family*, an *association*, a *club*, etc., can create symptomatic factors of differentiation. It would be easy to lengthen the list in this direction. In W. von Wartburg's family, for example, the word *konto* was used instead of the synonym *confiture* "marmalade" (W. von Wartburg, *Problems and Methods in Linguistics*, 1969, p. 112; *Problemas y métodos de la lingüística*, Madrid, 1951, p. 183).

dodo/dormir "sleep"; Spanish *guagua/perro* "dog", *pupu/coche* "car", Latin American *chavo/muchacho* "boy"; *momiza*, used by those under 25 to refer to those over 25.

16. Sex: for example, in Puebla de Don Fadrique (Andalucía, Spain) [*la riendah*] ("the reins," men)/[*la bridah*] (women), [*chico*] ("little finger")/[*margarite*], [*nochegüena*] "Christmas"/[*dia enacimjénto*] etc. (M. Alvar, "Diferencias en el habla de hombres y mujeres," *Revista do Livro* (Río de Janeiro) 12, 1958, 77–86, especially p. 80)[28]; see also *Orbis* 1, 10–86, 335–384; 2, 7–34[29]. I was told in Mexico that women prefer *lindo* for "pretty" and men prefer *bonito*.

17. There remains the problem of *archaisms*[30] and *modernisms*, of diachronic implications in synchrony[31], which I

---

[28]The same in M. Alvar, *Diferencias en el habla de Puebla de Don Fadrique (Granada)*, Granada (Publicaciones del Atlas lingüístico de Andalucía, I, 3), 1957, 34 pp. (especially p. 28).

Compare the remarks of Antonio Alatorre: "At this very moment the linguist interested in the phenomena of Mexican Spanish can see, for example, the increasing frequency with which a final -*r* of a word is unvoicing and assibilating, producing, in words such as *calor* and *cantar*, a sound that seems to be a mixture of *r* and *s*. He can check that this change began to occur in women's speech first; this is nothing odd, because in linguistic matters as in so many others women tend to be more revolutionary than men . . ." ("El Mexicano y su lengua", *Revista de la Universidad de México* 22, no. 10 (June), 1968, p. 4).

[29]Examples such as Neapolitan *spusarsi* "marry" (speaking of a man), *maritarsi* "marry" (speaking of a woman) (see also *FEW*, 6¹, 354) are not valid because there are differences between them on the symbolic level. The same is true of Spanish *barbero/peluquero* "barber".

[30]See, for ex., J.-M. Klinkenberg, *Style et archaïsme dans la Légende d'Ulenspiegel de Charles de Coster*, Bruxelles, 1973, I, pp. 93, ff.

[31]For example, *passing/death* (Ullmann, 1962, p. 143); Fr. *col* for *cou* in Gide (Ullmann, "Choix et expressivité", 1959, p. 220); "archaism is an important source of stylistic effects" (Ullmann, *Language*

am not yet able to classify satisfactorily[32], and

18. the problem of *learned words* (↔ *popular words*) and

19. the problem of *foreign words* (↔ *native words*)[33], which also seem to exercise a symptomatic function. Is it necessary to classify them under 11 or 12? Since they can also function as euphemisms (see 25), etc., I think it would be worth while to examine them separately. We should add, however, that in most cases different symptomatic factors are combined into a single lexeme.

FUNCTION OF SYMPTOM OR OF SIGNAL (AFFECTIVITY)

20. Intensification: French *beaucoup/une mer de* ("many/a sea of"), etc. (Wartburg, *Einführung*[2], 150 [= Problems and Methods in Linguistics, 1969, p. 150]; see also ib. 86 [p. 87]

---

and Style, 1964, p. 167). It is often a problem of generations. "Lorsqu'un vieil ami de la famille dit: *les fillettes partagent la même couche* (énoncé observé), il ne dit rien d'autre que: *mes petites filles couchent dans le même lit*, dans une langue vieillie" (Josette Rey-Debove, *CahLex*, 6, 1966, p. 87, n. 28: an old family friend observed to say something simple in an archaic manner. Both sentences mean "my young daughters sleep in the same bed"). This is a neat example of symbolic identity and symptomatic differentiation.

[32]Ullmann suggested that I put archaisms together with the age factor, under the heading "Time factor". I think, however, that it is necessary to distinguish between the *language of children – language of adults*, on one hand, and *archaisms*, on the other hand.

[33]Concerning **18** and **19**: for example French *vélocité* / *hâtiveté* "speed" (Oresme; Wartburg, *Problems and Methods in Linguistics*, 1969, p. 189 [= *Einführung*, [2]1962, p. 192; in the Span. translation, *Problemas y métodos de la lingüística*, Madrid, 1951, p. 328]); Ger. *Telephon* (foreign + pop.) / *Fernsprecher* (learned + native) "telephone" (see Söll, *GRM*, 16, 1966, p. 94); see also Ullmann, 1962, pp. 145 and 149; *Language and Style*, 1964, pp. 112, ff.; on the semantic process of "naturalization" see Josette Rey-Debove, "La sémiotique de l'emprunt lexical", *TraLiLi* XI, 1973, 109–123.

Madrid, 1951, 252 and 132)[34]. Spanish *llover/llover a cántaros* ("rain/rain cats and dogs"); *apuñalar/coser a puñaladas* ("stab/carve up").

21. Humour: French *tête/poire* ("head/pear")[35], *jambe/gigue*, etc., Spanish words for "leg", *pierna/pata*, *patita*, *zanca*, *remo*, *garra* (Wartburg, *Problems and Methods in Linguistics*, 1969, p. 14; *Problemas y métodos de la lingüística*, Madrid, 1951, p. 232); French *morir/fermer son parapluie* ("die/close his umbrella", compare English *kick the bucket*, etc.) (Ullmann, *Précis*[2] 1959, 190, = *Introducción a la semántica francesa*, Madrid, 1965, p. 259), *femme/animal porte-jupe* ("woman/ skirt-wearing animal") (Regnard, *Le Bal*, p. 7, Robert). (Compare English *chick*, *dish*, *doll*, etc.).

22. Irony and parody: see Ullmann, *Language and Style*, 1964, p. 108; for example, French *cacophonie/sérénade* ("cacophony/serenade") (Robert).

23. Laudatory affectivity: Spanish *esbelto/delgado*, "slim" (praiseworthy)/"thin".

24. Pejorative affectivity: Spanish *flaco/delgado*, "skinny" (not praiseworthy)/"thin": (see Ullmann, 1962, 143)[36].

25. Euphemism: *crétin* (cretin)/*benêt* (= benôit, blessed); see, for example, the designations for 'weasel', for a 'woman's

---

[34]See especially the studies by Olaf Deutschmann, "Untersuchungen zum volkstümlichen Ausdruck der Mengenvorstellung im Romanischen," in *Romanistisches Jahrbuch*, 4, 1951, pp. 221, ff., concerning Spanish *una barbaridad de cosas*, etc.; "Der Gebrauch von Bezeichnungen für "Haufen" zum Ausdruck der unbestimmten grossen Menge ("viel") und zur Steigerung ('viel, sehr') im Romanischen," in *Homenaje a Fritz Krüger*, vol. II, Mendoza, 1954, pp. 19–57; *Zum Adverb im Romanischen*, Tübingen (Niemeyer Verlag), 1959, 295 pp.

[35]See also my article "Designaciones de la cabeza en la América española", in *Anuario de Letras* (Universidad de México), 6, 1964, pp. 25–56, in which I mention more than 140 affective synonyms for *cabeza*, "head".

[36]In a concrete case it is not easy to distinguish between pejorative

breast', 'oaths' etc. (see Mansur Guerios, *Tabús lingüísticos*, Río, 1956; Ullmann, *Language and Style*, 1964, 89–91).

Through euphemism one makes an abstraction from the function of symptom or of signal which implies the word replaced by the euphemism.

Let us sum up: the factors we have just enumerated bring all the wealth of stylistic resources into the realm of synonymy and, through synonymy, into semantics[37]. The outstanding conclusion from our investigation is this: one must distinguish carefully between the different planes or levels. Two words may be *absolute synonyms* as far as their conceptual-symbolic content is concerned, but they are never such if we consider the wealth of external factors, which depend on the speaker, and internal factors which depend on the structure of the language itself. Synonymy exists on the conceptual-symbolic plane

---

symbolic and affective factors (functions of symptom and of signal): French *voiture* and *bagnole*, for the 'bourgeois' are differentiated on the symbolic level: *voiture* (normal word) – *bagnole* "vieille voiture, voiture dont on est mécontent" (old, unsatisfactory vehicle: with a value judgment on the symbolic level; see below, paragraph 1). On another social level (popular) *bagnole* is a normal word with no value judgment ("on achète une belle bagnole", we've bought a fine car). The same thing happens with *boulot* = *travail* "work" (popular) and *boulot* = "travail déplaisant ou malfait" "unsatisfactory or botched work" (bourgeois). See Josette Rey-Debove, *CahLex*, 8, 1966, p. 89.

[37]In the same sense, S. Ullmann: "For the student of style, 'expressiveness' covers a wide range of linguistic features which have one thing in common: they do not directly affect the meaning of the utterance, the actual information which it conveys" [= symbol, sememe]. "Everything that transcends the purely referential and communicative side of language belongs to the province of expressiveness: emotive overtones, emphasis, rhythm, symmetry, euphony, and also the so called 'evocative' elements which place our style in a particular register (literary, colloquial, slangy, etc.) or associate it with a particular milieu (historical, foreign, provincial, professional, etc.)" (*Language and Style*, 1964, p. 101).

as synonymy of *signifiés* or synonymy of sememes; synonymy does not exist on the semasiological level[38]. I agree with Heger's conclusions, summed up by Söll in the article already referred to: "Identity of meaning between two words does not exist, but identity of concepts does" ("Bedeutungsgleichheit für zwei Wortkörper gibt es nicht, wohl aber Begriffsgleichheit")[39]. In other words, there is no free variation in the realm of meaningful units (Heger, *TraLiLi* III[1], p. 27)[40]. When

---

[38]Wilhelm von Humboldt recognized the difference between symbolic function and symptomatic function when he wrote:

"Only on the basis of precise reflection, but then clearly and distinctly, does one find, joined to the value of the words, the character of the different conception of the world that peoples have. I have previously stated (pp. 197, 204, 205) that there hardly exists a word which is conceived of in the same way in the representation formed of it by each individual, except insofar as it is used momentarily *as the mere material sign of a concept*" [= symbolic value]. "For this reason it can even be maintained that in each word there is something that cannot be described in words, and that words of different languages, even when, broadly speaking, designating identical concepts, are never true *synonyms*" [differentiation by symptomatic values]. "Considered in an exact and strict manner, one definition cannot cover them, and often it only indicates, to a certain extent, their place in the field to which they belong" (*Über die Verschiedenheit* . . . , pp 221, ff.). See also the *Grammaire des Grammaires* by Girault-Duvivier ([10]1838, p. 597): "*Synonym* is applied to words that resemble each other in a *common idea*" (symbolic value) "but are even so distinguished from each other by some *accessory idea peculiar to each of them*" (differentiation by symptomatic values, etc.), "which nearly always leads to the necessity of choosing, to use them appropriately and speak accurately".

[39]Söll, "Synonymie und Bedeutungsgleichheit", in *GRM*, 16, 1966, p. 91, note 10.

[40]Just one exception: if the significative unit functions as a metalinguistic statement concerning the *form of expression* (Heger ib.). If I say: "The word *voler*, in French, is composed of the phonemes v/o/l/e," it doesn't matter whether *voler* means "fly" or "rob" (it has both meanings). But this is precisely because we have left the realm of significations, retaining only the form of the expression. In a paral-

I reintegrate the concepts with the monemes, the differentiating stylistic implications are inevitable, or, to use Ullmann's words "almost all the phenomena studied by this science" [semantics] "have stylistic extensions"[41]. The content of the moneme is necessarily composed of a sememe (which allows absolute synonymy) and a cluster of additional stylistic values (which, because of their complexity, do not allow absolute synonymy). English *almost* and *nearly*, the only example of absolute synonymy (even taking into account stylistic values) suggested by Collinson and quoted by Ullmann (*Semantics*, 1962, 142) does not stand the test (see Söll, *GRM* 16, 1966, 94)[42]. Onomasiology allows us to mark the boundaries between

---

lel manner one could also say "The concept 'remember' in position 2–3 can be realized by means of *se souvenir* or *se rappeler*; they are perfectly synonymous on the conceptual level." In this case, we only retain a part of the linguistic reality; it is a metalinguistic statement. Within the object language itself I only know of one case, which was pointed out to me by J. A. Suárez, cf. Jorge A. Suárez, "A Case of Absolute Synonyms," *International Journal of American Linguistics* 37, 1971, 192–195, where the author gives a list of 'absolute synonyms' in Tehuelche (southern Argentina). Even when the list is reduced by a different distribution (the case of two words for "dog") or by frequency (the case of two words for "horse") there remain examples such as *g'ót* and *'o.on* "head." "I do not see any reason to consider such forms . . . different until the lower morphemic alternation pattern is reached. They are the same sememically, lexemically, and partly morphemically; they begin to be different only as sign patterns" (p. 195). These cases are explained historically by taboo.

[41]S. Ullmann, "Sémantique et stylistique," in *Mélanges Delbouille*, 1964, p. 636.

[42]Only *nearly* is negatable or gradable (*not nearly*, *more nearly*, *very nearly*). The *absolutely perfect synonyms*, defended by Ducháček (*Orbis*, no. 13, pp 35–49) do not exist; I am in complete agreement with L. Söll, *GRM*, 16, 1966, p. 95. J. P. Rona (Montevideo) has directed my attention to *joya* and *alhaja* (both meaning "jewel") in Uruguay; they are synonymous in almost all their uses, but are clearly distinguished on the metaphorical level: *mi novia es una joya* ("my girl friend is a jewel") has a positive value, while *mi novia es una alhaja* has a pejorative value.

all the monemes, groups of monemes, etc., that is, between all the means of expression of *one* or of *several* given languages, those means which realize the same concept or the same conceptual system (capable of being expressed in formulae, if you wish), that is, those which have the same communicative value. It supplies us, then, with monemes (etc.) which realize the same sememes or semes. The analogy between *onomasiology* and *phonology* is impressive: both methods set the limits of their objects through the analysis of distinctive values (identity of the elements found). Both methods supply us with distinctive features. *Phonetics* and *semasiology* give us an infinite number of nuances which leave a greater margin of freedom[43]. A conclusion for those who like precision: monemes or groups of monemes can be absolute synonyms as to their conceptual-symbolic content, but not as to their stylistic values (which are derived from the previously established factors). A conclusion for those who like brief formulae: absolute synonymy does not exist on the level of monemes (linguistic signs)[44].

---

[43]Heger calls my attention to the fact that these comparisons (onomasiology–phonology; semasiology–phonetics), although interesting and fruitful, do not correspond entirely to the Hjelmslevian model which has served as our basis (according to this model, the comparison of phonetics and semasiology would be justified; but the companion of phonology would be a 'monosemistic' semantics of content–monemes or values (Weisgerber, Weinrich, Guillaume)). See K. Heger, "Temporale Deixis und Vorgansquantität ("Aspekt" und "Aktionsart")," in *ZRP*, 83, 1967, pp. 512–82.

[44]As early as 1694, the Académie Française showed that absolute synonyms do not exist: "Outre la Definition ou Description de chaque mot, on y a adjousté les Synonymes, c'est à dire les mots qui sont de mesme signification; sur quoy on croit devoir avertir que le Synonyme ne respond pas tousjours exactement à la signification du mot dont il est Synonyme, et qu'ainsi ils ne doivent pas estre employez indifferemment l'un pour l'autre" (Ac 1694; quote according to Ac 1695, Reprint 1968, Preface); see also B. Quemada, *Les Dictionnaires du français moderne* (1539–1863), Paris, 1967, p. 447. (As well as the definition or description of each word, we have

The theory we have just outlined implies a series of individual problems which will occupy our attention next.

(h) SYNONYMY AND SCIENTIFIC TERMINOLOGY

It has often been claimed (with greater or less conviction) that absolute synonymy exists in scientific terminology[45]. I do not think so. There is, so to speak, only a change of accent; the conceptual content – delimitable and definable – is situated on the highest level. One could even say that this is the only aspect which interests science. Stylistic implications are not altogether lacking, but they are not important, or at least they are much less important and, in general, so few as to be left out of consideration. *Lautlehre* and *Phonetik*, *Formenlehre* and *Morphologie* are scientific synonyms in German (phonetics, morphology); but one of the two words is motivated, while the other is a foreign word[46]. These stylistic implications are in abeyance, but, for example, a purist movement (rejection of

---

added the synonyms, i.e. the words with the same meaning; we feel we should point out in this connection that the synonym does not always correspond exactly to the meaning of the word to which it is synonymous, and also that they should not be used indiscriminately for each other).

[45]For example, Ullmann, *Semantics*, 1962, p. 141 ("The fact that scientific terms are precisely delimited and emotionally neutral enables us to find out quite definitely whether any two of them are completely interchangeable, and absolute synonymy is by no means infrequent"). But *semantics* and *semasiology*, for example, used as synonyms, are differentiated from the stylistic viewpoint due to the fact that *semasiology* is morphologically related to *onomasiology*. See also Ramón Trujillo, "El lenguaje de la técnica", in *Doce ensayos sobre lenguaje* Madrid, 1974, pp. 197–211.

[46]Cf. L. Söll, "Synonymie und Bedeutungsgleichheit", in *GRM*, 16, 1966, p. 94. On the other hand, relations of inclusion such as *moneme ⊃ morpheme*, to which Lothar Wolf, "Zur Diskussion über Terminologie und Semantik" (in *Übersetzer und Dolmetscher*, edited by Volker Knapp, Heidelberg, 1974, p. 58), refers, do not exclude, naturally, exact definitions.

Latinisms or foreign words, etc.) is all that is needed to activate them; often the symptomatic implications are absolutely necessary to guarantee understanding (*moneme* = Martinet's school, *morpheme* = Bloomfield's school). Frequently scientific terminology occupies a middle-of-the-road position between the general language and unambiguous terminology: *signification* or *meaning*, for example, is a scientific and unambiguous term for each investigator who uses it, once he defines it; its polysemy is only realized on another plane of metalanguage (this also applies to the terms *moneme*, etc.). Only artificial languages (Algol, etc.) contain unambiguous units, in opposition (by definition) to the scientific terminologies which use natural languages.

(i) SYNONYMY AND TRANSLATION

Our basic theory has immediate consequences for the theory of translation. Our results explain both the possibility and the impossibility of translation[47]. Translation is possible due to the

---

[47]I concur with the conclusions of Georges Mounin, *Problèmes théoriques de la traduction*, Paris, (Gallimard), 1963, 297 pp. See also E. A. Nida, *Toward a Science of Translating*: with special reference to principles and procedures involved in Bible translating, Leiden, 1964, x + 331 pp.; Ludwig Söll, "Zur Problematik des Übersetzens", in *Praxis des neusprachlichen Unterrichts*, 1966, pp. 9–16. Concerning the difficulty of translating German adverbs into a Romance language, see (as a concrete example) Mario de Carvalho, "Periphrastische Prädikatsformen mit Modalverben im Portugiesischen als Übersetzung von Adverbien und adverbiellen Bestimmungen bei finiten Verben im Deutschen", in *IRAL* (Julius Groos Verlag, Heidelberg), 5, 1967, pp. 53–70. "Even within the same language one is constantly translating", Karl Löwith, "Die Sprache als Vermittler von Mensch und Welt", in *Beiträge zu Philosophie und Wissenschaft, Wilhelm Szilasi zum 70. Geburtstag*, München (Francke), 1960, pp. 141–60 (p. 152). "By all the accepted theories of linguistics, it should be impossible to translate from one language to another. Fortunately the ordinary translator does not know this, and he goes ahead and translates anyhow" (William G. Moulton, *Romance Philology*, 20, 1967, p. 339). See also Jesús Neira Martínez "La

identical sememes of the units in question (with the reservation, however, that the "target language" must have means of
expression which correspond to the conceptual systems in question[48]). Exact translation is impossible, if by "exact translation"
we mean the equivalent, including all stylistic values. The translator faces the difficult task of finding the equivalent which
gives form to the same sememe and which, in addition, implies
the same stylistic values, something which is only possible to a
relative degree (because of the wealth of different stylistic factors brought together in one moneme). Conclusion: translation
continues to be an art which requires a great *linguistic* and
stylistic sensibility on the part of the translator; but it is an art
which has to be based on a linguistic theory.

My friend Weinrich believes that the context can compen-
sate for the absence of coordination that exists between
words: "Translated words always lie, translated texts only if
they are badly translated" ("Übersetzte Wörter lügen immer,
übersetzte Texte nur, wenn sie schlecht übersetzt sind")[49].

---

traducción: posibilidades y límites" *Archivum* (Oviedo) XXI, 1971,
337–57; Jaime Tur, "Sobre la teoría de la traducción", Bogotá
(Instituto Caro y Cuervo), 1974, 19 pp. (from *Thesaurus* 29, 1974: a
chapter of his book *Maragall; Goethe, Les traduccions del Faust*,
Barcelona, 1974).

[48]One may wonder whether Jakobson is not exaggerating when he
affirms that languages are not distinguished by what they *can* say, but
by what they *must* say.

[49]Harald Weinrich, *Linguistik der Lüge* [Linguistics of the Lie],
1966, pp. 24f.: "What exists first and always is *the word in the text*.
And if there is a primary interpretation of the world by means of the
words of different languages, such an interpretation – if it exists at
all – is always already overcome in the text. We are not slaves of the
words, since we are masters of the texts. Besides, we must emphasize
here that there is no reason to complain about languages, maintain-
ing, for example, that *Gemüt* is a typically German word, or that *business* is a typically Anglo-American word, and are thus untranslatable
into any other language. Such arguments by amateurs are of no value
and are, at the same time, annoying ["ärgerlich"]. Neither are the
words *Feuer* (German), *rue* (French), *car* (English) translatable. No

Although Weinrich finds it annoying (*ärgerlich*), there is only one possible conclusion: exact translation (which tries to take

_____

word is translatable. What we ought to be translating is sentences or whole speeches and texts. It does not matter at all that when one translates from one language to another, the different meanings of the words do not generally correspond. Within a text, what counts, and the only thing that counts, are the thoughts expressed; and these can be suitably adjusted without having to do anything more than suitably adjust the context. As a result, texts (as such) are translatable on principle. Now then, can it still be maintained that translations are lies? It will be best to stick to this rule: translated words always lie, translated texts, only if they are badly translated".

In the same sense, Gert Wotjak, "Zur Wahrung der semantischen Invarianz beim Übersetzen", in *Beiheft VII* of *Fremdsprachen*, Leipzig, 1973, 71–79 says:

"In translation one can arrive at semantic invariance, in spite of the different specific sememes of each language and of their differing association with formatives, since these groups of features are made up of universal elements of a noetic-conceptual character which make possible both reference (*den Referenzbezug*) and the expression of the personal perspective of the organizer of the text (*die Einschätzung des Textorganisators*), of his attitude towards what is communicated as well as of the emotion he wants to arouse, and does arouse, with what he communicates. In general, since it is a question of rendering semantic universals which participate equally in the formation of the sememes and allosemes of the target language, although, granted, with a different selection, ordering and number, we are simultaneously in the presence of the minimal semantic invariants", p. 78; we are in complete agreement, as long as we are dealing with symbolic-functional semes; equivalents for factors of symptoms and signals are at least more difficult to find, and those which are linked to one language are completely "untranslatable" [except that they can be paraphrased by symbolic-conceptual explanations, metaenunciations]. On the problematic nature of translation expressed with modern criteria on the basis of a *tertium comparationis*, cf. also Henry Vernay, "Elemente einer Übersetzungswissenschaft", in *Übersetzer und Dolmetscher*, Theoretische Grundlagen, Ausbildung, Berufspraxis, edited by Volker Knapp, Heidelberg (Quelle und Meyer) 1974, 26–37, especially p. 29.

into account all the stylistic implications) is theoretically impossible. Weinrich's thesis is still valid concerning the possibility
of finding the exact equivalent for the same sememe.

We agree in essence with Mario Wandruszka:

> How are our languages made up? They are instruments made
> of essentials and accidentals. In all languages there are some
> common elements that by general consent are called linguistic
> universals, and are a kind of common denominator of our human
> condition. To this extent, all languages are *translatable*. But each
> language also involves a particular view of the world, different
> mentalities and sensitivities, and to this extent they are *un-
> translatable*[50]. To a large extent they are made up of forms and
> structures that are arbitrary, accidental, conventional; of expedi-
> ents, of adjustments, of compensations, of functional equiva-
> lences, and all this part of the way it is used is translatable. Our
> languages are at once intranslatable and translatable, in-
> comparable and comparable, motivated and arbitrary, essential
> and accidental, necessary and contingent – our languages, these
> instruments that are so imperfect and so admirable ("Esquisse
> d'une critique comparée de quelques langues européennes,"
> *TraLiLi* V[1], 1967, 169–184, quote pp. 183, f.)[51].

The translator, like the speaker in general, can select freely
(from the conceptual viewpoint) among the designations which
realize the same concepts (an onomasiological position), but
when he chooses his moneme or monemes, at the same time
he chooses all those stylistic nuances implied by these monemes (a semasiological position). The hearer can activate these

---

[50]See also Ludwig Söll, "Traduisibilité et intraduisibilité", in *Meta*
(Montréal) 16, 1971, 25–31 (= Actes du Colloque Int. de Linguistique et de traduction, 30 sept.–3 oct. 1970) [The limits of a general
theory of translation "are not concerned with truth or translatability
or languages as systems, but with the language as a creative activity.
No original linguistic formulation can be transferred completely . . ."
30].

[51]See also Mario Wandruszka, *Sprachen – vergleichbar und unver-
gleichbar*, Munich (Piper) 1969, 542 pp.

implications even if the speaker should prefer to neutralize them. The scientific investigator, instead of translating, will often prefer to quote the foreign term, or, in order to avoid these implications, will create a new term (which contains a minimum of associations and stylistic implications). This latter solution, on the other hand, favours the growth of the labyrinth of scientific terminology.

(j) EXTENSIONAL SYNONYMY AND INTENSIONAL SYNONYMY

The conceptual system, as we have established it for "remember", a conceptual system which does not depend 'on the structure of a given language'[53], has been determined *intensionally*, that is, in a way which is not extralinguistic. This type of determination is opposed to *extensional* definitions which, in an ontologically relevant way, involve extralinguistic reality, as is illustrated by our example of *maníes/cacahuetes* and *cortado grande/capuchino chico* (see *d* above). These words are at the same time, and necessarily, intensional and extensional (conceptual) synonyms, since a synonym by intension is also one by extension. On the other hand, the synonym by extension is not always one by intension. Remember the case of *Mount Everest* and *Gaurisankar*, which are extensional synonyms, exclusively extensional, by definition, for those who know the two expressions refer to the same object. Ullmann has quoted Pascal's comment: "il y a des lieux où il faut appeler Paris, *Paris* et d'autres où on l'appellera '*capitale de la France*' " (sometimes one should call Paris *Paris*, other times *the capital of France*) (*Précis*[2] 1959, 196; = *Introducción a la semántica francesa*,

---

[52]See especially W. V. O. Quine, *Word and Object*, 1960, p. 49. My thanks to Heger for having directed my attention to this problem; see also his review in *ZRP*, 81, 1965, pp. 513–16. I use *intensional* in the sense of 'by comprehension', opposed to *extensional* 'by extension'.

[53]Translation of *aussereinzelsprachlich* in German and of *indépendant de la structure d'une langue donnée* in French; see Heger, in *TraLiLi* III[1], p. 19, n. 27.

Madrid, 1965, p. 266). *Paris* and *capitale de la France* are synonyms by extension, only for those who know that they are identical. The *morning star* (Morgenstern) and the *evening star* (Abendstern) are defined as two different objects when one proceeds intensionally; extensionally, however, they are synonyms (Venus). The two procedures for determining the conceptual system (starting from the language, by intension, or from reality, by extension), can arrive at divergent results. In the same way, the problem of conceptual synonymy is presented differently according to the two points of view.

(k) AFFECTIVITY AND VALUE JUDGMENT

We have classified affective values among the factors of symptom or of signal which have their origin in the speaker. One must distinguish between this affectivity and the *value judgments* which form part of the content of the linguistic sign ('representative function' according to Bühler) and, as a result, part of the conceptual system[54]. The realization of the conceptual systems in question (which contain semes of 'evaluation') implies value judgments inherent in the monemes: one needs only to think of words such as French *sot (foolish), heureux (happy), mauvais (bad), bon (good), impertinent, jaloux (jealous)*, etc. The value implied may be moral, material or whatever; the important point is that the value judgment forms part of the symbolic meaning of the monemes or groups of monemes in question. Affectivity which originates in the speaker, on the other hand, is *added* to the symbolic values of the monemes[55]. We must distinguish clearly between:

> *sot (foolish)* which contains a value judgment (as to someone's intellectual faculties) on the symbolic level; and

---

[54]S. Ullmann speaks of a 'permanent affective note' (*Mélanges Delbouille*, 1964, p. 643), but it is better to make a sharp distinction between *affectivity*, on one hand, and *value judgement*, on the other.

[55]"Undoubtedly, the emotive overtones of words are largely dependent on speech-contexts. We have already seen that in most

poire [lit. "pear"; cf. Eng. *bean*], in the sense of "head", which realizes the same conceptual system as the lexeme *tête*, but which adds an affective value which comes at the same time from polysemy (cf. 1) and the personality of the speaker (cf. 2).

The concept 'foolish' is unthinkable without a value judgment; the concept 'head,' as long as it has no seme of 'evaluation', can be realized in French by the moneme *tête*, which contains no value judgment or affectivity. The affectivity which originates in the speaker can be added to the symbolic content in both cases. It can be *implicit* or *explicit*. If it is implicit, the affectivity is evident only from the context. It becomes explicit if we replace the customary moneme (lexeme), the normal word, with a moneme (lexeme) which underlines the affectivity; *sot* is replaced by *cornichon*, 'gherkin', *cruche* 'jug', both sometimes meaning 'foolish'; compare English *half-baked*, Spanish *alcornoque*, literally 'cork tree'; *avaricious* is replaced by *mingy* (see Ullmann, *Semantics*, 1962, 143, etc.), similarly *amarrete* in Argentina and Perú, *coñete* in Chile and Perú for Spanish *avaro*; or if we reinforce it with supplementary monemes (*sot comme un cornichon*, daft as a gherkin (English 'daft as a brush'); Spanish *terco como una mula*, as the English,

---

cases the situation alone can tell us whether a term is used *referentially* or *affectively*, as 'langage-signe' or as 'langage-suggestion' (Paulhan, *Revue Philosophique*, 104, p. 28 e.o.). Even the most prosaic object can suddenly acquire unexpected sentimental overtones . . ." (S. Ullmann, *The Principles of Semantics*. 2nd. ed., Glasgow (Jackson) – Oxford (Blackwell), 1957, p. 99). See also Jürgen Scharnhorst, "Die emotionale Komponente der Wortbedeutung und Methoden zu ihrer Bestimmung", Actes du Xe Congr. Int. des Linguistes (Bucharest 1967), t. III, Bucharest, 1970, pp. 475–478 [for example, Ger. *Fahrrad* "bicycle" (normal word)/ *Drahtesel* (literally) "wire donkey" (affective). The author distinguishes between six variants of emotionality and proposes "tests" for its determination]; Elena Slave, "La hiérarchie des niveaux expressifs de la langue", ib., pp. 365–369, gives a fuller picture.

Table 24

	value judgment (symbolic level)	affectivity (level of symptom and of signal)	
		implicit	explicit
sot	+	−	−
sot (+ context)	+	+	−
archi (sot)	+	−	+
sot comme un cornichon	+	+ sot (comme)	+ un cornichon
cornichon "foolish"	+	−	+
tête	−	−	−
tête (+ context)	−	+	−
poire "head"	−	−	+

stubborn as a mule', etc.; *tête* is replaced by *poire*, etc. Prefixes such as *archi-[sot]* can reinforce value judgment, but at the same time they add an affective element [in *archiphoneme* the prefix has another function; besides, it is a term from the meta-language of linguists][56].) Table 24 can therefore be drawn up.

It will not always be easy to distinguish between the value judgment (a function of the symbol) and effectivity (a function of the symptom and of the signal), but this does not invalidate the theoretical need for the distinction.

(l) CONCLUSIONS

Absolute synonymy (identity of content between two mone-mes) does not exist except on the level of the symbol, of the *Darstellungsfunktion* (the function of representation), *synonyms of sememes* or *synonyms of signifiés*. Synonymy of seme-mes involves differentiation on the level of monemes first: the potential presence of other sememes (that is, the potentialities

---

[56]Concerning *archi–* see, for example, H. Marchand, *The Categories and Types of Present-day English Word-Formation*, Wiesbaden, 1960, pp. 96, ff.

present in the semasiological field, for the lexemes or morphemes) (**1**).. On the level of the form of expression, a formal similarity of a third moneme with one of the two synonyms may intervene, which constitutes a second differentiating factor (**2**). A third differentiating factor arises from the fact that two synonyms evoke (or can evoke) two different families of words (**3**). If there is a combination of monemes (derivation, composition) the synonymy of *signifiés* and of sememes is combined with the phenomenon of *motivation* (*Gehweg*, motivated; *Trottoir*, not motivated in German) on the level of the form of content, which constitutes a fourth differentiating factor (**4**). These four differentiating factors are due to the structure of the linguistic sign itself (polysemy = semasiological field; motivated combination of monemes), to its formal similarity to another sign or to its relationship with the word family to which it belongs: 1, on the level of the substance of content (with symbolic function), 2, on the level of the form of expression, 3, on the level of the form of content. The differentiation continues in the framework of more complex structures, which go beyond the moneme and the lexeme; phonostylistics, syntagmatic factors, context, intonation and rhythm, the level of style, conventional stylistic principles (factors **5–9** previously mentioned without detailed examination).

Along with those differentiating factors which depend on the structure of the linguistic sign and on the more complex structures which we have just mentioned, there are completely different factors which also destroy absolute synonymy: this second group of factors is due to the functions of symptom and of signal (*Symptom-* and *Signalfunktion*, in K. Bühler's terminology, see §f). These two functions depend on the speaker (*Symptom-* or *Ausdrucksfunktion*) who addresses a hearer (*Signal-* or *Appellfunktion*). Since the speaker belongs to one or more social groups (profession, religion, etc.), the linguistic sign may reflect his group membership (**10–19**). Furthermore, the speaker can add his own feelings, his affectivity, which 'appeals' to the hearer (affectivity as a function of symptom or signal, **20–25**), to the communicative value of the language (symbolic function).

Let us return to our original question: Does absolute synonymy exist? Our answer is precise: absolute synonymy does exist, but only on the level of sememes (or on that of the *signifiés*, if, and only if, the *signifié* has only one symbolic sememe and if we ignore its non-symbolic components); in other words: absolute synonymy does not exist except on the level of onomasiological analysis. Two different monemes may realize the same conceptual-symbolic system (there are, therefore, absolute synonyms from the onomasiological viewpoint)[57]. But when I give a form to a concept or a conceptual system, I unite in one linguistic sign a series of stylistic implications of non-linguistic origin (symptom and signal values) and of internal origin (structure of the language), both on the level of the form of expression or of content or on the level of the substance of content, and on the level of any other aspect of the language, including context and intonation; the stylistic level is added like a halo to the conceptual content. The complexity of this 'halo' of stylistic values differentiates and individualizes the synonyms. On the level of linguistic signs, that is, on the semasiological level, absolute synonymy does not exist, neither in the ordinary language nor in scientific terminology, even if in this latter case the emphasis is placed on the absolute synonymy that derives from the conceptual system.

The synonymy of the monemes is shown in Figure 34.

The determination of the conceptual system can be made both intensionally, starting from a non-extralinguistic base, and extensionally, starting from an extralinguistic base; intensional synonymy is at the same time extensional, but the reverse is not always so. In fact, translation is nothing more than a problem of synonymy. It can be exact as regards con-

---

[57]Ch. Bally had already noticed both identity on the conceptual level (absolute synonymy) and the difference due to stylistic-affective values: "It is true that the two adverbs, *très* and *bien*, are conceptually identical" [in *c'est très bon* and *c'est bien beau*], "but they are fundamentally different in their affective value" (quoted in Jaberg, *Sprachwiss. Forschungen und Erlebnisse*, 1965, p. 16).

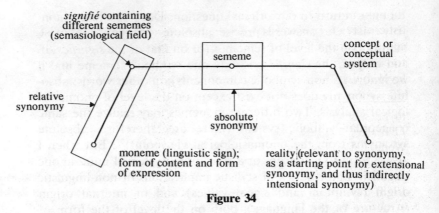

Figure 34

ceptual content, but it will never be completely exact as regards the 'halo' of stylistic implications which surround the content. Translation, as a result, is not a mathematical equation, but a work of art. The good translator will try to find the exact equivalent as regards the conceptual content and a maximum of stylistic equivalences as regards the 'halo'. Language always serves for communication. But this communication may be combined with affective values which originate in the speaker. One must avoid confusion between affectivity and value judgments which have a symbolic function and form part of the conceptual system. *Sot* contains a value judgment; *sot comme un cornichon* contains at the same time a value judgment and an affective element.

I have limited myself to the problem of synonymy with identity of sememe, but it would be necessary to extend the subject and talk about quasi-synonyms (see Ullmann, *Précis*, 1959, p. 193; = *Introducción a la semántica francesa*, Madrid, 1965, p. 262). In practice, it often happens that the speaker, for stylistic reasons, prefers a conceptually neighbouring word, for example *volume* for *book* (which are not synonyms on the conceptual level, since a *book* may have several *volumes*; see Söll, *GRM*, 16, 1966, 98)[58]. In such cases, stylistic selection is

---

[58]It would be necessary to examine the problems of quasi-synonyms more closely (it appears that French *tome* and *volume* have been able

thought more important than the difference in sememes[59]. Stylistic effect is preferred to communicative precision. This procedure (conscious on the stylistic level; unconscious if it is due to confusion or ignorance) is very important on the diachronic level, being one of the sources of change of meaning[60].

---

to be sememe-symbolic synonyms since the sixteenth century; see *FEW* 13^2, 22b and 14, 612a). One of my former students, Lothar Wolf, has discovered in his thesis *Sprachgeographische Untersuchungen zu den Bezeichnungen für Haustiere im Massif Central* (Beiheft zur Zeitschrift für Romanische Philologie 117, Tübingen, 1968) that literary language tends to neutralize the distinctive semes of quasi-synonyms. ("The unmotivated lexical variation shows how much literary linguistic usage exploits the possibility here of neutralising distinctive features. As a result, we can see, within the framework of the literary references quoted, synonyms in the true sense of the word" p. 111). But the phenomenon of *neutralization* – which would deserve a detailed study – also quite frequently occurs in the spoken language: ". . . two words which are not synonymous in the *langue* can become so in speech. If I say to a friend at the dinnertable *pass me the salt* or *pass me the salt-cellar,* he is likely to consider these two messages to be identical. One would have to conclude from this that *salt* and *salt-cellar* are synonyms" (Josette Rey-Debove, "La définition lexicographique, recherches sur l'équation sémique", in *CahLex*, 8, 1966, pp. 71–94; concerning *synonymy*, 86–90, with very sensible observations). Most of the difficulties are solved if we distinguish between symbolic and symptomatic functions. In the case of *salt / salt-cellar* there is neutralization on the symbolic level [as to the *message*], but symptomatic differences remain.

[59]Even the language of advertising makes use of this resource to suggest the superiority of a product: the Larousse firm has distributed a prospectus – *Larousse synonyme de Dictionnaire*!

[60]About this, see also Karl Bühler, *Sprachtheorie*, p. 66 ("Freiheitsgrade der Bedeutungsverteilung") [= *Teoría del lenguaje*, 2nd. ed., p. 93; "the degrees of freedom of meaning-distribution"].

6

Functions of Symbol, Symptom and Signal in the Trapezium

The study of synonymy has shown us the true complexity of the linguistic sign, the multitude of factors which come into play when we speak. Heger's trapezium, already complicated enough, becomes even more so. The trapezium as a working model for onomasiological methodology took into account the symbolic function of language; it was also valuable as a model for semasiological methodology, if we considered no more than communicative symbolic values, the representative function of language (see our diagrams in Part II, Chapter 2). But if we start from the linguistic sign in all its aspects, including the three functions established by Bühler (functions of symbol, symptom and signal); if we start from the linguistic sign as a sign which communicates something (function of symbol), which has its origin in a speaker (function of symptom, or expression) and which is directed to someone (function of signal, appeal to the hearer); then we have to expand the trapezium, by distinguishing between the three functions (for practical reasons we shall not separate the functions of symptom and of signal, which originate in the speaker and in the hearer). At the same time, we must draw a fine line of distinction between concepts that are not dependent on a given language and those concepts that are linked to a particular language (at least in the matter of symbolic sememes; see Figure 34).

Figure 35 represents the following structure: the moneme is the union of a form of expression and a form of content. Semantics analyses the substance of the content on the level of the *signifié* which covers everything which, as content, is joined to a moneme; in the *signifié* are brought together not only several meanings, but also the three functions of symbol, symptom and signal. If we analyse the *signifié*, we arrive at each one of the meanings contained in the one *signifié*. These meanings are

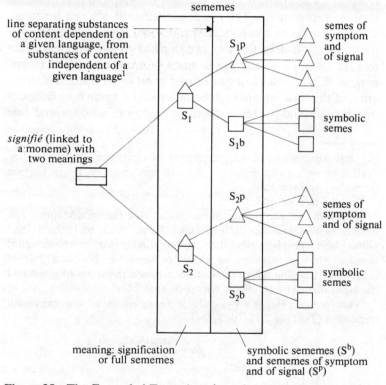

Figure 35 The Expanded Trapezium (top view, hypothetical case)

---

[1]See the next chapter.

sememes which we can call "full", because the functions of symbol, symptom and signal are still together[2]; here ends – at least as far as the symbolic content is concerned – the realm of what is linked to one particular language. The full sememe can be analysed as the combination of a symbolic sememe and a sememe of symptom/signal which is analysed in its turn as the sum of the semes on the right hand side. Symbolic semes (and, therefore, a combination of semes, = conceptual system, = symbolic sememe) do not depend on a given language (Heger)[3]. The character of the semes of symptom and of signal is more problematic. Their independence of a given language seems often to be quite clear (profession, social level, political party, etc., but does this fact not depend on extralinguistic factors?)[4]; in other cases this is much less obvious (French *septante* = "70" [= symbolic sememe] + /a/ [= symptomatic sememe, in this case meaning "characteristic of French in Belgium and Switzerland"][5]. Since there is only one Belgium and one

---

[2]Thus we come to a new definition of *signification (meaning)* = "full sememe", and precision in the relationship between signification (meaning) and sememe.

[3]See the next chapter.

[4]This is the subject matter of *pragmatics*; see Georges Mounin, *Les problèmes théoriques de la traduction*, Paris, 1963, p. 159: "I shall admit here provisionally that connotations, for methodological reasons, are not regarded as a part of semantics but as a part of *pragmatics* (dealing with the relation between the users of signs and the signs themselves)." See Chapter 5, note 21.

[5]This is how Heger's example is represented in the expanded trapezium (*TraLiLi* III[1], 1965, 24):

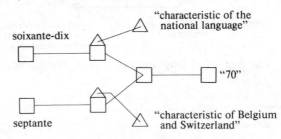

French Switzerland, this is a borderline case (with a possible extensional definition); what does not, in this case, depend on a concrete and unique situation is the seme of 'regionality.' I do not propose to discuss here the nature of symptom and signal sememes; the study of these factors has hardly started.

In previous chapters we have given methodological diagrams illustrating *semasiology* and *onomasiology*, the two most important methods of semantics (Chapters I 3a; 7; 10; II 2; 4). The diagrams keep getting more complicated, thanks to an ever subtler and more detailed analysis. Now, at the end of this section, we have to complicate it yet more, adding the functions

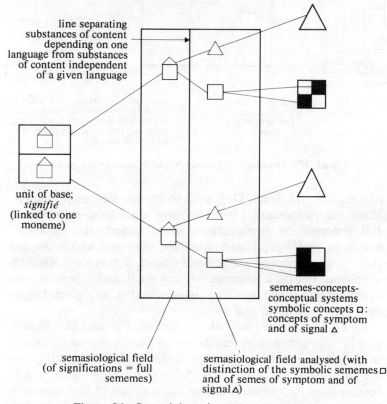

line separating substances of content depending on one language from substances of content independent of a given language

unit of base;
signifié
(linked to one moneme)

sememes-concepts-conceptual systems
symbolic concepts □:
concepts of symptom and of signal △

semasiological field
(of significations = full sememes)

semasiological field analysed (with distinction of the symbolic sememes □ and of semes of symptom and of signal △)

Figure 36   Semasiology (top view, hypothetical case)

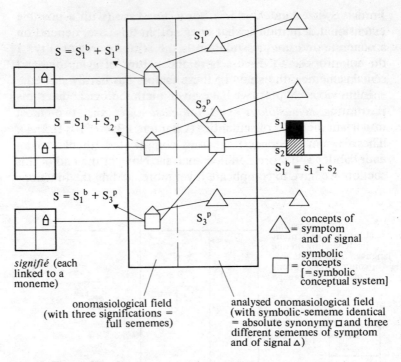

Figure 37   Onomasiology (top view, hypothetical case)

of symptom and signal. Only with this last model can we understand the phenomenon of synonymy, distinguishing between full sememes (= significations which include the values of symbol and signal) and symbolic sememes which do not depend on a given language (and only here there are absolute synonyms; but these sememes are not yet linked to sememes of symptom and signal, nor to a *signifié*, that is, to a given language) (see Figures 36 and 37).

As we come to the end of this section, I should like to emphasize that semantic research, which studies the entire aspect of the content of language, has made revolutionary strides in the last ten or fifteen years. Several methodological roads remain open and promising. The investigation of the structures in this area has only just begun. In conclusion, I recall the last words spoken by John Orr to the Conference at Madrid in 1965. He was afraid that the *geometric spirit*, the realm of the structuralists, would prevail over the *spirit of finesse*, realm of the traditionalists. I have tried to show that language, tool of objective communication and subjective expression, is quite capable of uniting the two aspects: the geometric spirit, which guarantees mutual understanding, and the spirit of finesse, which guarantees stylistic wealth. The problem of synonymy has shown us both aspects. Let us hope that the structuralists and the traditionalists follow this fine example of peaceful coexistence which the very object of their studies offers them.

7

The Present Form of the Trapezium

The trapezoidal model acquired its present form in 1969, in an article by Klaus Heger, "Die Semantik und die Dichotomie von Langue und Parole"[1] (Figure 38).

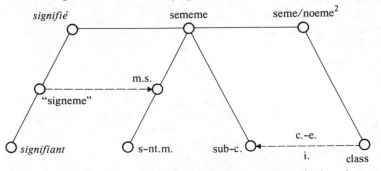

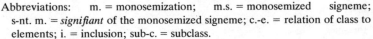

Abbreviations: m. = monosemization; m.s. = monosemized signeme; s-nt. m. = *signifiant* of the monosemized signeme; c.-e. = relation of class to elements; i. = inclusion; sub-c. = subclass.

Figure 38

---

[1]Klaus Heger, "La sémantique et la dichotomie de langue et parole. Nouvelles contributions à la discussion sur les bases théoriques de la sémasiologie et de l'onomasiologie", in *TraLiLi* VII, I, 1969, 47–111. The original German version appeared the same year under the title of "Die Semantik und die Dichotomie von Langue und Parole, Neue Beiträge zur theoretischen Standortbestimmung von Semasiologie

Comparing this model[3] with the one presented in 1965 (see above II, 2, p. 156), we can see that important changes have been

---

und Onomasiologie", in *ZrP* 85, 1969, 114–215. There is a Spanish version, somewhat modified, in Klaus Heger, *Teoría semántica. Hacia una semántica moderna II,* Madrid (Alcalá) 1974, 135–209 (= *TS*). Quotations from Heger in this chapter are based, with occasional modifications, on the Spanish.

[2]In the 1969 model (*TraLiLi* VII, I, 1969, 75) Heger puts only the *noeme* in this place, but in the text (p. 68; 77) he clearly distinguishes between the two notions; in *Monem, Wort und Satz* (Tübingen 1971, 39) and *Monem, Wort, Satz und Text,* (1976, 51) Heger puts both terms in this place: also in the *TS* (p. 168), which contains some of the modifications introduced in *Monem, Wort und Satz*. Heger speaks for the first time of the terms *seme* and *noeme* in *ZrP* 83, 1967, 527 n. 32; he established the definitive difference in *TraLiLi* VII, 1, 1969, 68, 77 and *Monem, Wort und Satz*, 30, ff. (cf. also *TS*, 160, and *Monem, Wort, Satz und Text*, 43).

[3]Růžená Ostrá, *Structure onomasiologique de travail en français,* Etude diachronique d'un champ conceptuel (Opera Universitatis Purkynianae Brunensis Facultas Philosophica, 191), Brno, 1974, p. 112, adopts the trapezium, modifying it:

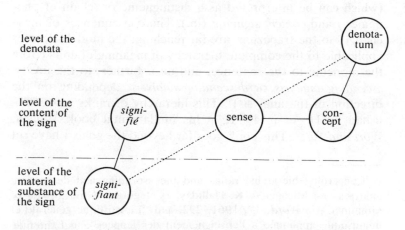

On the intermediate level, in order to be consistent, there should also be included a *level of the substance of the content of the sign*.

introduced:

(1) The term *signifiant* replaces *phonic substance*. "The 'phonic substance' refers to an occurrence on the level of speech rather than the unit of language which is under consideration here, and, in addition, implies an undesirable limitation of 'expression' to oral expression alone" (*TS*, 158; *TraLiLi* 1969, 67).

(2) The term *signeme* replaces *moneme*:

This new term introduced by Heger marks a new important stage in the conception of the trapezium: "it is obvious that the model should be usable not only for the analysis of minimal meaningful units (monemes) but also for the analysis of meaningful units of higher hierarchical ranks" (*TS*, 158; *TraLiLi* 1969, 67). Based on André Martinet's 'double articulation', Heger distinguishes between *meaningful linguemes* (= signemes) and *distinctive linguemes* (= distinguemes). The corresponding minimal units are the *moneme* in the case of the signeme and the *phoneme* in the case of the phonic distingueme (ib.). Signemes, significative units of all ranks, in turn, can be the object of a distinction between *expression-signeme* (which can be interpreted as a distingueme or 'chain of phonemes') and *content-signeme* (ib.). The consequences of these changes in the trapezium are far reaching: the model becomes applicable to the complete hierarchy of meaningful units (from the moneme to the sentence, and even further, to the text = *ascending analysis* or *descending analysis*, depending on the direction of the analysis)[4]. This hierarchy of ranks was established by Heger in 1971, in his fundamental book *Monem, Wort und Satz*[5]. This book goes far beyond the goals I have set

---

[4]Concerning hierarchic ranks and the ascending and descending analyses, see Michael A. K. Halliday, "Categories of the Theory of Grammar", in *Word*, 17, 1961, 292, and "Linguistique générale et linguistique appliquée à l'enseignement des langues", in *Etudes de Linguistique Appliquée*, 1, 1962, 5–42.

[5]Klaus Heger, *Monem, Wort und Satz*, Tübingen (Niemeyer) 1971;

myself here, so I shall be satisfied with simply pointing out the ranks established by Heger:

R 1[6]: *moneme*. The *moneme*, minimal meaningful unit, can be a *lexeme* or a *grammeme*. Lexemes form an open paradigm, grammemes a closed paradigm. Both can be free forms or bound forms, that is, they may or may not figure as autonomous signemes at the immediately higher rank. Both can contain a sememe which is *exclusively* or *non-exclusively reflexive-metalinguistic*[7]: Latin *cant-a-ba-nt*, for example, is composed of

cant- :	lexeme, with a non-exclusively reflexive-metalinguistic sememe,
-a- :	grammeme, with an exclusively reflexive-metalinguistic sememe (*a* indicates that this verbal form belongs to the class of verbs in *-are*),
-ba- : *-n-* *-t-*	grammemes with non-exclusively reflexive-metalinguistic sememes (all three have their own meaning at the object language level: *-ba-* indicates the 'past imperfect of process', *-n-* the 'plurality of the actant designated by the nominative' and *-t-* the 'not-I, non-participant in the act of communication, in this same actant' (*TraLiLi* 1969, 83; *TS* 178; *Monem, Wort, Satz und Text*, 1976, 75 ff.)[8].

The three classifications to which we have just referred are

---

in 1976 the second corrected and enlarged edition appeared under the title of *Monem, Wort, Satz und Text*.

[6]R 1 = unit of the first rank.

[7]This distinction corresponds approximately to the one made by Joe Larochette, "La signification", in *Linguistica Antverpiensia* 1, 127–169, espec. 149, between *meaningful sign* and *mark*; see also Heger, *TraLiLi* 1969, 85 and 88, *Monem, Wort und Satz* 1971, 51; *TS*, 178–179; *Monem, Wort, Satz und Text* 1976, 75.

[8]This exemplification can be completed with the case of *pomme* in *pomme de terre*, which represents a lexeme with an exclusively reflexive–metalinguistic sememe (cf. *TraLiLi* 1969, 87).

Table 25

	free		bound
	with a non-exclusively reflexive-metalinguistic sememe		with an exclusively reflexive-metalinguistic sememe
lexeme	free lexeme *now*	bound lexeme *cant-*	metalinguistic bound lexeme *pomme* (S_2)
grammeme	free grammeme *I*	bound grammeme *-ba-, -n-, -t*	metalinguistic bound grammeme *-a-*

summarized in Table 25[9], in which the six possible cases are marked with the corresponding simplified terms and by examples.

R 2: *Minimal autosemic unit*[10]. For example, Fr. *pomme* has two sememes: one (S_1) non-exclusively reflexive-metalinguistic, when it is to be translated by "apple", and the other (S_2) exclusively reflexive-metalinguistic, when it forms part of the unit of rank higher than R 1 *pomme de terre*, "potato". S_2 is *heterosemic*, that is, the semantic functions are delegated to it by a unit of superior rank only on the base of its rôle as a component of this unit (*ZrP* 83, 1967, 528–530; *TS* 180; *TraLiLi* 1969, 84, f.)[11].

---

[9]*TraLiLi* 1969, 88, (= *ZrP* 85, 1969, 190); *Monem, Wort und Satz* 1971, 57; *TS*, 184; *Monem, Wort, Satz und Text*, 1976, 82.

[10]Concerning the terms *autosemic* and *heterosemic*, see Heger, "Temporale Deixis und Vorgangsquantität ('Aspekt' und 'Aktionsart')", *ZrP* 83, 1967, 512–582, esp. 528–530; there is a summary in Spanish of this article under the title of "Problemas y métodos del análisis onomasiológico del "tiempo" verbal", included in *TS*, 107–134.

[11]The distinction between *autosemy* and *heterosemy* allows resolution of the old problem of the "word"; it explains the fact that both *pomme* and *pomme de terre* can be considered, without there being any contradiction, as "words": both are autosemic, *pomme* (sememe

R 3: *flectional form*, e.g., *cant-a-ba-nt* but also examples like Ger. *er hat's ihr gegeben*, Sp. *se lo ha dado*, Fr. *il le lui a donné*, Engl. *he has given it to her*. The flectional form is the "combination of the minimal autosemic unit with grammemes bound to lexemes". But, at least on the level of the language system, one can also establish a more abstract unit of rank R 3, definable as the "combination of a minimal autosemic unit and the paradigms of grammemes which, in the possible occurrences of this minimal autosemic unit, can be bound to it, – that is, the paradigm of the flectional forms which have the same minimal autosemic unit" (*vocable*), e.g., Latin *cantare* with the entirety of its paradigm (*TraLiLi* 1969, 91; *TS* 187; *Monem, Wort, Satz und Text* 1976, 85 f.). This is why in dictionaries the *infinitive* is regarded as the representative of the whole paradigm[12].

The units of ranks 1 to 3 make up the principal domain of lexicology[13] and of morphology (including the study of prefixes and suffixes). As for higher ranks (the domain of syntax and even of textual analysis) which presuppose a noematic system of actants[14], I shall only refer the reader to Heger's book

---

S_1) on rank 1, *pomme* (sememe S_2) *de terre* on rank 2 (see *TraLiLi* 1969, 85).

[12]Heger proposes calling this unit in the language level *vocable*, while he designates the same unit in the speech level with the term *word*, that is, the occurrence of the flectional form which is at the same time an occurrence of the vocable. In this way, *vocable* and *word* become well-defined terms (which do not entirely correspond to their normal usage). See Part I, Chapter I, n. 4.

[13]Only compounds (compounds of lexemes) belong to a higher level.

[14]Heger's system is, in my opinion, superior to Fillmore's grammar of cases (excellent in its own right) since, thanks to the noematic analysis on the level of the deep structure, it shows all the theoretically possible cases; cf., Charles J. Fillmore, "The Case for Case", in *Universals in Linguistic Theory*, ed. E. Bach and R. Harms, New York 1968, 1–88; "Some Problems for Case Grammar", in *Report of the 22nd Annual Round Table Meeting on Language Studies*, ed. Richard J. O'Brien, S. J., Washington 1971, 35–56.

(*Monem, Wort, Satz und Text* 1976); however, I shall summarize the conclusions (cf. *Monem, Wort, Satz und Text*, 1976, 330 ff.):

Rank (=R) 4	: compositional form
R 5	: proposition
R 6	: specified proposition
R 7	: proposition specified by speech act
R 8	: sentence
R 9	: presuppositional group
R 10	: specified presuppositional group with assertion (the occurrence of which on the level of speech is the *text*)
R 11	: hyper-sentence of the text
etc[15].	

(3) The terms *seme/noeme* replace *concept*: The description of the relations between the *signifié* (Si), the sememe (S), and the component of the sememe (= c, as a non-specified unit of the upper right side of the trapezium) can be made clearer using the logical terms

conjunction (A + B, therefore A and B, therefore, neither A alone, nor B alone, nor neither of the two),

adjunction (A v B, therefore either A alone, or B alone, or both, therefore, not neither of the two) and

disjunction (A / B, therefore, either A alone, or B alone, therefore, not both and not neither of the two):

– the *signifié* can be described as a disjunctive combination of sememes (Si = $S_1/S_2 \ldots S_j$)

– the *signifié* can be described as adjunctive combination of components of sememes (Si = c_1 v c_2 v $\ldots$ v c_k)

---

[15]For higher levels, see also K. Heger, "Signemränge und Textanalyse", in Elisabeth Gülich/Klaus Heger/Wolfgang Raible, *Linguistische Textanalyse – Überlegungen zur Gliederung von Texten*, Hamburg 1974, 1–71; E. Gülich/Walter Raible, *Linguistische Textmodelle* (Uni-Taschenbücher 130), Munich (Fink) 1977 (Heger's theory 136–150).

– the sememe can be described as a conjunctive combination of components of sememes ($S = c_1 + c_2 \ldots + c_1$).

The component of the sememe (c) can be a *seme* or a *noeme*:

The *seme* [a term originating with B. Pottier] is defined as the minimal distinctive unit (of the content substance) with reference to the sememe, which is bound to the structure of a given language, and it, too, consequently depends on this structure (*TraLiLi* 1969, 68; *TS*, 160; and above all *Monem, Wort, Satz und Text* 1976, 42 and 339).

·"*Noeme* = unit of the content substance, a concept intensionally defined, which does not depend on the structure of a given language" (*TraLiLi* 1969, 111; *TS*, 209; *Monem, Wort, Satz und Text* 1976, 338). *Noemes* are defined by the place each one of them occupies in a logical system of relations ruled by axiomatic premises (*TS* 16; *TraLiLi* III, 1, 1965, 19, where one only need replace *concept* by *noeme*): "species are defined by *genus proximum* and *differentia specifica*; a *genus* is divided in an exhaustive manner into two *species* by the introduction of a *differentia specifica* and its negation, which thus form a binary opposition" (ib.).

The distinction between *seme* and *noeme* helps avoid misunderstanding. *Seme* corresponds to an internal analysis of a given language; *noeme* corresponds to a comparative analysis, whether of two different languages or of two different stages of the same language. "It is true that 'independent of the structure of a given language' and 'minimal-distinctive' do not reciprocally exclude each other and that, consequently, their intersection is not necessarily an empty class – there can be noemes, then, which are at the same time semes, and vice versa – but it was ill advised to identify the two" (*TraLiLi* 1969, 68; *TS*, 160; *Monem, Wort, Satz und Text* 1976, 47).

The distinction between *seme* and *noeme*, for example, allows us to differentiate between *polysemy* and *homonymy* (on the synchronic level). What is common to *homonymy* and *polysemy* (what Heger calls sememic disjunction), appears when a *signifié* is analysed as a disjunctive combination of two or more sememes. This sememic disjunction is called *homonomy* when two sememes have no common seme[16], that is, when it is true for all possible pairs formed by sememes S_i to S_n that their intersection $S_i \cap S_k = 0$ semes; on the other hand, it is called *polysemy* when the sememes of one *signifié* have at least one seme in common, that is, when it is true for all possible pairs formed by them that their intersection $S_i \cap S_k \geqslant 1$ seme. These two definitions, however, only account for extreme and unambiguous cases; "Along with these there are hybrid cases such as those illustrated by J. Larochette [17] with the example of French *chou* and its sememes S_1 ("cabbage"), S_2 (a kind of "cake") and S_3 ("darling"). Here $S_1 \cap S_2 \geqslant 1$ seme (s_i = round) and $S_2 \cap S_3 \geqslant 1$ seme (s_k = sweet), but $S_1 \cap S_3 = 0$ semes. Such a case can be described without ambiguity by saying that there exist relationships of polysemy between the sememes "cabbage" and "cake", and between the sememes "cake" and "darling", and that there exists a relationship of homonymy between the sememes "cabbage" and "darling". Even so, this description leaves open the question (which is all-important in lexicography) of whether the signeme *chou* should be classified as a polysemic or a homonymic signeme. Unless a third category is introduced by the side of polysemy and homonymy, this problem cannot be resolved except by a decision which is essentially arbitrary. The decision best suited to practical needs is the one taken by Larochette, who classi-

---

[16]Except for sememes S_Σ which contain all the semes of two or more sememes which are normally different (which occurs in plays on words, e.g., *une langue bien cuite et mal parlée; a well cooked and poorly spoken tongue*), cf. *TraLiLi* 1969, 73, ff., *TS*, 66, ff., *Monem, Wort und Satz*, 1971, 37 ff., *Monem, Wort, Satz und Text* 1976, 53 ff.

[17]Joe Larochette, "La signification", in *Linguistica Antverpiensia* 1, 1967, § 7; Joe Larochette himself, "A propos du livre de Klaus Heger «Monem, Wort und Satz»", *Linguistica Antverpiensia* 6, 1972, 155–179; esp. 167 ff., points out that in fact in the case of *chou* it is not a question of *semes*, since these "components of the sememe" establish no opposition between a cabbage and an identical vegetable that is not round, so another example is needed.

fied these hybrid cases as cases of polysemy; and because of these cases the definition of polysemy has to be made more general, in that it is said to be polysemy when each sememe of a *signifié* is linked to at least one of the other sememes through a common seme – that is, by the relationship $S_i \cap S_k \geqslant I$ seme – and when this kind of linking establishes indirect links between all the semes in question" (*TS* 171–2; *TraLiLi* 1969, 77 ff; cp. also *Monem, Wort und Satz* 1971, 42 ff; *Monem, Wort, Satz und Text* 1976, 61 ff, using Spanish *lengua*).

(4) *Class* replaces *thing* or *reality*. At the language level, on the right hand side of the trapezium, the intensionally defined units *semes* or *noemes* are opposed to the extensionally de-fined *class of things* or *class of classes* of things[18] as non-linguistic "referent". I repeat that concepts defined by exten-sion have no ontological implication concerning, for instance, the distinction between "real" and "fictitious" referents. Uni-corns can appear as a class of things with as much right to be there as horses. (Cf. *TraLiLi* 1969, 64; *Monem, Wort und Satz* 1971, 25; *Monem, Wort Satz und Text* 1976, 35).

(5) *Insertion of the triangle inside the trapezium*:
The signeme with its *signifié* (normally complex, i.e., with several sememes) is *monosemized* (although not so elegant, a more exact term would be *monosememized*!) by the context (reduction of polysemy, necessary for the mutual comprehen-sion between speaker and hearer); in other words, the signeme is monosemized when it is integrated into units of a higher rank. In this case, the *signifié* of the monosemized signeme is reduced to one only of its sememes, while keeping the same *signifiant* and the same form of expression (*signifiant of the monosemized signeme*).

---

[18]See now in this regard the excellent thesis by Hartmut Kubczak, *Das Verhältnis von Intension und Extension als Sprachwissenschaft-liches Problem*, Tübingen 1975. Based on this work Heger has modi-fied in the second edition of *Monem, Wort und Satz* § 2.3.1.3. (pp. 32 ff.) of the 1971 edition [1976, 47 ff.].

If the model is applied on the first meta-level it will normally – and especially in the case of semasiological analysis – be adequate to read the upper part of the trapezium as representing the relationship of one signifié to n sememes (with $n \geq 1$) and p semes or q noemes (with $q \geq p \geq n$). This reading of the upper part allows for two different interpretations of the lower right corner: according to the first one of them, this corner of the trapezium would stand for the intersection of the n classes which correspond to the n sememes of the signifié and thus would only result in a superfluous duplication of the class which corresponds to the most comprehensive S_Σ-sememe. Of much higher interest for application of the above mentioned kind, therefore, is the second interpretation according to which the lower right corner of the trapezium is regarded not as the intersection, but as the union of the n classes corresponding to the n sememes. If, in the case of monosemization, the signifié is reduced to one of its sememes, which are in disjunctive combination with each other, this will mean that automatically that union of n classes, too, is reduced to that one of its possible sub-classes that corresponds to the remaining sememe[19].

If, on the other hand, the model is applied on the second meta-level it will often be useful to consider the respective units as such, i.e. without any reference to, among other things, their possible quantifications. Here – just as in the case of applying the model on the first meta-level for certain onomasiological problems –, it will be more adequate to read the upper part of the trapezium in the sense of the series "1 signifié – 1 sememe – 1 seme/noeme". As for the class appearing at the lower right corner of the trapezium, this interpretation means that the smaller number of defining features in the intensional definition of the noeme or the seme, as compared with the definition of the sememe, necessarily implies a greater extension of the class corresponding to the noeme or the seme, given that a less wide intension entails a more general concept and hence wider extension. Since, furthermore, the sememe has been defined as a conjunctive combination of those noemes/semes for which the one

---

[19]It is in this sense that we have made use of the trapezium in our analysis of *se souvenir*, etc. (cf. above, II 3). To distinguish this interpretation from the other possible one, we have called it a "top view".

noeme/seme of this reading stands as a representative, the more extensive class corresponding to this noeme/seme necessarily includes as a sub-class the class corresponding to the sememe.

The extended trapezium model, just as its predecessors, refers to the level of langue and allows for being used there for paradigmatic as well as for syntagmatic analyses of signemes. Thus it contrasts on the one hand with the simple trapezium model (II. 2) which is applicable only to paradigmatic analyses of signemes of one given rank, and on the other hand with other variants which could be reduced from it in order to represent what might be taken as the corresponding semantic relations on the levels of parole and Σ-parole (*Monem, Wort, Satz und Text* 1976, 58–59; translation revised by Klaus Heger):

Between *langue* (language) and *parole* (speech) Heger has introduced a third level, that of the Σ-speech (sigma-speech), based on the opposition of type and occurrence (token). We here can only mention this opposition and refer to Heger (*TraLiLi* VII, 1, 1969, 65 and 76; *TS*, 147 and 170; *Monem, Wort und Satz* 1971, 16 ff and 41; *Monem, Wort, Satz und Text* 1976, 35 ff and 60)[20]. On the level of Σ-speech, we need only use the reduced form of the trapezium in Figure 39.

The fundamental work by Heger, *Monem, Wort und Satz* of 1971, and its revised and enlarged edition of 1976 *Monem, Wort, Satz und Text*, begins with the trapezoidal model constructed in 1964[21], which was originally conceived for the mini-

---

[20]In *Monem, Wort, Satz und Text*, 16 ff., Heger takes into account different degrees of abstraction, taking as a basis the work of H. H. Lieb, *Sprachstudium und Sprachsystem*, Stuttgart 1970 (see the review by Heger in *ZrP* 87, 1971, 550–560).

[21]Gerold Hilty's trapezoidal model (for the first time in *RF* 75, 1963, 148 ff.) is different in fundamental respects from Heger's. For Heger, Hilty's trapezium was no more than a "geometric suggestion". The two models have as much in common as a sack of cement and a sack of nuts. Among other things, Hilty also rejects the distinction between seme and noeme, since, according to him, there is "no essential difference" between the two (*Vox Romanica* 31, 51 n. 23), which is not so, if only because every seme can become a noeme, if it is incorporated into a logically coherent system, but not every noeme

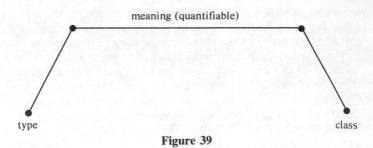

Figure 39

mal meanginful unit, the moneme (now represented by the three lower ranks of the hierarchy). But this model subsequently has grown considerably (1969). The replacement of the moneme with any meaningful unit entails the transformation of the trapezium from a lexicological‚model into a general linguistic model, which implies a definition of all the meaningful units which might be established in the framework of a hierarchy of the different possible ranks.

The trapezium, combined with an actantial model (of which we have not spoken because we have limited ourselves to the lexicologically interesting first three ranks) thus constitutes a solid basis for a semantics of all the ranks, and supplies the noematic background for lexicology, morphology, word-formation, syntax and text linguistics. Against this background may be mapped the surface structures of individual languages. It is these structures which serve as a basis for semasiological investigations, with the orientation of signeme-*signifié*-sememes-semes. The results which are attained in these investigations, however, can only be compared with the results of other investigations of immanent structures of geographically and/or chronologically different languages if one makes use of a *noematic* system, – that is, independent of the immanent

---

can become a seme. – Cf. G. Hilty, "Bedeutung als Semstruktur?", *Vox Romanica* 30, 1971, 242–263, see also H. M. Gauger, "Bedeutung als Semstruktur?" *VR* 31, 1972, 24–39; G. Hilty, "Und dennoch: Bedeutung als Semstruktur", ib. 40–54. In reality, our semantics is much further from Gauger's than it is from Hilty's.

structures of the individual languages – which allows the comparison in its function as tertium comparationis[22]. The *semasiological* and *onomasiological* approaches complement each other just as speaker and hearer: they ask and answer different questions. The substitution of the *moneme* by the *signeme* in the trapezium is the ultimate consequence of having recognized that semasiology and onomasiology are methods which have validity for all the ranks, and that onomasiology has advanced since its origin long ago, linked to the investigation of «Wörter und Sachen», words and things.

---

[21]I should also refer here to the work of Henry Vernay (of Heger's school): "Un système logique comme cadre d'une étude comparative de deux structures", in *La Linguistique* 1 (Presses Universitaires de France), 1967, 39–62 [I. La "deixis" des personnes, II. Le système des concepts temporels et aspectuels chez Heger]; "Die Bedeutung der Semantik für eine Übersetzungstheorie", in *Ruperto–Carola* (Universität Heidelberg) XX. Jahrgang (Band 43/44), Heidelberg, 1968, 152–163; "Sémantique, structure conceptuelle et traduction", in *Linguistica Antverpiensia* 2, 1968, 429–457 [on the trapezium and on Bühler's model in relation to the problems of translation]; "Zur semantischen Struktur des Verbalknotens und des Nominalknotens", in *Sprachwissenschaft und Übersetzen*, Symposium an der Universität Heidelberg 24.2.–26.2.1969 (Commentationes Societatis Linguisticae Europaeae, III), Munich (Hueber) 1970, 93–103; "Zur sprachlichen Realisierung lokaler Begriffskategorien", in *Interlinguistica* (Festschrift Wandruszka) 1971 (Niemeyer), 326–339 [the noematic theory from which Vernay starts in his thesis *Essai sur l'organisation de l'espace par divers systèmes linguistiques*, Munich (Fink) 1974, 214 pp.]. Very near Heger's semantic model and mine is Gerd Wotjak, *Untersuchungen zur Struktur der Bedeutung*, Berlin (Akademie-Verlag), 1971, 343 pp. (see especially pp. 34 ff., and pp. 38 ff., on G. F. Meier's noematics); "Zur Wahrung der semantischen Invarianz beim Übersetzen", in *Beiheft* VIII of *Fremdsprachen*, Leipzig, 1973, 71–79.

Appendix

SEMASIOLOGY AND ONOMASIOLOGY IN DIACHRONY (THE CONCEPT "WORK" AND ITS REPRESENTATIONS IN FRENCH AND PROVENÇAL)*

*Translation of the article, "Sémasiologie et onomasiologie", in *Revue de linguistique romane*, 28, 1964, pp. 249–72.

1

Outline of its Historical Development

The evolution of linguistics from the nineteenth century to the twentieth – leaving aside numerous other new aspects – is characterized by two essential tendencies: the focus has shifted from the *sound* to the *word* (from historical phonetics to historical lexicology) and, at the same time, the way of approaching problems, atomistic at first – unidimensional – has become structural, that is, bi- and tridimensional. Linguistic atlases have contributed a great deal to this development. Even the linguistic atlas of Gilliéron began with the *sound* and ended, almost against the author's wishes, in lexical studies, in the founding of linguistic geography. The new etymology of the French word *aune* ("alder") proposed in 1908 by Jakob Jud, caused a sensation. The etymology of Latin ALNUS> French *aune*, indisputable from the phonetic viewpoint, was no longer valid, although the new etymology presented some important difficulties from precisely the phonetic angle[1]. This meant the triumph of the new school (that of linguistic geography) over the old (that of phonetic laws). While Gilliéron was publishing in Paris his first works on linguistic geography in 1905, at the

---

[1]Cf. Th. Frings, "Erle und Aune", in *Etymologica* (*Festschrift Wartburg*), Tübingen, 1958, pp. 238–59, and lately L. Remacle, "Remarques sur l'étymologie du fr. aune", *RLiR* 36, 1972, pp. 305–310.

University of Geneva de Saussure was giving theoretical courses of considerable importance. As against the previous way of approaching problems, until then linear and historical, he proposed a synchronic study of language viewed as a system of expression, as a structure[2]. From de Saussure on, we distinguish synchronic linguistics and diachronic linguistics.

Let us remember:

1. From the nineteenth century to the twentieth, the centre of study has changed from the *sound* to the *word*; phonetics, nevertheless, has, fortunately, continued to exist, and has split into two parts, phonetics and phonology.

2. Change to a *structural vision* of linguistic phenomena.

The basis and development of these two methods in about 1900 and a little later reflect the primacy of the *word* over the *sound*. Both methods – Semasiology[3] and Onomasiology – are at the disposal of historical lexicology, but are, at the same time, influenced by the second tendency, the primacy of *structure*. Semasiology, it is true, considers the isolated word and the way its meanings are manifested, while Onomasiology looks at the designations of a particular concept, that is, at a multiplicity of expressions which form a whole. From the outset, then, Onomasiology implies concern with structural ordering. Dornseiff puts it precisely: "Onomasiology and Semasiology have the same relation to one another as that between a dictionary arranged according to themes and an alphabetical dictionary". And the same author adds: "Both are necessary . . ."[4], but his whole introduction is a polemic against an alphabetical dictionary, in which "the child is placed between the cheese and the coal" (in German, *Kind* between *Käse* and

---

[2]"The great originality and the great revolution of Saussurian linguistics has been to show that language is a structure" (Pierre Guiraud, *La sémantique*, Paris, 1955, p. 68).

[3]We distinguish between *Semasiology* "science of significations" and *Semantics* "science of the content of language" (a much broader sense which includes Semasiology as well as Onomasiology).

[4]Franz Dornseiff, *Der deutsche Wortschatz nach Sachgruppen*, 2nd ed., 1940, Introduction, p. 25.

Kohle). In fact, systematic opposition to the alphabetical dictionary began during the third decade of the twentieth century, in the belief that it distorted the organic system of the vocabulary. Similar severe criticism has been directed against Semasiology. One may observe how Dornseiff classifies as "a modest compilation" the *Essai de Sémantique*, by Bréal (Paris, 1899), which set the pattern (Dornseiff, ib. 17). Those who have "considered it to be one of the monuments of French science", continues Dornseiff, "have only done so through ignorance or through chauvinism" (terms which he repeats in the revised edition of 1957).

In 1919, Vossler contrasts Semasiology with Onomasiology, which latter he considers to represent one of the greatest advances in linguistics[5]; later, in 1927, Leo Weisgerber goes even further in his "Semasiology, a wrong way for linguistics?" (the title of an article which constitutes a whole programme)[6]. We read there: "Thus, Semasiology cannot help us to arrive at the sense of the linguistic form, or to understand change, transformation, and evolution of the linguistic content; on the contrary, Semasiology, which boasts of being a scientific discipline, is more of an obstacle. In effect, Semasiology is a mistake, the last sprout of antiquated linguistic conception. In short, it lacks the requisites of a science". Again, Dornseiff, in 1934, maintained:

> With Semasiology, linguistics is still tied to medieval Aristotelian verbalism. From the Renaissance on, the modern turn of the Natural Sciences toward reality, the liberation from academic Peripatetic ideas and entelechies toward the causal and geneticobiological investigation of reality, considered as far as possible without presuppositions, all this up to now has been able

---

[5]Karl Vossler, "Französische Philologie", in *Wissenschaftliche Forschungsberichte*, 1, Gotha, 1919, p. 43; Dornseiff's complete quote, *loc. cit.*, p. 20.

[6]Leo Weisgerber, "Die Bedeutungslehre – Ein Irrweg der Sprachwissenschaft?", in *Germanisch–romanische Monatsschrift* (= *GRM*) 15, 1927, pp. 161–83.

to produce fewer changes in the study of language than in any
other science. Apparently, as far as linguistics is concerned,
Bacon lived in vain . . ." (*loc. cit.*, p. 20).

In spite of this and many other attacks, *Semasiology* has not
died; far from it!

Onomasiology asserted itself more easily: in an excellent
exposition Bruno Quadri has given documentary evidence of
its development[7]. In his already cited work, Leo Weisgerber
turns continually not only against Semasiology, but also against
Onomasiology, and this in defence of a *science of concepts*[8].
According to him, Onomasiology tries to link the object and
the name directly, thus omitting the linguistic content or concept (*GRM* 15, 178). Two students of Weisgerber and of Trier,
Gipper and Schwarz, have published the first fascicules of a
manual of the Weisgerber school, *Bibliographical Manual of
the Investigation of Linguistic Content*[9]. The preface of the first
fascicule takes up a position against both Semasiology and
Onomasiology: "This end [the investigation of the content of
language] is accessible neither by means of traditional Semasiology (theory of significations) nor through Onomasiology
(theory of designations) . . . neither really gets at the problem
of the content of the language". Moreover, the two authors
deliver an unmannerly attack on my little 1957 résumé on
Semasiology, while *advising the reader to consult it for its
bibliographical references!*[10]

---

[7]Bruno Quadri, "Aufgaben und Methoden der onomasiologischen
Forschung. Eine entwicklungsgeschichtliche Darstellung", Bern, 1952
(*Romanica Helvetica*, vol. 37).

[8]See Quadri, *loc. cit.,* pp. 159, ff.

[9]Helmut Gipper und Hans Schwarz, *Bibliographisches Handbuch
zur Sprachinhaltsforschung.* Teil I. Schrifttum zur Sprachinhaltsforschung in alphabetischer Folge nach Verfassern mit Besprechungen
und Inhaltshinweisen, Band I: Buchstabe A–K, Köln and Opladen
(Westdeutscher Verlag), 1962–1972, ccvii + 1902 pp.

[10]Original title of the German, *Die Semasiologie. Versuch eines
Überblicks* (= Vorträge und Schrifttum der Deutschen Akademie

I should add that in about 1930 Trier established his *theory of the field*[11], which provided fruitful results, but also mis-understandings. In 1957, in Strasbourg, Wandruszka called the *theory of the field* a "brilliant failure".

This rapid and very succinct sketch of the principal phases of this evolution shows that there are controversial positions on both sides, and it seems to me that the moment has come to reflect on the essence and the ends of semasiological and onomasiological methods. It is not the theoretical consider-ations which seem decisive to me, but rather the linguistic facts. It is, then, towards them that we must turn. Let us choose as our starting-point a concrete example used by Dornseiff him-self against Semasiology. To quote him:

> Greek πόνος, Latin *labor*, Old High German *arebeit*, for example, mean first "toil, drudgery, exertion, suffering", later "an effort directed toward a specific end". The semanticist will discover an improved evaluation in the meaning, and if he can he will conclude that there has been ethical progress of this sort: "Ha! He who once merely suffered has been transformed into a worker" (Dornseiff refers to Lazarus Geiger, *Ursprung und Entwicklung der menschlichen Sprache und Vernunft*, II, Stutt-gart, 1872, pp. 191, ff.). This conclusion suggests that good men also improve the words. But in reality, men use words when they want to express an idea, and under these circumstances they have to use existing words. When men wanted to express, make some-one understand, for the first time, that a conscious activity fatigued them, they had to resort to one of the normal desig-nations for suffering. The notion 'suffering, with index' (meaning

---

der Wissenschaften zu Berlin, Heft 61), Berlin (Akademie-Verlag), 1957; there is a Spanish translation by Graciela García Montaño de Gardella: *La Semasiología. Ensayo de un cuadro de conjunto* (= Instituto de Filología Moderna, Cuaderno 1), Rosario (Uni-versidad Nacional del Litoral, Facultad de Filosofía y Letras), 1964, 55 pp. In fact there are not so many fundamental differences between my own views and those of the Weisgerber school. I think it is rather a case of misunderstanding.

[11]See Quadri, *loc. cit.*, pp. 149, ff.

'work') was understood and prevailed. But this creative act shows man to be at a rather low level of the ethics of work. Anyone who studies the means of designation finds out that everywhere man has first experienced work as suffering" (*Der deutsche Wortschatz nach Sachgruppen*, 2nd. ed., Introduction, p. 19).

Dornseiff accuses Semasiology of drawing conclusions that should be drawn by Onomasiology. On the other hand, we must say that the reverse is also true; Onomasiology is not capable of finding more satisfactory solutions to the problems of Semasiology. In order to study both methods, we take Dornseiff's own example: the words *trebalh, trebalhar* in Old Provençal (semasiological field) and the designations of the concept "work" (onomasiological field).

2

The Field of Significations (Semasiological Field)

Old Provençal *trebalh, trebalhar*.

First of all, let us consider the area of semasiology, and tackle an explanation of the Old Provençal noun *trebalh* and verb *trebalhar*, "work". A glance at the two fundamental works by Raynouard and Levy is sufficient to show that we are confronted with a *multiplicity* of meanings; and a more thorough study reveals that these different meanings are not entirely unrelated. They are clustered around a *nucleus of meanings*: "suffering, torment". The conclusion quickly emerges that this is a matter of a semasiological structure, a field of significations. Levy, in fact, lists some thirty references for *trebalh*, classifying them under 14 different definitions:

The meanings of Old Prov. *trebalh* (as in Levy's list)

1. "anguish, torture". Levy cites just one context, and he gives this meaning with a question mark. Jeanroy translates (correctly, in our opinion) "souci", that is, "anxiety, worry"; it thus comes under meaning 3.
2. "torment, misery, fatigue": «auem establit per lo profiit dous todz e per esquiuar grans *tribailhs* e *mortz* e *dampnadges*, que . . .» (Bayonne, 1275): "to avoid great misery, death and damage, we have established that . . ." Very frequently attested.
3. "destitution, grief, worry, displeasure" (a semantic weakening of meaning 2, and difficult to separate from it): «chens auer

regoart . . . aus *tribailhs* et *vexations* que lodit supplicant donne a le ciutat» (Bayonne, 1518): "without considering the displeasure and the bother said plaintiff causes the city". Frequently attested.

4. "labour pains": «Verges humils, aysi cum sens *tribalh* vos enfantetz» (Joyas): "Humble virgen, just as you gave birth without pain . . ." Similarly, the verb *trebalhar*: «A femna quant *trebalha* de enfan que no pot enfantar . . .» (formula for a difficult childbirth, in a treatise on medicine from about 1441). Also attested in Old Fr.

5. *trebal de la mar* "seasickness": «La dona es greujada per lo *trebal de la mar*»: "The lady is afflicted with seasickness". The only reference. Levy believes it could also be a case of meaning 9.

6. "fighting, combat, struggle". «Recomensa la *guerra* el *trebalhs* el *chapliers*» (Toulouse, thirteenth century): "The war, the *fighting*, the slaughter began again". Frequently attested.

7. "lawsuit, litigation": «cum *contente* e *tribalh* fosse enter na R. bescomps et l'affar d'Orte de une part, et los ciutadantz et lo commun d'Ax de l'autre» (Dax, around 1480): "since there have arisen disputes and litigation between . . ." Frequent in legal documents.

8. "quarrel, disturbance, tumult": «avian contrast plenier li frayre de Lerins denfra lo monestier, car volian elegir lur aministrador, e menavan antr'ellz e *trebayll* e *cridor*» (documented from about 1300): "the monks of Lérins had a great quarrel in the monastery, because they wanted to elect their administrator, and there was a great disturbance and outcry among them". Only one reference.

9. "agitation (of the sea)" «La mar, que esson luoc esta fera, e tal *trebalh* fa e tal guerra . . .»; "The sea, which is generally rough in this place, is so agitated and so turbulent . . ." (Literally; "makes such a noise of *battle* and such a war . . .") Only one reference.

10. "racket, clamour (of birds)": «non aug d'auzelhs lo *trebalh*» (B. de Venzac.): "I do not hear the racket (clamour) of the birds". Only one reference. Metaphor of meaning 6.

11. "work": «Tot medge . . . prenen son salari . . . segon son *tribailh*» (Bayonne, 1336): "Each doctor receives his pay according to his work" (that is, "according to the trouble he has taken", "the effort he has made on his part"). Levy's definition does not express the affective element.

12. "trouble, bother": «per lo *trebalh*, so que vos playra» (B. Alpes 1420): "for your concern (bother), whatever seems right to you (as compensation)". Weakening of meaning 11.

13. "payment for one's bother": «desduth lo *trebalh* del governador» (Rodez, 1392): "(having) deducted the payment due to the governor".

14. "salary" (?): «Los deutors agen terme entro a Sent-Johan, exceptat de logueys de hostaus, de *tribalh*, de cens e rendas» (Bordeaux, 1409): "the debtors receive a postponement to St. John's Day, except for rents, salaries, royal tributes and taxes". The meaning given by Levy is confirmed by the frequent combination *salari et trebalh*. Between 13 and 14 there is only a gradual distinction.

In passing, it must be said that the ordering of significations as given by Levy requires some modification. The establishment of semasiological fields is the principal task of every alphabetical and synchronic lexicon. This is basically a truism, which, like so many truisms, is often forgotten, at least as regards its consequences. For many years, we have been systematically gathering all the examples of Old Gascon *trebalh*, *trebalhar*, for our dictionary of Old Gascon, now under preparation. We have already gathered more than 1500 references (including the regional French), which, in general, confirms the order of the meanings established by Levy on the basis of some thirty references; but since our material is infinitely wider, it allows us to distinguish in addition those applications or meanings which are normal from those which are only sporadically attested, and which are due, in part, to stylistic factors in the source. Only the context allows us to select one from these 14 meanings; the context then, plays a decisive rôle.

The dictionary can replace a context with a *definition*. But – and I should like to insist on this point – introducing the context is not always enough when we are dealing with a historical text, because our modern sense of the language tends to interfere with our interpretation of the historical texts. This is the reason we are tempted, in the following phrase taken from the *Etablissements de Bayona* (1336), to translate *tribailh* simply as "work":

> *Tot medge . . . prenen son salari . . ., segon son tribailh.* "Every
> doctor receives his salary according to his work".

We do not doubt for a moment that Levy should have included this reference under number 11, "work". Of course, it
actually does mean "work", but with this additional element *x*
which comes neither from the context nor from Levy's definition. And we only recognize this *x* element if we examine all
the references given under definition number 11 of "work", in
relation with the total structure of the semasiological field of
Old Prov. *trebalh*, and above all in relation to the semasiological centre "suffering, torment". Only the knowledge of the
semantic structure makes us immediately aware of a complementary affective element. We should not, then, translate this
by the word "work", taken in its modern objective sense, but,
for example, as Modern French:

> "Tout médecin reçoit son salaire selon sa *peine*".
> "Each doctor receives his pay according to his *toil* (effort, exer-
> tion)".

In fact, Fr. *peine*, Old Prov. *pena*, is often found with *travail*
in Middle Fr., and the combination *pena et trebalh* is cited so
often in Old Prov. that one may call it a stereotyped expression[12].

This example shows us two things. First, that knowledge of
the structure of the semasiological field is very important for
the interpretation of every context. Only in this way can we
unmask "false friends", that is, words that are familiar to us

---

[12]See my article "Vom Affektwort zum Normalwort. Das
Bedeutungsfeld von agask. *trebalh* 'Plage; Arbeit' ", in *Etymologica.
Walther von Wartburg zum 70. Geburtstag*, Tübingen, 1958, pp.
59–93.

today and which we accept gladly when we find them in a historical context, but which we interpret incorrectly because, so
to speak, their "spirit" has changed in the course of time.

Secondly, this example directs our attention to the problem
of words combined in the same context. I have deliberately
preferred "combined" references to illustrate Levy's 14 meanings. The words combined with *trebalh* are not synonyms, it is
true – there are no synonyms, in the strict sense of the word –
but they relate the word that interests us to a particular semantic field.

Let us take, for example, meaning 6 "combat, struggle":

> *Recomensa la guerra el trabalhs el chapliers* (thirteenth century,
> Toulouse, Crois, 8, 386).

Trebalh is flanked by *guerra* "war" and *chapliers* "slaughter,
massacre". An examination of this evidence, furthermore,
brings us to another problem: the specific meaning is given to
us by the use of the word with the meaning "suffering, torment", in a specific situation; in other words, "suffering, torment" becomes in warlike environments "struggle, combat"
(definition 6). The use of the same word with the same nucleus
of meaning of "suffering, torment", in a completely different
specific situation, gives the meaning "labour pains" (definition
4). The general signification or base, then, becomes limited or
restricted by the use of the word in a very precise situation.
The use of the word in a precise situation produces a new
meaning which requires a new definition in the dictionary.
This delimitation of the meaning which is due to the use of the
word in a particular situation corresponds to the well-known
fact of the restriction of the meaning when a word passes from
the ordinary language to a professional language or a special
terminology. We see here at very close range how language
works. If we use a word in a particular situation (which is very
frequent), for this very reason the word acquires a nuance
which is derived from the situation. Is it, at this point, a stylistic nuance, or a new meaning? There is, in practice no precise
border between stylistics and semantics. The difference be-

tween a stylistic nuance and a new meaning is a matter of degree and not of principle[13].

If there is still much to be said about the semasiological structure of a word – for example, it would be possible to arrive at more results concerning stylistics – one thing has been achieved: we have a semasiological structure, a semasiological field. It is no accident that Pierre Guiraud affirms, specifically concerning stylistics: "Every word is made up of a semantic *nucleus*, more or less dense or more or less voluminous, surrounded by a halo of secondary affective or social associations" (*La sémantique*, Paris, 1955, p. 112). The particular meaning is incorporated organically within the field of the signification. The structure of this field cannot be established until after a thorough study has been made of a great number of contexts. I have organized the results of our study of the meanings of *trebalh* in Figure 40.

If we compare this synchronic cross-section with a corresponding cross-section in Old French, we shall then discover the same nucleus, but definite differences as to specific uses; that is, secondary meanings can appear spontaneously and at any moment in the use of the word in a particular situation. There is, however, a sector of the semasiological field which is to be of decisive importance for the later development, but which is only weakly outlined in Old Fr.: it is the meaning of "toil, effort and exertion in expectation of remuneration" (which has become the present-day sense)[14].

---

[13]Cp. E. Coseriu: "what we call 'polysemy' is often just the list of contextually determined variants" (*Act. Ier Cong. Int. Linguist. appliquée*, Nancy 1966, p. 204).

[14]We already find in one of the first versions of the *Oxford Psaltery* the following passage: «Si nostre Sire ne edifieried la maisun, en vain *travaillerent* qui edifient li» [translated from Latin *in vanum laboraverunt*] but the idea of (paid) work is missing, as in the documents of Old Prov.; *travailler* means no more than "strive toward a certain goal". See also Guido Keel, *Laborare und operari. Verwendungs- und Bedeutungsgeschichte zweier Verben für "arbeiten" im Lateinischen und Galloromanischen*, Thesis, Bern, 1932 [appeared in 1942],

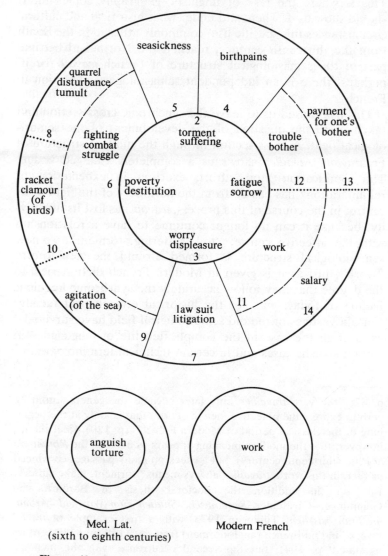

Figure 40 Semasiological field of Old Provençal *trebalh*

This is where the task of linguistic geography comes in. It should show us if, when, and under what historical and cultural circumstances this specific use, commonly attested in the South from the thirteenth century, reached the North and became part of the semasiological structure of French *travail* (or if, perhaps, there is an independent semasiological evolution in French).

This has caused us to leave the synchronic cross-section and taken us to the question of the development of the semasiological field. A cross-section through the modern structure of Fr. *travail*, *travailler* shows us a completely changed image. The signification "toil, effort, exertion in expectation of remuneration" has passed from the periphery of the field to its centre; in the course of this process, *travail* has lost its affectivity, because it can no longer continue to have a relationship with the affective centre, "toil, suffering, torment". A new semasiological structure is formed around the new centre "work", just as it is given in Modern French dictionaries, to the degree that they follow accurately the synchronic linguistic feeling of today, and not the historical etymological feeling. Certain vestiges of the old semasiological field have survived – as is often the case in the complicated life of language – in certain stylistic cases and in certain technical terminologies.

---

p. 87; "the verb *travailler* only later became the general ordinary verb to express the objective idea of 'work', that is, only at the beginning of the classical period of Modern French" (p. 120). Keel claims, however, that the modern meaning appears as early as the *Roman de la Rose* (thirteenth century), but a check on many passages convinced us that, in this work, *travailler* always means "torment, make suffer". But see in addition the doctoral thesis of Barbara von Gemmingen–Obstfelder, *Semantische Studien zum Wortfeld 'Arbeit' im Französischen*, Tübingen 1973, with a first example of *travail* "work" in Old French (anglonorman) from *ca.* 1150 (not 11th century as stated, p. 104); but the second occurrence with the meaning "work" is as late as 1288); see also Růžená Ostrá, *Structure onomasiologique du travail en français, Etude diachronique d'un champ conceptuel*, Brno, 1974, 127 pp. (esp. pp. 46, ff.).

Today there are only three of these vestiges for a word like Fr. *muer* "change" (it means "change the voice", "shed hair or feathers" and "shed antlers"). Nowadays, these three vestiges no longer have any bond between them, because the semantic centre "transform" (Latin *mutare*) has disappeared and been replaced by *changer* "change". *Muer* has not created a new centre, and as a result, has lost its coherent structure. Nothing is left except isolated remains. *Travailler*, on the other hand, has created a new semasiological centre: it is the central meaning "work". But – when a new centre is formed – what happens to the vestiges of the old semasiological field? They are orientated towards the new centre. Their motivations change, and something like popular etymologies are produced. Thus we find today – in the Larousse of 1949 – phrases such as *la fièvre le travaille* "the fever torments him", or *travailler un cheval* "fatigue a horse" registered as illustrations of the central meaning "work". This undoubtedly conforms to today's linguistic instinct, which is undistorted by knowledge of historical linguistics. The French interpret *travailler un cheval* "fatigue a horse" in the sense of making it work too much, weakening it through work. In fact, this is something left over from the old semasiological field (with "torment" in the centre), kept as a technical term. It is very significant that in the 1933 Larousse, for *travailler un cheval*, "fatigue a horse" is preceded by a first sense "exercise it, manoeuvre it". (This also occurs for Spanish *trabajar*; the Academy Dictionary, vol. 18 (1956), def. 9, "ejercitar y amaestrar el caballo"). Historically and genetically, the first meaning ("exercise it") is derived from the second; today linguistic instinct explains the second by the first. The relation has become reversed. In a parallel manner, the French interpret the phrase *la fièvre le travaille* as "the fever acts (works) on him". The remnants of the old semasiological field are orientated, as a result, towards the new centre, and they change their motivation.

Our previous considerations have presented the main attitudes of Semasiology, as well as its most urgent tasks. In the first place, *Semasiology* has no individual linear character; it is concerned with a *structure*, the semasiological structure, to be precise, which, depending on the circumstances, can be very complicated or very simple. It completely confirms the theory that has increasingly prevailed since de Saussure, that one must get to the bottom of the structural relations of the language. It is in this way that Semasiology is incorporated at the same time into de Saussure's synchronic-diachronic axis: the initial aim is always to get to the bottom of the synchronic structure, or, more precisely, the synchronic structures which differ as to time and place.

Only by getting to the bottom of the semasiological structure can we arrive at a sure interpretation of texts. Remember: to the base word and its central meaning, a special nuance is added according to the situation in which it is used, or, if one prefers, a meaning more or less remote from the nucleus of the meaning. When I say that this depends on the *situation*, I mean that it also depends on the medium (*milieu*), on the social situation or the occupation of the speaker.

Our task consists in trying to determine in what kind of style, on what social level, or in what profession a new meaning is born, and to what historical and cultural factors it is related. At this point, then, we move on from the problem of synchrony directly to the problem of diachrony, that is, to the second principal task of Semasiology: the study of the modification of the semasiological structure – in the case of *travail*, the step from the field that has as its centre "suffering, torment", to the field whose centre is "work". The development comes about first on certain social or trade levels. Only the semasiological method allows one to study thoroughly, on the basis of a great number of contexts, the generalization of the meaning, that is, its progress from the periphery to the centre, and thus, the modification of the semasiological structure[15]. One certainly cannot speak of Semasiology, then, as a

---

[15]My reflections are similar to those of P. Guiraud (*La Sémantique*, 1955, pp. 30, ff.). He distinguishes between four types of associations: *base sense* (cp. our semasiological nucleus) and *contextual sense*, on the semasiological level; *social–contextual value* and *expressive*

"wrong road, the last extension of an antiquated linguistic concept", nor can we say that it is "still linked to the Aristotelian verbalism of the Middle Ages", as Weisgerber and Dornseiff have tried to make us believe.

But from the moment we examine the step from the old to the new semasiological centre, or, to express ourselves more specifically, the development from the old central signification "torment" to the new central signification "work", we face a new problem which we have not dealt with up to now, which consists in knowing *if* this development of the meaning has modified or affected the lexical system, and, if so, how it has done it. What used to be said for "work", and what is said now to express the idea contained in "torment, punish"? We are no longer asking about meanings, but about designations, and we are directing our attention to considerations of the same problem from the *onomasiological* viewpoint.

---

value on the stylistic level. "According to the individuals and the circumstances, there are produced within the word constant changes between its different associations. The function of the three subsidiary associations is to specify and colour the base sense, but as they develop they may deform it, stifle it or even replace it completely; this is the problem of shifts of sense" (ib., p. 31; see also pp. 26, ff., and pp. 61, ff.).

3

The Field of Designations (Onomasiological Field)

While it is easy to recognize the semasiological field of Old Prov. *trebalh, trebalhar*, or at least its elementary structure – it is only necessary, in fact, to open Levy's dictionary to begin to get the idea – it is very difficult to obtain a clear view of the onomasiological structure. What is needed is a dictionary of Old Prov. – as well as a dictionary of Old Fr. – based on Onomasiology. In Belgium an onomasiological dictionary of Old Fr. is being prepared (see *RLiR* 21, 1957, 330; at present in the form of onomasiological monographs in Liège)[16], and in Heidelberg we are working on an onomasiological dictionary of Old Prov.[17]. For the present, it is necessary to read all eight volumes of Levy and five volumes of Raynouard to get an idea of the onomasiological field in Old Prov. Well, we have done it, and we have found seven or eight different designations for

---

[16]From this project there has appeared: A. Grisay, G. Lavis, M. Dubois-Stasse, *Les dénominations de la femme dans les anciens textes littéraires français*, Gembloux (Duculot) 1969 (Introduction p. IX ff. on the state of the project).

[17]Kurt Baldinger, *Dictionnaire onomasiologique de l'ancien occitan* (DAO), rédigé avec le concours de Inge Popelar, Tübingen 1975 (fasc. I); *Dictionnaire onomasiologique de l'ancien gascon* (DAG), Tübingen 1975 (fasc. I), 1977 (fasc. 2/3).

"work": along with *trebalhar*, we also have *obrar, laborar, manobrar, besonhar, brasseyar, afanar*[18].

The designations for the concept "work" in Old Provençal.

1. *obrar*: «que no isquen de le biele per *hobrar* aulhor, sober peie de . . .» (Bayonne, 1306): "for they are not permitted to leave the city to work elsewhere, under penalty of . . ." It refers especially to manual labour.

2. *laborar, laorar, laurar*: «Dreitz ditz: Qu'om *labor* et aura ricor e be» (P. Cardinal). Raynouard translates: "Justice says: that man should work and he will have power and wealth". Most of the quotes refer to rural work.

3. *trebalhar*: «biuer en bone uite e *tribailhar* e gadeinhar lor pan» (Bayonne, 1336): "lead a good life, work and earn their bread". With affective value.

---

[18]Levy also translates Old Prov. *manejar* (in Guiraut de Bornelh, published by A. Kolsen, 1, 1910, p. 424) as "manage, work", but I have checked the passage and it is clear that this is a figurative and isolated use which has nothing to do with our field of designations (for this reason, no doubt, this definition is not found in Levy's *Petit dict. prov.-fr.*).

Old Prov. *vacar* "have time to do something, be busy at something" (*FEW* defines "be busy, work", 14, 95a) comes closer to our field.

It is also necessary to include in the onomasiological field "work" Old Prov. *maltrach* (m.) "effort, suffering, work, remuneration obtained from work" (which corresponds perfectly to the semasiological field of *trebalh*). *Maltrach* is found many times in the documents of Limoux (Languedoc). To Levy's references may be added "Item can le sestier del froment costa de comprar .ii. sols, et hom dona azaquel o ad aquela que'l vol pastar per far pa vendal, .ii. sols per so *maltrayt* et per so guazanh" (about 1300, *Les manuscrits consulaires de Limoux*, 222); «Item can le sestier del froment costa .iij. sols, hom dona entre *gazanh* e *maltrayt* .ij. sols» (ib. and often); we also find, but much less frequently, *entre maltrayt e guasanh*; in the same documents of Limoux we find the synonym *trebalh*: «enclus lo *trebalh* de .ij. sols que hom dona» (1459, ib. 226). The editor comments "tant pour son travail (*maltrayt* = sa peine) que pour son profit" (p. 221), "as much for his work as for his profit".

4. *afanar*: «Lo jorn per *afanar*, la nuegz per pauzamens». (P. de Corbiac): "the day to work, the night to rest". With affective value? Raynouard translates "fatiguer". Cf. also, in Levy, *afanier* "worker", *gen d'afan* "workers".

5. *manobrar*: «ayan a obrar e a *manobrar* tot lo jorn» (Gironde, 1336): "that they might have all day to work and render service" (in general, feudal service or construction work).

6. *brasseyar*: «A II frays, l'un va *brasseyan*» (Béarn, fourteenth century): "he has two brothers, one of whom works". Properly, "work with one's arms"; cf. "viven de lor brasse" ("they live by the work of their arms").

7. *besonhar*: «Johan . . . *besonhant* a Pau» (Old Bearnese). Affective in its origin. In Old Prov. it is only found (and frequently) from 1480; it is probably a loan-word from Middle French.

As for *trebalh, trebalhar*, we have seen that as a matter of fact *trebalhar* could already mean "work" in Old Prov. but that, at the same time, it was not yet the normal, objective word for "work"; that is, it also underlines affectively the pain and suffering associated with work. It was a marginal meaning of the semasiological field "torment, suffering". This semasiological place at the same time determines the place *trebalhar* occupies in the onomasiological field; as a matter of fact, *this semasiological determination is the condition for the onomasiological determination*. In other words, to determine more precisely the reciprocal relationships of the seven verbs mentioned for "work", in order to be able to recognize the onomasiological structure, it is absolutely necessary to determine for each verb the semasiological place of the meaning "work" in the totality of each semasiological field. We shall not do that here – we have explained the principle in the case of *trebalh* –. I shall only characterize briefly the completely different semasiological structure of Old Prov. *obrar*, according to the meanings given by Levy, in Figure 41.

In this case the meaning "work, produce, manufacture" is found in the centre of the field. From Pliny's time on, in fact, *operari* had the sense "work", especially for manual labour and commerce, as, for example, engraving and weaving (see

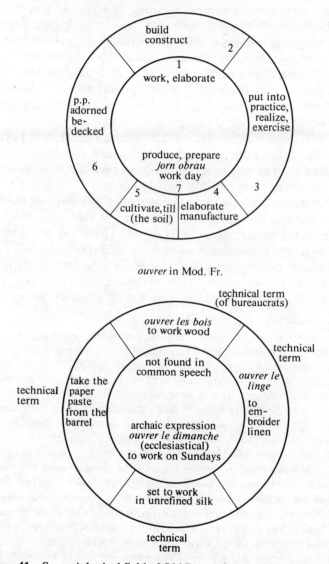

Figure 41 Semasiological field of Old Prov. *obrar* and Mod. Fr. *ouvrer*

FEW 7, 368)[19]. The meanings "adorn, bedeck, construct, till, etc.", which move around the centre, are explained by the use of the verb with its central meaning in a certain situation or environment. We said before that the semasiological position determines at the same time the onomasiological position. In our case, we find the meaning "work" in the centre of the semasiological field; as a result, we shall again find *obrar* with this meaning in the centre of the onomasiological field. An analysis of the semasiological fields of the seven designations of "work" allows us to recognize an onomasiological structure which is relatively similar to the semasiological structure we already know, with a centre, and elements (this time lexical) situated around the centre; that is, this time the basic elements are no longer meanings but designations.

Our analysis allows us to discover that by means of this diagram we can recognize that there are at the same time two verbs in the centre: *obrar* and *laborar*. There are, it is true, no synonyms; the text shows us that the spheres of the two verbs do, in fact, often overlap, but that *obrar* refers primarily to the work of craftsmen, and *laborar* designates particularly the work of country people[20]. The words situated around the

---

[19]"*Operari*, unlike *laborare*, possesses from the beginning, the sense 'work' ", Keel, *op. cit.*, p. 31 (see also p. 52: "*Operari* in the sense of 'work' belonged especially to the urban sphere, that is, to the language of the city population working in industry and commerce. In the urban sphere, it was used by everyone in the sense of 'daily work'; later, both transitively and intransitively, especially for the 'work of a craftsman' in some specialized branches of industry, such as weaving, sculpture, and artistic ironwork. Even the agricultural type is an urbanism or Hellenism quite rare among country people").

[20]*Laborare*, which in Italian became the regular word for "work" (*lavorare*), followed the same path later, as "work" moved from a peripheral, affective meaning, to the central objective meaning; see Guido Keel, *Laborare und operari*, pp. 3, ff.: "*Laborare* is formed on the base of the noun *labor* which, in turn, comes from *labi*, with the original meaning of 'physical movement which requires an effort' (slipping, coming and going). The earliest content of this verb, then, was the fact of finding oneself in the difficult situation designated by

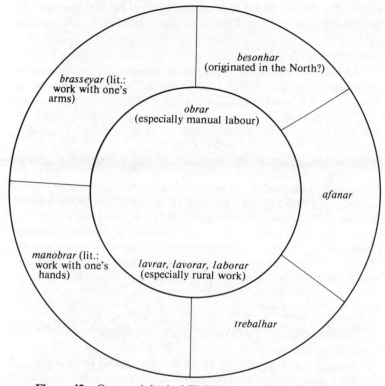

Figure 42 Onomasiological Field "work" in Old Provençal

labor; but it was soon used in the more general sense of 'endure the effort, tire, be harassed' . . ." (p. 6). "Medieval Lat. *laborare* can have the secondary meaning of "combat", just as *trebalhar* in Old Prov. (ib. p. 10). *Laborare* in the sense of "work" (affective) is attested to as early as Plautus, Cato and Varro (ib., p. 19). At first, among the lower classes, the verb designated the occupation that was felt as a private "affliction". Naturally, this concerned less city work, craftsmanship and industry (see *operari*), than work in the country – both of men and of animals – which fatigues the whole body. We discover, then, that most of the colloquial evidence of *laborare* in the sense of "work" is of rural character" (p. 19, see also p. 60 for the influence of the Church). For the relationships between the forms *laurar, laorar, lavorar* and the form *laborar*, a loan-word, see Keel, p. 54, ff.

centre can be classified into two groups. The first group with
trebalhar[21], *afanar*[22], and perhaps also *besonhar*[23], adds to the

---

[21]An exact parallel to the ancient phase of development of
*trepaliare is the ecclesiastical Slavic *maciti* "martyrize, torture" >
Roum. *a munci* "work (hard)"; see Keel, p. 20.

[22]The origin of **afannare* has not been very well clarified; see
Vittore Pisani, "Relitti lessicali oscoumbri nelle lingue romanze",
in *Romanica* (Festschrift *Rohlfs*), 1958, pp. 377, ff. "In the sense of
'work' and to designate field work, it is known neither in Italy nor in
the Iberian Peninsula, but it is found, on the other hand, in the sense
of 'torment, affliction' . . . The origin of **afannare* is not at present
known", in *FEW* 24, 243 (see now H. Stimm, *Zeitschrift für franz.
Sprache und Literatur* 87, 1977, 180–182 (got **AF-HANNAN*)). Old
Prov. *afanar* means "fatiguer, chagriner, prendre peine"
(Raynouard), as well as "gagner quelque chose à grand peine"
(Levy); *afanier* "travailleur", *gen d'afan* "travailleurs, gens qui
travaillent" (alongside *afan* "peine, chagrin", *afanamen* "fatigue,
peine", *sobrafan* "grand chagrin", Raynouard). The meaning "become
fatigued with hard work" is also attested in dialects, *FEW*, 24, 241.
According to Keel, *op. cit.*, p. 19, **afannare* is "the most exact parallel to *laborare* concerning the change of meaning from 'suffer pain' to
'work, do country tasks' ".

[23]According to Gamillscheg, the direct root of Old Fr. *besogne* and
Old Prov. *besogna* would be the Frankish **BISUNNJA*, in the sense of
"cares"; in this case, the objectivisation of the concept would have
led to the medieval use as "need, necessity". From there – as with
Latin *labor* – came the sense of "hard work", and finally, just
"work". On the noun – again, as in the case of Lat. *laborare* derived
from *labor* – the verb *besognier* would have been formed, already in
the preliterary Gallo-Roman period, with the first meaning of "to be
in need, in poverty" or of "to need care", Keel, *op. cit.*, p. 119.
(According to Keel, in the same way, the original content of a state of
"need, torment, suffering, poverty" evolved to mean "work" ib.);
Wartburg criticizes this opinion, *FEW*, 17, p. 282, n. 24. *Besonhar*
and *besonha*, in the sense of "work" and in others, are only attested
to at a late date in Old Prov. (lacking in Levy; Raynouard quotes only
one passage in the Albigensian Chronicle, which has no great linguistic value; the attestations in our Old Gascon material only begin in
1483; Meyer, *Doc.*, p. 637, attested from 1607). Since in Middle

signification "work" an affective element of "pain, suffering"; the second group specifies the central meaning in an objective, precise way. *Brasseyar*[24] means "work with one's arms", *man-obrar*[25] originally "work with one's hands", later especially "work on a construction", or "lend feudal service" in the sense of the Middle Ages, in spite of the general meaning of

---

French *besogne, besogner* becomes the first serious competitor of *ouvrer* (see Keel, p. 119, ff.), one would have to ask if there is an influence from the North of France (the pressure of the written language of the French of the North on the South becomes very strongly felt after 1450, see A. Brun, *Recherches historiques sur l'introduction du français dans les provinces du Midi*, Thèse Lettres, Paris, 1923, xv + 505 pp.). For this reason, *besogner* would not only be a semantic parallel of *travailler*, but also its linguistic–geographic equivalent; *travailler* took over the central sense in the South and perhaps went up to the North; *besogner* took it over in the North and went down to the South. In both cases, careful investigation is necessary. The origin in the North of France is now confirmed by the *FEW*, 17, pp. 275, ff., as is the Frankish origin; but for *travailler* in Old French see also the work by B. von Gemmingen, mentioned in note 14.

[24]*Brasseyar* in this sense is found only in OBearn., and rarely attested, the same as *brasse* fem. noun, "manual labour" (*viven de lor brasse*, fourteenth century, Lespy-Raymond); however, much more extended, *brassier* "worker, one who works with his arms, manual labourer" (Coutumes Condom y V. y Vert., Raynouard., *FEW* 1, p. 486a).

[25]*FEW*, 6¹, p. 283: OFr. *manovrer* v. n. "travailler" BenSMaure, *menovrer* (1303, DC), MFr. *manouvrer* (Tournai, 1422–1434), OGasc. *manaobrá* (1411) ..., MFr. *manœuvrier* m. "worker who works with his hands and for daily pay" (from 1189; 'archaic' *Ac* 1935) ..., OPr. *manobrier* (Martel, thirteenth century, *RPh*, 8, p. 289), OLim. *manobreir*, OGasc. *manobrey, manaobrer*, OBearn. *manobrè* etc. In Old Gasc., for example; *ayan a obrar e a manobrar tot lo jorn* (in the sense of "drudgery"), 1366, *Arch Gir*, 51, p. 199; *IX jorns de manaobra* ("drudgery"), 1412 Gers. *Arch Gir*, 29, p. 305; *foc ordenat que hom agos manahobra a la carrera deu C.* 1448, *Arch Gir*, 32, p. 73; etc.

"work" given by Levy. This double aspect of the designations which surround the normal words of the centre reminds us of the two outlines given by von Wartburg in 1937, dealing with a different matter: the normal word is surrounded, on the one hand, "by other normal words which designate secondary notions of the same semantic space"; on the other hand, "by synonyms which are charged with emotion"[26].

The onomasiological field "work" of Old French is similar to that of Old Provençal, but up to the fourteenth century the word *travailler* was lacking, and was absent from the ono-masiological field in the same way that the signification "work" was missing in its semasiological field (but see foot-note 14).

In modern French, *travailler* is in the centre of the ono-masiological field "work", and this notion has taken over the position of the central meaning in the semasiological field of *travailler*. On the other hand, *ouvrer* only occurs today in a semasiological field which is in a state of ruin; old vestiges are still found, such as, for example, the expression *ouvrer le dim-anche* (which, in addition, has a special stylistic value), or *ouv-rer les bois* "les préparer en forêt", as a technical term (Eaux et Forêts). Another old vestige – *jours ouvrables* – has taken refuge in another family of words: for the French, *les jours ouvrables* are the days on which the shops are open (*ouvrir*), which coincides with work days. This popular etymology is due to the fact that the semasiological field of *ouvrer* "work" has remained in the centre of the onomasiological field, and this fact would lead us to the morphological structure, to new prob-lems which would be no less interesting. On the other hand, the new central designation *travailler* is surrounded by a great number of affective words: *turbiner, trimer, piocher, bûcher, boulonner, bosser*, etc. (slang would give us a score more); the same is true of *obrar* and *laborar* in Old Prov., or *arbeiten* in

---

[26]W. von Wartburg, "Betrachtungen über die Gliederung des Wortschatzes und die Gestaltung des Wörterbuchs", in *ZRP*, 57, 1937, pp. 297, ff.

German (surrounded by *krüppeln*, *schuften*, *schanzen*, *ochsen*, *schinden*, Swiss-German *chrampfe* alongside the central designation *schaffe*).

It is easy to see the consequences of these considerations on the development of the onomasiological field "work"; one can immediately see the parallelism with Semasiology. Onomasiology also studies a structure, that is, the reciprocal positions of different designations, and for this reason we recognize, as in the case of the semasiological structure, a centre of one or more poles surrounded by a field which is objective, affective, or mixed – the objective differences concern symbolic functions; the affective differences concern functions of symptom and of signal, see Part II, Chap. 5. In the same way, there are synchronic and diachronic problems related to both fields.

4

The Interdependence of the Two Structures

Only now that we have formed an idea of the two structures, taking as an example the word *travailler* with its semasiological structure, and the notion "work" with its onomasiological structure, can we pose the question of their interdependence, and, at the same time, the need for their existence, their possibilities and their borders. The two structures interlock. Old Prov. *trebalh*, to be specific, because of its secondary signification "suffering → paid work", invades the onomasiological field "work". The position in the semasiological field (characterized by the affective element which appears in its relationship with the centre of the semasiological field, that is, with the central meaning of "suffering, torment") determines, at the same time, its position in the onomasiological field: there too, *trebalh* is found on the circumference with an affective value. This fact, once discovered on the synchronic plane, can be of decisive importance when one moves from the synchronic to the diachronic point of view. W. von Wartburg has often insisted, and especially since his "quarrel" with Gilliéron, on the creative factors that are always at work in the language, even when there are no conflicts, homonymic or otherwise[27]. He insists on the fact that the affective or objective

---

[27]W. von Wartburg, "Das Ineinandergreifen von historischer und deskriptiver Sprachwissenschaft" [The Interrelationship of Historical

words that accompany a normal word are always liable to replace it if something happens to it. Remember the famous case
of *gallus* and *cattus*, 'cockerel' and 'cat', in Old Gascon. The
cockerel and the cat became homonyms (*gat*); a word from the
affective periphery (*bigey*< VICARIUS) 'beadle of a village' is
what saved the situation[28]. The affective word, which already
existed before there was any conflict, became the normal word
when the need arose. In the same way, *chef* has been replaced
by *tête*, the affective word, etc., etc ... These changes were
possible only because of the interdependence of the semasiological and onomasiological structures. The semasiological
field of *bigey* 'beadle' thanks to its secondary and affective
metaphorical meaning 'cockerel', forms at the same time part
of the onomasiological structure of designations for the 'cockerel'. In the onomasiological field, *bigey* was originally a marginal, affective designation. It acquired the central position when
people began to avoid *gat* 'cockerel', previously the normal
word, because it was on bad terms with the cat. Let us return
to our subject, that is, to our *work*. *Trebalhar*, from the fourteenth to the seventeenth centuries, was slowly shifting towards the centre of the onomasiological field "work". At the
same time, and in a parallel manner, the meaning "work" was
slowly shifting toward the centre of the semasiological field of
travailler. The fact is that diachronic shifts are produced in the
same way simultaneously in both structures. This interdependence of two structures, as discovered in the case of
travailler, must have profound reasons, reasons that spring from
the very structure of the language. It concerns the two micro-

---

and Descriptive Linguistics], in *Berichte über die Verhandlungen der
Sächsischen Akademie der Wissenschaften zu Leipzig*, Philol. hist.
Klasse 83, 1 (1931), 1–23.

[28]See W. von Wartburg, *Problems and Methods in Linguistics*,
Revised ed. with the collaboration of Stephen Ullmann, translated by
Joyce M. H. Reid, Oxford (Blackwell) 1969, p. 139; (the beadle in the
village is compared with the cockerel in the chicken run; see *FEW*,
14, p. 408).

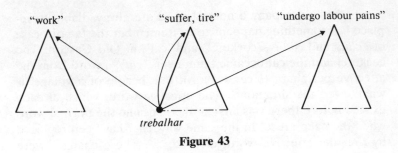

Figure 43

structures of which we spoke in the first part of this book (Chap. 3a; 7; 10)[29]. Applied to our case, see Figure 43.

Conversely, the concept "work" is designated by many designations (Figure 44).

In this way, both structures, onomasiological and semasiological, interlock, as we have discovered with *travailler*.

The *onomasiological* structure is based on "synonymy", the *semasiological* structure is based on "polysemy". Onomasiology approaches problems from the viewpoint of the

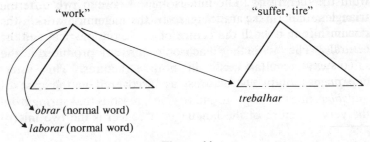

Figure 44

---

[29]I wrote the article, published here as an appendix, in 1957 (it was published in 1964), that is, before analysing conceptual systems. According to everything presented in the second part (with the analysis of the concept "remember"), we would ask today for a preliminary analysis of the concept "work", and of the other concepts related to it, that is, an analysis made much more rigorously on the level of the substance of content.

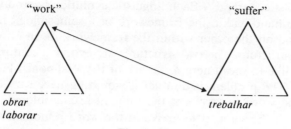

Figure 45

speaker, who has to choose between different means of expression. Semasiology approaches problems from the viewpoint of the *listener*, who has to determine the meaning of the word he hears, from among all the possible meanings.

The fact, now discovered, that the position of a word in the semasiological field determines at the same time its position in the onomasiological field, also finds an explanation in Figure 45.

We see that it is a question of the same relationship; the difference only arises from the way it is approached, that is, from the direction[30]. The link is made between two different triangles; that is, the meaning and the designation are on the circumference in both cases, since the central meaning and the central designation are always found in the same triangle.

To summarize: the double aspect of the linguistic sign (form of *expression* and form of *content*) conditions a double aspect

---

[30]Compare P. Guiraud, *La sémantique*, Paris, 1955, pp. 108–09: "in studying words one may start either from the *signifiant* form (semasiology), or from the thing signified (onomasiology), which constitutes, rather than two autonomous parts of semantics under its different forms, two different points of view". Guiraud, ib., insists on the need for clarifying terminology (which we do in this book). Concerning the double meaning (now outdated) of the word "semasiology", see also our summary *Die Semasiologie*, 1957, p. 11, n. 22 (Span. translation *La Semasiología*, Rosario, 1964, translated by Graciela García Montaño de Gardella, p. 13, n. 22).

of linguistic method[31]. Each linguistic evolution is produced on the one hand within the framework of a semasiological structure, and on the other within the framework of an onomasiological structure. The two structures are evolving continually. I should like to recall here a remark of the Walloonist Feller, in 1926: «The problem is double: it would be necessary to start with the word to arrive at the thought [Semasiology], and to start with the thought to arrive at the word [Onomasiology]». That is what we have been trying to show.

However, I do not wish to come to a close without insisting on the fact that we have been concerned only with internal linguistic problems. Language lives only through man. A semasiological and onomasiological inquiry is nothing more than a skeleton, until it is completed with human relations, with historical, cultural, sociological and economic questions. The more we delve into the complexity of linguistic evolution, the more humble we become. We have not touched the historical, sociological or economic aspects, even though it is basically by starting with these problems that the story of the development of *travail* becomes interesting, since, in this way, we grasp the relationship between language and man. The very notion of etymology has changed since Gilliéron and de Saussure. As Gilliéron said, the old concept of etymology corresponded to a biography of Balzac consisting of no more than

---

[31]On each level (name and content), with a double aspect. Thus, Ullmann distinguishes, on each of the two levels, two kinds of associations (cp. the lexical solidarities of Coseriu), *association by similarity* (Guiraud) and *association by contiguity*. "A 'chapeau'" (hat) "reminds me: Ia of *casque*, of *béret*, etc., similarity of sense; Ib of *tête*, of *veston*, etc., contiguity of sense; IIa of *chapelle*, *chapon*, *drapeau*, *crapaud*, similarity of name; IIb of *claque*, of *melon* by contiguity of name in expressions of the type *chapeau-claque*, *chapeau-melon*" (Guiraud, *op. cit.*, p. 45). Let us add to this the change of the thing while the designation continues to be the same, an extralinguistic development which has as consequence changes of a conceptual, and therefore also semasiological, order.

two sentences: "Balzac, sitting on his nurse's knees, wore a blue suit with red stripes. He wrote the *Comédie Humaine*".

I think it is Wartburg who has best defined the new concept of etymology[32], which covers at the same time both aspects, semasiological as well as onomasiological. Both should be placed under its banner, and with this I shall close:

> Etymology in the modern sense follows words and groups of words in their numerous ramifications, in all their relationships with other words, during all the time in which they live in the whole structure of the language. It discovers in the word the footprints of an age-old and ancient evolution in humanity, and discovers in it the history of the unceasing efforts of the human spirit, which in a way fitting to it, with the help of language, transmits continually to succeeding generations the chaos which surrounds it in an organized world, for its preservation and convenient transformation. To know the vocabulary in its relationship with everything that constitutes the development of humanity, to grasp it as the most immediate and universal expression of the most elevated as well as of the most humble matters that life involves – this is the direction of modern etymological investigation.

---

[32]See my article "L'étymologie hier et aujourd'hui", in *Cahiers de l'Association Internationale des Etudes françaises*, 11, 1959, pp. 233–64 [republished in *Etymologie*, Darmstadt (Wissenschaftliche Buchgesellschaft) 1977, 213–246].

Index